AF522245

Industrial Management

Industrial Management

Dominic Pepall

Industrial Management

ISBN 978-93-5111-447-5

Published in 2014 in India by

RANDOM PUBLICATIONS

4376-A/4B, Gali Murari Lal, Ansari Road
New Delhi-110 002
Phone : +91-11-43580356, +91-11-23289044
e-mail: randomexports@gmail.com, sales@randompublications.com,
info@randompublications.com

Type Setting by: Friends Media, Delhi-110089
Printed at Thomson Press (India) Ltd

Preface

Industrial Management can be defined as the effective and efficient running of an industry using its human and non-human resources in order to achieve its set goals and objectives. It can also be defined as the effective and efficient utilization of organizational resources to achieve an industry set goals. Top of Form Industrial management is that deals with people in industry, material and energy leading towards production growth. Our country is fast growing in industrial sector. Due to its economic policies many companies are coming forward to develop factories and production facilities in our country. Every company is in need of an industrial management person. They have much career opportunities now days. Some industries they give training to the qualified persons, and some they appoint experiences, skilled person.

The various topics concerning industrial engineers include management science, work-study, financial engineering, engineering management, supply chain management, process engineering, operations research, systems engineering, ergonomics / safety engineering, cost and value engineering, quality engineering, facilities planning, and the engineering design process. Traditionally, a major aspect of industrial engineering was planning the layouts of factories and designing assembly lines and other manufacturing paradigms. And now, in so-called lean manufacturing systems, industrial engineers work to eliminate wastes of time, money, materials, energy, and other resources. Examples of where industrial engineering might be used include flow process charting, process mapping, designing an assembly workstation, strategizing for various operational logistics, consulting as an efficiency expert, developing a new financial algorithm or loan system for a bank, streamlining operation and emergency room location or usage in a hospital, planning complex distribution schemes for materials or products (referred to as Supply Chain Management), and shortening lines (or queues) at a bank, hospital, or a theme park.

Modern Industrial Engineers typically use Predetermined motion time system, computer simulation (especially discrete event simulation), along with extensive mathematical tools and modelling and computational methods for system analysis, evaluation, and optimization. Depending on the subspecialties involved, industrial engineering may also be known as, or overlap with, operations management, management science, operations research, systems engineering, manufacturing engineering, ergonomics or human factors engineering, safety engineering, or others, depending on the viewpoint or motives of the user. For example, in health care, the engineers known as health management engineers or health systems engineers are, in essence, industrial engineers by another name.

The book provides readers with of some of the basic principles of this subject.

I thank all members of my team who have helped in the preparation of the book. My special thanks go to "Random Publication" who have published the book.

—Dominic Pepall

Contents

1

Introduction

Industrial psychology is a relatively new branch of psychology that was created for corporations and organizations that needed more structure. Industrial psychology is able to provide this structure by evaluating employee behaviour for the good of the company. It is often referred to as *organizational psychology* because of its emphasis on analysing individuals who work for various organizations. Essentially, industrial psychologists study the behaviour of employees in a work setting. Although industrial psychology didn't begin until the 1920's, the discipline has evolved rapidly and revolutionized the workplace within the last century. Because the workplace is a social system, the application of industrial psychology is useful in understanding its complexity. For years, psychologists have studied how human beings have interacted with their environments and each other, but industrial psychology begins to evaluate the interaction between people and their jobs. Industrial psychologists can be used to improve job satisfaction as well as company productivity and is becoming vital to the success of many organizations.

There are certain things that industrial psychologists focus on when evaluating the relationship a person has with their work. They analyse the way a person works, their skills, duties, obligations, and general satisfaction with their job on a day-to-day basis. This information is extremely helpful to human resources departments and company overseers who must create training programs, feedback and rewards systems, and make hiring decisions as well as engage in recruitment practices. Most companies use industrial psychologists to train their own staff so that the organizations can run smoothly and at peak capacity.

One of the most interesting aspects of industrial psychology is how employee behaviour affects others individuals on the job and organization in general. Industrial psychology can be used to reduce counterproductive behaviour, enhance team effectiveness, and boost morale. It is also vital in conflict resolution. Many individuals find the brunt of their work dissatisfaction rooted in their relationships with managers and colleagues. Fortunately, industrial psychology provides solutions for this.

Although industrial psychology is a mixture of anthropology, counselling, sociology and industrial management, there are key components used in this type of psychology. Some of the key components include the evaluation of employee's personalities, perceptions, as well the biological side of their behaviour. By documenting these key points, industrial psychologists have the ability to help organizations improve their functionality and set up a system that promotes growth for the company and employees.

Industrial psychology also helps CEOs and executives adjust their way of thinking and their management style, which can impact the stress levels of the employees that they manage. By using psychology, many companies are able to retain their employees because they understand how to keep them happy. Organizations with a low retention rate and employee dissatisfaction benefit from the work and assessment of industrial psychologists.

Impact of Industrialization

Industrialisatioon (British English) or Industrialization (Canadian & American English) is the process of social and economic change that transforms a human group from a pre-industrial society into an industrial one. It is a part of a wider modernisation process, where social change and economic development are closely related with technological innovation, particularly with the development of large-scale energy and metallurgy production. It is the extensive organisation of an economy for the purpose of manufacturing.

Industrialisation also introduces a form of philosophical change where people obtain a different attitude towards their perception of nature, and a sociological process of ubiquitous rationalisation. There is considerable literature on the factors facilitating industrial modernisation and enterprise development. Key positive factors identified by researchers have ranged from favourable political-legal environments for industry and commerce, through abundant natural resources of various kinds, to plentiful supplies of relatively low-cost, skilled and adaptable labour. One survey of countries in Africa, Latin America, the Caribbean, and the Middle East and the rest of Asia in the late 20th century found that high levels of structural differentiation, functional specialisation, and autonomy of economic systems from government were likely to contribute greatly to industrial-commercial growth and prosperity. Amongst other things, relatively open trading systems with zero or low duties on imported goods tended to stimulate industrial cost-efficiency and innovation across the board. Free and flexible labour and other markets also helped raise general business-economic performance levels, as did rapid popular learning capabilities.

Positive work ethics in populations at large combined with skills in quickly utilising new technologies and scientific discoveries were likely to boost production and income levels – and as the latter rose, markets for consumer goods and services of all kinds tended to expand and provide a further stimulus to industrial investment and economic growth.

By the end of the century, East Asia was one of the most economically successful regions of the world – with free market countries such as Hong Kong being widely seen as models for other, less developed countries around the world to emulate.

The first country to industrialise was Great Britain during the Industrial Revolution. According to the original sector classification of Jean Fourastié, an economy consists of a "Primary sector" of commodity production (farming, livestock breeding, exploitation of mineral resources), a "secondary sector" of manufacturing and processing, and a "Tertiary Sector" of service industries. The industrialisation process is historically based on the expansion of the secondary sector in an economy dominated by primary activities.

The first ever transformation to an industrial economy from an agrarian one was called the Industrial Revolution and this took place in the late 18th and early 19th centuries in a few countries of Western Europe and North America, beginning in Great Britain. This was the first industrialization in the world's history.

The Second Industrial Revolution describes a later, somewhat less dramatic change that came about in the late 19th century with the widespread availability of electric power, internal combustion engines, and assembly lines to the already industrialised nations. The lack of an industrial sector in a country is widely seen as a major handicap in improving a country's economy, and power, pushing many governments to encourage or enforce industrialisation.

History of Industrialisation

Most pre-industrial economies had standards of living not much above subsistence, aming that the majority of the population were focused on producing their means of survival. For example, in medieval Europe, 80% of the labour force was employed in subsistence agriculture. Some pre-industrial economies, such as classical Athens, had trade and commerce as significant factors, so native Greeks could enjoy wealth far beyond a sustenance standard of living through the use of slavery. Famines were frequent in most pre-industrial societies, although some, such as the Netherlands and England of the seventeenth and eighteenth centuries, the Italian city states of the fifteenth century, the medieval Islamic Caliphate, and the ancient Greek and Roman civilisations were able to escape the famine cycle through increasing trade and commercialisation of the agricultural sector. It is estimated that during the seventeenth century Netherlands imported nearly 70% of its grain supply and in the fifth century BC Athens imported three quarters of its total food supply. Industrialisation through innovation in manufacturing processes first started with the Industrial Revolution in the northwest and Midlands of England in the eighteenth century. It spread to Europe and North America in the nineteenth century, and to the rest of the world in the twentieth.

Industrial Revolution in Western Europe

In the eighteenth and nineteenth centuries, Great Britain experienced a massive increase in agricultural productivity known as the British Agricultural Revolution, which enabled an unprecedented population growth, freeing a significant percentage of the workforce from farming, and helping to drive the Industrial Revolution.

Due to the limited amount of arable land and the overwhelming efficiency of mechanised farming, the increased population could not be dedicated to agriculture. New agricultural techniques allowed a single peasant to feed more workers than previously; however, these techniques also increased the demand for machines and other hardwares, which had traditionally been provided by the urban artisans. Artisans, collectively called bourgeoisie, employed rural exodus workers to increase their output and meet the country's needs. The growth of their business coupled with the lack of experience of the new workers pushed a rationalisation and standardisation of the duties the in workshops, thus leading to a division of labour, that is, a primitive form of Fordism. The process of creating a good was divided into simple tasks, each one of them being gradually mechanized in order to boost productivity and thus increase income. The accumulation of capital allowed investments in the conception and application of new technologies, enabling the industrialisation process to continue to evolve. The industrialisation process formed a class of industrial workers who had more money to spend than their agricultural cousins. They spent this on items such as tobacco and sugar, creating new mass markets that stimulated more investment as merchants sought to exploit them.

The mechanisation of production spread to the countries surrounding England in western and northern Europe and to British settler colonies, helping to make those areas the wealthiest, and shaping what is now known as the Western world.

Some economic historians argue that the possession of so-called 'exploitation colonies' eased the accumulation of capital to the countries that possessed them, speeding up their development. The consequence was that the subject country integrated a bigger economic system in a subaltern position, emulating the countryside, which demands manufactured goods and offers raw materials, while the colonial power stressed its urban posture, providing goods and importing food. A classical example of this mechanism is said to be the triangular trade, which involved England, southern United States and western Africa. Critics argue that this polarity still affects the world, and has deeply retarded industrialisation of what is now known as the Third World.

Some have stressed the importance of natural or financial resources that Britain received from its many overseas colonies or that profits from the British slave trade between Africa and the Caribbean helped fuel industrial investment.

Early Industrialisation in other Countries

After the Convention of Kanagawa issued by Commodore Matthew C. Perry forced Japan to open the ports of Shimoda and Hakodate to American trade, the Japanese government realised that drastic reforms were necessary to stave off Western influence. The Tokugawa shogunate abolished the feudal system. The government instituted military reforms to modernise the Japanese army and also constructed the base for industrialisation. In the 1870s, the Meiji government vigorously promoted technological and industrial development that eventually changed Japan to a powerful modern country.

In a similar way, Russia suffered during the Allied intervention in the Russian Civil War. The Soviet Union's centrally controlled economy decided to invest a big part of its resources to enhance its industrial production and infrastructures to assure its survival, thus becoming a world superpower. During the Cold war, the other European socialist countries, organised under the Comecon framework, followed the same developing scheme, albeit with a less emphasis on heavy industry. Southern European countries saw a moderate industrialisation during the 1950s-1970s, caused by a healthy integration of the European economy, though their level of development, as well as those of eastern countries, doesn't match the western standards.

The Third World

A similar state-led developing programme was pursued in virtually all the Third World countries during the Cold War, including the socialist ones, but especially in Sub-Saharan Africa after the decolonisation period. The primary scope of those projects was to achieve self-sufficiency through the local production of previously imported goods, the mechanisation of agriculture and the spread of education and health care. However, all those experiences failed bitterly due to a lack of realism: most countries didn't have a pre-industrial bourgeoisie able to carry on a capitalistic development or even a stable and peaceful state. Those aborted experiences left huge debts toward western countries and fuelled public corruption.

Petrol Producing Countries

Oil-rich countries saw similar failures in their economic choices. An EIA report stated that OPEC member nations were projected to earn a net amount of $1.251 trillion in 2008 from their oil exports. Because oil is both important and expensive, regions that had big reserves of oil had huge liquidity incomes. However, this was rarely followed by economic development. Experience shows that local elites were unable to re-invest the petrodollars obtained through oil export, and currency is wasted in luxury goods.

This is particularly evident in the Persian Gulf states, where the per capita income is comparable to those of western nations, but where no industrialisation has started. Apart from two little countries (Bahrain and the United Arab Emirates), Arab states have not diversified their economies, and no replacement for the upcoming end of oil reserves is envisaged.

Industrialisation in Asia

Apart from Japan, where industrialisation began in the late 19th century, a different pattern of industrialisation followed in East Asia. One of the fastest rates of industrialisation occurred in the late 20th century across four countries known as the Asian tigers thanks to the existence of stable governments and well structured societies, strategic locations, heavy foreign investments, a low cost skilled and motivated workforce, a competitive exchange rate, and low custom duties.

In the case of South Korea, the largest of the four Asian tigers, a very fast paced industrialisation took place as it quickly moved away from the manufacturing of value added goods in the 1950s and 60s into the more advanced steel, shipbuilding and automobile industry in the 1970s and 80s, focusing on the high-tech and service industry in the 1990s and 2000s. As a result, South Korea became a major economic power and today is one of the wealthiest countries in Asia.

This starting model was afterwards successfully copied in other larger Eastern and Southern Asian countries, including communist ones. The success of this phenomenon led to a huge wave of offshoring – i.e., Western factories or Tertiary Sector corporations choosing to move their activities to countries where the workforce was less expensive and less collectively organised.

China and India, while roughly following this development pattern, made adaptations in line with their own histories and cultures, their major size and importance in the world, and the geo-political ambitions of their governments (etc.).

Currently, China's government is actively investing in expanding its own infrastructures and securing the required energy and raw materials supply channels, is supporting its exports by financing the United States balance payment deficit through the purchase of US treasury bonds, and is strengthening its military in order to endorse a major geopolitical role. Meanwhile, India's government is investing in specific vanguard economic sectors such as bioengineering, nuclear technology, pharmaceutics, informatics, and technologically-oriented higher education, openly overpassing its needs, with the goal of creating several specialisation poles able to conquer foreign markets.

Both Chinese and Indian corporations have also started to make huge investments in Third World countries, making them significant players in today's world economy.

Newly Industrialised Countries

In recent decades, a few countries in Latin America, Asia, and Africa, such as Turkey, South Africa, Malaysia, Philippines and Mexico have experienced substantial industrial growth, fuelled by exportations going to countries that have bigger economies: the United States, Japan,

China, India and the EU. They are sometimes called newly-industrialised countries. Despite this trend being artificially influenced by the oil price increases since 2003, the phenomenon is not entirely new nor totally speculative. Most analysts conclude in the next few decades the whole world will experience industrialisation, and international inequality will be replaced with worldwide social inequality.

Other Outcomes

Urbanisation

Urbanization, Urbanisation or Urban Drift is the physical growth of urban areas as a result of global change. Urbanization is also defined by the United Nations as movement of people from rural to urban areas with population growth equating to urban migration. The United Nations projected that half of the world's population would live in urban areas at the end of 2008.

Urbanization is closely linked to modernization, industrialization, and the sociological process of rationalization.

Movement

As more and more people leave villages and farms to live in cities, urban growth results. The rapid growth of cities like Chicago in the late 19th century and Mumbai a century later can be attributed largely to rural-urban migration. This kind of growth is especially commonplace in developing countries. The rapid urbanization of the world's population over the twentieth century is described in the 2005 Revision of the UN World Urbanization Prospects report. The global proportion of urban population rose dramatically from 13% (220 million) in 1900, to 29% (732 million) in 1950, to 49% (3.2 billion) in 2005. The same report projected that the figure is likely to rise to 60% (4.9 billion) by 2030. However, French economist Philippe Bocquier, writing in THE FUTURIST magazine, has calculated that "the proportion of the world population living in cities and towns in the year 2030 would be roughly 50%, substantially less than the 60% forecast by the United Nations (UN), because the messiness of rapid urbanization is unsustainable. Both Bocquier and the UN see more people flocking to cities, but Bocquier sees many of them likely to leave upon discovering that there's no work for them and no place to live."

According to the UN State of the World Population 2007 report, sometime in the middle of 2007, the majority of people worldwide will be living in towns or cities, for the first time in history; this is referred to as the arrival of the "Urban Millennium" or the 'tipping point'. In regard to future trends, it is estimated 93% of urban growth will occur in developing nations, with 80% of urban growth occurring in Asia and Africa. Urbanization rates vary between countries. The United States and United Kingdom have a far higher urbanization level than China, India, Swaziland or Niger, but a far slower annual urbanization rate, since much less of the population is living in a rural area.

- Urbanization in the United States never reached the Rocky Mountains in locations such as Jackson Hole, Wyoming; Telluride, Colorado; Taos, New Mexico; Douglas County, Colorado and Aspen, Colorado. The state of Vermont has also been affected, as has the coast of Florida, the Birmingham-Jefferson County, AL area, the Pacific Northwest and the barrier islands of North Carolina.
- In the United Kingdom, two major examples of new urbanization can be seen in Swindon, Wiltshire and Milton Keynes, Buckinghamshire. These two towns show some of the quickest growth rates in Europe.

Urbanization occurs naturally from individual and corporate efforts to reduce time and expense in commuting and transportation while improving opportunities for jobs, education, housing, and transportation. Living in cities permits individuals and families to take advantage of the opportunities of proximity, diversity, and marketplace competition. People move into cities to seek economic opportunities. A major contributing factor is known as "rural flight". In rural areas, often on small family farms, it is difficult to improve one's standard of living beyond basic sustenance. Farm living is dependent on unpredictable environmental conditions, and in times of drought, flood or pestilence, survival becomes extremely problematic. In modern times, industrialization of agriculture has negatively affected the economy of small and middle-sized farms and strongly reduced the size of the rural labour market. Cities, in contrast, are known to be places where money, services and wealth are centralized. Cities are where fortunes are made and where social mobility is possible. Businesses, which generate jobs and capital, are usually located in urban areas. Whether the source is trade or tourism, it is also through the cities that foreign money flows into a country. It is easy to see why someone living on a farm might wish to take their chance moving to the city and trying to make enough money to send back home to their struggling family. There are better basic services as well as other specialist services that aren't found in rural areas. There are more job opportunities and a greater variety of jobs. Health is another major factor. People, especially the elderly are often forced to move to cities where there are doctors and hospitals that can cater for their health needs. Other factors include a greater variety of entertainment (restaurants, movie theaters, theme parks, etc.) and a better quality of education, namely universities. Due to their high populations, urban areas can also have much more diverse social communities allowing others to find people like them when they might not be able to in rural areas. These conditions are heightened during times of change from a pre-industrial society to an industrial one. It is at this time that many new commercial enterprises are made possible, thus creating new jobs in cities. It is also a result of industrialization that farms become more mechanized, putting many labourers out of work. This is currently occurring fastest in India.

Economic Effects

In recent years, urbanization of rural areas has increased. As agriculture, more traditional local services, and small-scale industry give way to modern industry the urban and related commerce with the city drawing on the resources of an ever-widening area for its own sustenance and goods to be traded or processed into manufactures.

Research in urban ecology finds that larger cities provide more specialized goods and services to the local market and surrounding areas, function as a transportation and wholesale hub for smaller places, and accumulate more capital, financial service provision, and an educated labour force, as well as often concentrating administrative functions for the area in which they lie. This relation among places of different sizes is called the urban hierarchy.

As cities develop, effects can include a dramatic increase in costs, often pricing the local working class out of the market, including such functionaries as employees of the local municipalities. The almost universal European division into a 'good' west end and a 'poor' east end of large cities developed in this period." This is likely due the prevailing southwest wind which carries coal smoke and other airborne pollutants downwind, making the western edges of towns preferable to the eastern ones. Similar problems now affect the developing world, rising inequality resulting from rapid urbanisation trends. The drive for rapid urban growth and often efficiency can lead to less equitable urban development, think tanks such as the Overseas Development Institute have even proposed policies that encourage labour intensive growth as a means of absorbing the influx of low skilled and unskilled labour. Urbanization is often viewed as a negative trend, but can in fact, be perceived simply as a natural occurrence from individual and corporate efforts to reduce expense in commuting and transportation while improving opportunities for jobs, education, housing, and transportation. Living in cities permits individuals and families to take advantage of the opportunities of proximity, diversity, and marketplace competition.

Environmental Effects

The urban heat island has become a growing concern and is increasing over the years. The urban heat island is formed when industrial and urban areas are developed and heat becomes more abundant. In rural areas, a large part of the incoming solar energy is used to evaporate water from vegetation and soil. In cities, where less vegetation and exposed soil exists, the majority of the sun's energy is absorbed by urban structures and asphalt. Hence, during warm daylight hours, less evaporative cooling in cities allows surface temperatures to rise higher than in rural areas. Additional city heat is given off by vehicles and factories, as well as by industrial and domestic heating and cooling units. This effect causes the city to become 2 to 10° F (1 to 6° C) warmer than surrounding landscapes.. Impacts also include reducing soil moisture and intensification of carbon dioxide emissions.

In his book *Whole Earth Discipline*, Stewart Brand argues that the effects of urbanization are on the overall positive for the environment. Firstly, the birth rate of new urban dwellers falls immediately to replacement rate, and keeps falling. This can prevent overpopulation in the future. Secondly, it puts a stop to destructive subsistence farming techniques, like slash and burn agriculture. Finally, it minimizes land use by humans, leaving more for nature.

Changing Forms

Different forms of urbanization can be classified depending on the style of architecture and planning methods as well as historic growth of areas. In cities of the developed world urbanization traditionally exhibited a concentration of human activities and settlements around the downtown area, the so-called *in-migration*. In-migration refers to migration from former colonies and similar places. The fact that many immigrants settle in impoverished city centres led to the notion of the "peripheralization of the core", which simply describes that people who used to be at the periphery of the former empires now live right in the centre.

Recent developments, such as inner-city redevelopment schemes, mean that new arrivals in cities no longer necessarily settle in the centre. In some developed regions, the reverse effect, originally called counter urbanisation has occurred, with cities losing population to rural areas, and is particularly common for richer families. This has been possible because of improved communications, and has been caused by factors such as the fear of crime and poor urban environments. Later termed *"white flight"*, the effect is not restricted to cities with a high ethnic minority population.

When the residential area shifts outward, this is called suburbanization. A number of researchers and writers suggest that suburbanization has gone so far to form new points of concentration outside the downtown both in developed and developing countries such as India. This networked, poly-centric form of concentration is considered by some an emerging pattern of urbanization. It is called variously exurbia, edge city (Garreau, 1991), network city (Batten, 1995), or postmodern city (Dear, 2000). Los Angeles is the best-known example of this type of urbanization.

Rural migrants are attracted by the possibilities that cities can offer, but often settle in shanty towns and experience extreme poverty. In the 1980s, this was attempted to be tackled with the urban bias theory which was promoted by Michael Lipton who wrote: "...the most important class conflict in the poor countries of the world today is not between labour and capital. Nor is it between foreign and national interests. It is between rural classes and urban classes. The rural sector contains most of the poverty and most of the low-cost sources of potential advance; but the urban sector contains most of the articulateness, organization and power. So the urban classes have been able to win most of the rounds of the struggle with the countryside...". Most of the urban poor in developing countries able to find work can spend their lives in insecure, poorly paid jobs. According to research by the Overseas Development Institute pro-poor urbanisation will require labour intensive growth, supported by labour protection, flexible land use regulation and investments in basic services.'

Urbanization can be planned urbanization or organic. Planned urbanization, i.e. planned community or the garden city movement, is based on an advance plan, which can be prepared for military, aesthetic, economic or urban design reasons. Examples can be seen in many ancient cities; although with exploration came the collision of nations, which meant that many invaded cities took on the desired planned characteristics of their occupiers. Many ancient organic cities experienced redevelopment for military and economic purposes, new roads carved through the cities, and new parcels of land were cordoned off serving various planned purposes giving cities distinctive geometric designs.

UN agencies prefer to see urban infrastructure installed before urbanization occurs. Landscape planners are responsible for landscape infrastructure (public parks, sustainable urban drainage systems, greenways etc.) which can be planned before urbanization takes place, or afterward to revitalize an area and create greater livability within a region. Concepts of control of the urban expansion are considered in the American Institute of Planners.

Exploitation

Most often, the word *exploitation* is used to refer to economic exploitation; that is, the act of using another person's labour without offering them an adequate compensation. There are two major perspectives on economic exploitation:

- Organizational or "micro-level" exploitation: in the broad tradition of liberal economic thinking, most theories of exploitation centre on the market power of economic *organizations* within a market setting. Some neoclassical theory points to exploitation not based on market power.
- Structural or "macro-level" exploitation: "new liberal" theories focus on exploitation by large sections of society even (or *especially*) in the context of free markets. Marxist theory points to the entire capitalist class as an exploitative entity, and to capitalism as a system based on exploitation.

Developing nations (commonly called "third world countries" or "poor countries") are the focus of much debate over the issue of exploitation, particularly in the context of the global economy.

Critics of foreign companies allege, for instance, that firms such as Nike and Gap Inc. resort to child labour and sweatshops in developing nations, paying their workers wages far lower than those that prevail in developed nations (where the products are sold). This, it is argued, is insufficient to allow workers to attain the local subsistence standard of living if working hours common in the first world are observed, so that working hours much longer than in the first world are necessary. It is also argued that work conditions in these developing-world factories are much less safe and much more unhealthy than in the first world. For example, observers point to cases where employees were unable to escape factories burning down—and thus dying—because of locked doors, a common signal that sweatshop conditions exist. The Triangle Shirtwaist Factory fire of 1911 was another example, but it occurred in the US, so the first world of then is the equivalent of the third world of today. Others argue that, in the absence of compulsion, the only way that corporations are able to secure adequate supplies of labour is to offer wages and benefits superior to preexisting options, and that the presence of workers in corporate factories indicates that the factories present options which are seen as better—by the workers themselves—than the other options available to them.

A common response is that this is disingenuous, as the companies are in fact *exploiting* people by the terms of unequal human standards (applying lower standards to their third world workers than to their first world ones). Furthermore, the argument goes, if people choose to work for low wages and in unsafe conditions because it is their only alternative to starvation or scavenging from garbage dumps (the "preexisting options"), this cannot be seen as any kind of "free choice" on their part. It also argued that if a company intends to sell its products in the first world, it should pay its workers by first world standards. Following such a view, some in the United States propose that the U.S. government should mandate that businesses in foreign countries adhere to the same labour, environmental, health, and safety standards as the U.S. before they are allowed to trade with businesses in the U.S. (this has been advocated by Howard Dean, for example). They believe that such standards would improve the quality of life in less developed nations. According to others, however, this would harm the economies of less developed nations by discouraging the U.S. from trading with them. Milton Friedman is an economist who thinks that such a policy would have that effect. However, the common response to the argument that corporations exploit poor labourers by lowering working standards, wages, etc. is that the corporation only has an incentive to do business in these nations if there is this alleged "exploitation." If activists were to achieve their goal of raising work standards, it is likely that the corporation would no longer have a profit incentive to invest in that nation. The result would probably the corporation pulling back to its developed nation, leaving their former workers out of the job. Groups who see themselves as fighting against global exploitation also point to secondary effects such as the dumping of government-subsidized corn on developing world markets which forces subsistence farmers off of their lands, sending them into the cities or across borders in order to survive. More generally, some sort of international regulation of transnational corporations is called for, such as the enforcement of the International Labour Organization's labour standards.

Exploitation of Natural Resources

Some exploitation of natural resources is an essential condition of the human existence. This refers primarily to food production and necessities. The exploitation of nature is often done unsustainably and is of increasing concern as the depletion of natural resources from economic growth and population growth ultimately threatens human existence.

Why Resources are under Pressure

- Increase in sophistication of technology enabling natural resources to be extracted quickly and efficiently. *For Example*: In the past, it could take long hours just to cut down one tree only using saws. Due to increased technology, rates of deforestation have greatly increased
- A rapidly increasing population. This leads to greater demand for natural resources.
- Cultures of consumerism. Materialistic views lead to gold and diamonds mined and used for jewellery—something unnecessary for human life or advancement.
- Excessive demand often leads to conflicts due to intense competition. Organizations, such as Global Witness and the United Nations have documented the connections.
- Another reason maybe because of non-equitable distribution of resources.

Problems arising from exploitation of natural resources;

- Deforestation
- Desertification
- Extinction of species
- Soil erosion
- Oil depletion
- Ozone depletion
- Greenhouse gas increase
- Butt Depletion.

Workers have to leave their family in order to come to work in the towns and cities where the industries are found..

Change to Family Structure

The family structure changes with industrialisation. The sociologist Talcott Parsons noted that in pre-industrial societies there is an extended family structure spanning many generations who robably remained in the same location for generations.

In industrialised societies the nuclear family, consisting of only of parents and their growing children, predominates. Families and children reaching adulthood are more mobile and tend to relocate to where jobs exist.

Extended family bonds become more tenuous.

Environment

Industrialisation has spawned its own health problems. Modern stressors include noise, air, water pollution, poor nutrition, dangerous machinery, impersonal work, isolation, poverty, homelessness, and substance abuse. Health problems in industrial nations are as much caused by economic, social, political, and cultural factors as by pathogens. Industrialisation has become a major medical issue world wide.

Current Situation

In 2005, the USA was the largest producer of industrial output followed by Japan and China, according to International Monetary Fund.

Currently the "international development community" (World Bank, OECD, many United Nations departments, and some other organisations) endorses development policies like water purification or primary education.

The community does not recognise traditional industrialisation policies as being adequate to the Third World or beneficial in the longer term, with the perception that it could only create inefficient local industries unable to compete in a free-trade dominated world.

Methodology

Psychometrics

Psychometrics is the field of study concerned with the theory and technique of educational and psychological measurement, which includes the measurement of knowledge, abilities, attitudes, and personality traits. The field is primarily concerned with the construction and validation of measurement instruments, such as questionnaires, tests, and personality assessments.

It involves two major research tasks, namely: (i) the construction of instruments and procedures for measurement; and (ii) the development and refinement of theoretical approaches to measurement. Those who practice psychometrics are known as psychometricians and although they may also be clinical psychologists, they are not obliged to be so and could instead be (for example) human resources or learning and development professionals. Either way specific, separate, qualifications in psychometrics are required.

Origins and Background

Much of the early theoretical and applied work in psychometrics was undertaken in an attempt to measure intelligence. Francis Galton, often referred to as "the father of psychometrics", devised and included mental tests among his anthropometric measures. However, the origin of psychometrics also has connections to the related field of psychophysics. Two other pioneers of psychometrics obtained doctorates in the Leipzig Psychophysics Laboratory under Wilhelm Wundt: James McKeen Cattell in 1886 and Charles Spearman in 1906.

The psychometrician L. L. Thurstone, founder and first president of the Psychometric Society in 1936, developed and applied a theoretical approach to measurement referred to as the law of comparative judgment, an approach that has close connections to the psychophysical theory of Ernst Heinrich Weber and Gustav Fechner. In addition, Spearman and Thurstone both made important contributions to the theory and application of factor analysis, a statistical method developed and used extensively in psychometrics.

More recently, psychometric theory has been applied in the measurement of personality, attitudes, and beliefs, and academic achievement. Measurement of these unobservable phenomena is difficult, and much of the research and accumulated science in this discipline has been developed in an attempt to properly define and quantify such phenomena. Critics, including practitioners in the physical sciences and social activists, have argued that such definition and quantification is impossibly difficult, and that such measurements are often misused, such as with psychometric personality tests used in employment procedures:

> *"For example, an employer wanting someone for a role requiring consistent attention to repetitive detail will probably not want to give that job to someone who is very creative and gets bored easily."*

Definition of Measurement in the Social Sciences

The definition of measurement in the social sciences has a long history. A currently widespread definition, proposed by Stanley Smith Stevens (1946), is that measurement is "the assignment of numerals to objects or events according to some rule". This definition was introduced in the paper in which Stevens proposed four levels of measurement. Although widely adopted, this definition differs in important respects from the more classical definition of measurement adopted in the physical sciences, which is that *measurement is the numerical estimation and expression of the magnitude of one quantity relative to another.*

Indeed, Stevens's definition of measurement was put forward in response to the British Ferguson Committee, whose chair, A. Ferguson, was a physicist. The committee was appointed in 1932 by the British Association for the Advancement of Science to investigate the possibility of quantitatively estimating sensory events. Although its chair and other members were physicists, the committee also included several psychologists. The committee's report highlighted the importance of the definition of measurement. While Stevens's response was to propose a new definition, which has had considerable influence in the field, this was by no means the only response to the report. Another, notably different, response was to accept the classical definition, as reflected in the following statement:

> *"Measurement in psychology and physics are in no sense different. Physicists can measure when they can find the operations by which they may meet the necessary criteria; psychologists have but to do the same. They need not worry about the mysterious differences between the meaning of measurement in the two sciences."*

These divergent responses are reflected in alternative approaches to measurement. For example, methods based on covariance matrices are typically employed on the premise that numbers, such as raw scores derived from assessments, are measurements.

Such approaches implicitly entail Stevens's definition of measurement, which requires only that numbers are *assigned* according to some rule. The main research task, then, is generally considered to be the discovery of associations between scores, and of factors posited to underlie such associations.

On the other hand, when measurement models such as the Rasch model are employed, numbers are not assigned based on a rule. Instead, in keeping with Reese's statement above, specific criteria for measurement are stated, and the goal is to construct procedures or operations that provide data that meet the relevant criteria. Measurements are estimated based on the models, and tests are conducted to ascertain whether the relevant criteria have been met.

Instruments and Procedures

The first psychometric instruments were designed to measure the concept of intelligence. The best known historical approach involved the Stanford-Binet IQ test, developed originally by the French psychologist Alfred Binet. Contrary to a fairly widespread misconception, there is no compelling evidence that it is possible to measure innate intelligence through such instruments, in the sense of an innate learning capacity unaffected by experience, nor was this the original intention when they were developed. Nevertheless, intelligence tests are useful tools for various purposes. An alternative conception of intelligence is that cognitive capacities within individuals are a manifestation of a general component, or general intelligence factor, as well as cognitive capacity specific to a given domain.

Psychometrics is applied widely in educational assessment to measure abilities in domains such as reading, writing, and mathematics. The main approaches in applying tests in these domains have been Classical Test Theory and the more recent Item Response Theory and Rasch measurement models. These latter approaches permit joint scaling of persons and assessment items, which provides a basis for mapping of developmental continua by allowing descriptions of the skills displayed at various points along a continuum. Such approaches provide powerful information regarding the nature of developmental growth within various domains. Another major focus in psychometrics has been on personality testing. There have been a range of theoretical approaches to conceptualizing and measuring personality. Some of the better known instruments include the Minnesota Multiphasic Personality Inventory, the Five-Factor Model (or "Big 5") and tools such as Personality and Preference Inventory and the Myers-Briggs Type Indicator. Attitudes have also been studied extensively using psychometric approaches. A common method in the measurement of attitudes is the use of the Likert scale. An alternative method involves the application of unfolding measurement models, the most general being the Hyperbolic Cosine Model.

Theoretical Approaches

Psychometricians have developed a number of different measurement theories. These include classical test theory (CTT) and item response theory (IRT) An approach which seems mathematically to be similar to IRT but also quite distinctive, in terms of its origins and features, is represented by the Rasch model for measurement. The development of the Rasch model, and the broader class of models to which it belongs, was explicitly founded on requirements of measurement in the physical sciences.

Psychometricians have also developed methods for working with large matrices of correlations and covariances. Techniques in this general tradition include: factor analysis, a method of determining the underlying dimensions of data; multidimensional scaling, a method for finding a simple representation for data with a large number of latent dimensions; and data clustering, an approach to finding objects that are like each other. All these multivariate descriptive methods try to distill large amounts of data into simpler structures. More recently, structural equation modeling and path analysis represent more sophisticated approaches to working with large covariance matrices. These methods allow statistically sophisticated models to be fitted to data and tested to determine if they are adequate fits.

One of the main deficiencies in various factor analysis is a lack of consensus in cutting points for determining the number of latent factors. A usual procedure is to stop factoring when eigenvalues drop below one because the original sphere shrinks. The lack of the cutting points concerns other multivariate methods, also.

Key Concepts

Key concepts in classical test theory are reliability and validity. A reliable measure is one that measures a construct consistently across time, individuals, and situations. A valid measure is one that measures what it is intended to measure. A measure may be reliable without being valid. However, reliability is necessary, but not sufficient, for validity. Both reliability and validity can be assessed statistically. Consistency over repeated measures of the same test can be assessed with the Pearson correlation coefficient, and is often called *test-retest reliability*. Similarly, the equivalence of different versions of the same measure can be indexed by a Pearson correlation, and is called *equivalent forms reliability* or a similar term.

Internal consistency, which addresses the homogeneity of a single test form, may be assessed by correlating performance on two halves of a test, which is termed *split-half reliability*; the value of this Pearson product-moment correlation coefficient for two half-tests is adjusted with the Spearman-Brown prediction formula to correspond to the correlation between two full-length tests. Perhaps the most commonly used index of reliability is Cronbach's á, which is equivalent to the mean of all possible split-half coefficients. Other approaches include the intra-class correlation, which is the ratio of variance of measurements of a given target to the variance of all targets.

There are a number of different forms of validity. Criterion-related validity can be assessed by correlating a measure with a criterion measure known to be valid. When the criterion measure is collected at the same time as the measure being validated the goal is to establish *concurrent validity*; when the criterion is collected later the goal is to establish *predictive validity.* A measure has *construct validity* if it is related to measures of other constructs as required by theory. *Content validity* is a demonstration that the items of a test are drawn from the domain being measured. In a personnel selection example, test content is based on a defined statement or set of statements of knowledge, skill, ability, or other characteristics obtained from a *job analysis.* Item response theory models the relationship between latent traits and responses to test items. Among other advantages, IRT provides a basis for obtaining an estimate of the location of a test-taker on a given latent trait as well as the standard error of measurement of that location. For example, a university student's knowledge of history can be deduced from his or her score on a university test and then be compared reliably with a high school student's knowledge deduced from a less difficult test. Scores derived by classical test theory do not have this characteristic, and assessment of actual ability (rather than ability relative to other test-takers) must be assessed by comparing scores to those of a "norm group" randomly selected from the population. In fact, all measures derived from classical test theory are dependent on the sample tested, while, in principle, those derived from item response theory are not.

Standards of Quality

The considerations of validity and reliability typically are viewed as essential elements for determining the quality of any test. However, professional and practitioner associations frequently have placed these concerns within broader contexts when developing standards and making overall judgments about the quality of any test as a whole within a given context. A consideration of concern in many applied research settings is whether or not the metric of a given psychological inventory is meaningful or arbitrary.

Testing Standards

In this field, the *Standards for Educational and Psychological Testing* place standards about validity and reliability, along with errors of measurement and related considerations under the general topic of test construction, evaluation and documentation. The second major topic covers standards related to fairness in testing, including fairness in testing and test use, the rights and responsibilities of test takers, testing individuals of diverse linguistic backgrounds, and testing individuals with disabilities. The third and final major topic covers standards related to testing applications, including the responsibilities of test users, psychological testing and assessment, educational testing and assessment, testing in employment and credentialing, plus testing in program evaluation and public policy.

Evaluation Standards

In the field of evaluation, and in particular educational evaluation, the Joint Committee on Standards for Educational Evaluation has published three sets of standards for evaluations. *The Personnel Evaluation Standards* was published in 1988, *The Program Evaluation Standards* (2nd edition) was published in 1994, and *The Student Evaluation Standards* was published in 2003. Each publication presents and elaborates a set of standards for use in a variety of educational settings. The standards provide guidelines for designing, implementing, assessing and improving the identified form of evaluation. Each of the standards has been placed in one of four fundamental categories to promote educational evaluations that are proper, useful, feasible, and accurate. In these sets of standards, validity and reliability considerations are covered under the accuracy topic. For example, the student accuracy standards help ensure that student evaluations will provide sound, accurate, and credible information about student learning and performance.

Public Relations

Public relations (PR) is a field concerned with maintaining public image for businesses, non-profit organizations or high-profile people, such as celebrities and politicians. An earlier definition of public relations, by The first World Assembly of Public Relations Associations held in Mexico City in August 1978, was “the art and social science of analysing trends, predicting their consequences, counselling organizational leaders, and implementing planned programs of action, which will serve both the organization and the public interest.” Others define it as the practice of managing communication between an organization and its publics. Public relations provides an organization or individual exposure to their audiences using topics of public interest and news items that provide a third-party endorsement and do not direct payment. Once common activities include speaking at conferences, working with the media, crisis communications and social media engagement, and employee communication. The European view of public relations notes that besides a relational form of interactivity there is also a reflective paradigm that is concerned with publics and the public sphere; not only with relational, which can in principle be private, but also with public consequences of organizational behaviour. A much broader view of neo-ubiquitous interactive communication using the Internet, as outlined by Phillips and Young in Online Public Relations Second Edition (2009), describes the form and nature of Internet-mediated public relations. It encompasses social media and other channels for communication and many platforms for communication such as personal computers (PCs), mobile phones and video game consoles with Internet access.

Public relations is used to build rapport with employees, customers, investors, voters, or the general public. Almost any organization that has a stake in how it is portrayed in the public arena employs some level of public relations. There are a number of public relations disciplines falling under the banner of corporate communications, such as analyst relations, media relations, investor relations, internal communications and labour relations.

Other public relations disciplines include:

- Financial public relations-providing information mainly to business reporters
- Consumer/lifestyle public relations-gaining publicity for a particular product or service, rather than using advertising
- Crisis public relations-responding to negative accusations or information
- Industry relations-providing information to trade bodies
- Government relations-engaging government departments to influence policymaking.

In the United States of America, Edward L. Bernays, nephew of Sigmund Freud, is widely recognized as the father of public relations. In Europe and in antiquity there are many more contenders as the founders of the practice. Most notably, according to Bournemouth academic, Dr Kevin Moloney, Georgiana Cavendish, Duchess of

Devonshire with her political activism, use of printed news outlets, events management and social gatherings in the late 18th century in favour of her, predominantly, political clients, has a claim to be an early practitioner.

Two hundred years after the death of the Duchess, Bernays graduated from Cornell University in 1912 and opened the first recognized public-relations firm with Doris Fleischman in 1919. As Harold Lasswell explained in 1928, "public relations" was a term used as a way of shielding the profession from the ill repute increasingly associated with the word "propaganda": "Propaganda has become an epithet of contempt and hate, and the propagandists have sought protective coloration in such names 'public relations council,' 'specialist in public education,' 'public relations adviser.'

Global Alliance for Public Relations and Communication Management

Globally, the profession is represented by The Global Alliance for Public Relations and Communication Management, which is the umbrella organisation linking public relations professional associations worldwide. At its World Public Relations Forum in 2010, the Alliance accepted the Stockholm Accord for public relations. These accords present the practice of public relations in the following terms:

The Communicative Organisation

The concept of the communicative organisation was conceived as a result of the five-year research programme "Business Effective Communication" a collaboration between the Swedish Public Relations Association, Mälardalen University and the Stockholm School of Economics. During the project a number of cases were studied to define how information and communication can be used in the leadership of organisations in order to achieve a higher degree of external effectiveness.

The Value-creation Networks

The world is no longer a straight line from company to consumer. The organization holds a position in a network full of different stakeholders, and the network decides if you are valuable enough to keep your position. You can be replaced anytime. Your organization needs to find the perfect position where it is so valuable that the network cannot do without you. The key to this is to develop the organisation's communicative skills. This is where the communicator comes in to save the day.

The Contextual Leadership

The communicator needs to take on leadership in the communicative organization. It is his or her task to put the ideological leadership (i.e. the business idea or purpose) into the correct context. However the saying goes, perhaps selling sand in Sahara is not the best of ideas. The leadership can take different forms; as system building, mediation, coaching or influencing. The important thing is, communication is an organizational quality, rather than a function.

The Industry Today

The need for public relations personnel is growing at a fast pace. The types of clients for whom public relations people work include the government, educational institutions, nonprofit organizations, specific industries, corporations, athletic teams, entertainment companies, and even countries. The title public relations is a broad description of the field because careers that one can have in the public relations field include a publicist, media specialist, analyst, and communications specialist.

The practice of public relations is spread widely. On the professional level, there is an organization called Public Relations Society of America (PRSA), the world's largest public relations organization. PRSA is a community of more than 21,000 professionals that work to advance the skill set of public relations. PRSA also fosters a national student organization called Public Relations Student Society of America (PRSSA). In the USA, public relations professionals earn an average annual salary of $49,800 which compares with £40,000 for a practitioner with a similar job in the UK. Top earners bring home around $89,220 annually, while entry-level public relations specialists earn around $28,080. In the industry today, it is very critical for public relations professionals to learn and know the importance of new media outlets. New media outlets include blogs, social networking sites, as well as Internet radio. Public relations professionals must know that using these new media outlets are ways to directly send messages to their key publicians, also known as target audiences.

Methods, Tools and Tactics

Public relations and publicity are not synonymous, but many public relations campaigns include provisions for publicity. Publicity is the spreading of information to gain public awareness for a product, person, service, cause or organization, and can be seen as a result of effective public relations planning. More recently in public relations, professionals are using technology as their main tool to get their messages to target audiences. With the creation of social networks, blogs, and even Internet radio public relations professionals are able to send direct messages through these mediums that attract the target audiences. Methods used to find out what is appealing to target audiences include the use of surveys, conducting research or even focus groups. Tactics are the ways to attract target audiences by using the information gathered about that audience and directing a message to them using tools such as social mediums or other technology. Another emerging theme is the application of psychological theories of impression management.

Tools

There are various tools that can be used in the practice of public relations. Traditional tools include press releases and media kits which are sent out to generate positive press on behalf of the organization. Other widely-used tools include brochures, newsletters and annual reports. Increasingly, companies are utilizing interactive social media outlets, such as blogs, Twitter and Facebook, as tools in their public relations campaigns. Unlike the traditional tools which allowed for only one-way communication, social media outlets allow the organization to engage in two-way communication, and receive immediate feedback from their various stakeholders and publics.

One of the most popular and traditional tools used by public relations professionals is a press kit, also known as a media kit. A press kit is usually a folder that consists of promotional materials that give information about an event, organization, business, or even a person. What are included would be backgrounders or biographies, fact sheets, press releases (or media releases), media alerts, brochures, newsletters, photographs with captions, copies of any media clips, and social mediums. With the way that the industry has changed, many organizations may have a website with a link, "Press Room" which would have online versions of these pieces.

Targeting Publics

A fundamental technique used in public relations is to identify the target audience, and to tailor every message to appeal to that audience. It can be a general, nationwide or worldwide audience, but it is more often a segment of a population. A good elevator pitch can help tailor messaging to each target audience. Marketers often refer to socio-economically-driven "demographics", such as "black males 18-49". However, in public relations an audience is more fluid, being whoever someone wants to reach. Or, in the new paradigm of value based networked social groups, the values based social segment could be a trending audience. For example, recent political audiences seduce such buzzword monikers as "soccer moms" and "NASCAR dads."

An alternative and less flexible, more simplistic, approach uses stakeholders theory to identify people who have a stake in a given institution or issue. All audiences are stakeholders (or presumptive stakeholders), but not all stakeholders are audiences. For example, if a charity commissions a public relations agency to create an advertising campaign to raise money to find a cure for a disease, the charity and the people with the disease are stakeholders, but the audience is anyone who is likely to donate money.

Sometimes the interests of differing audiences and stakeholders common to a public relations effort necessitate the creation of several distinct but complementary messages. This is not always easy to do, and sometimes, especially in politics, a spokesperson or client says something to one audience that creates dissonance with another audience or group of stakeholders.

Lobby Groups

Lobby groups are established to influence government policy, corporate policy, or public opinion. An example of this is the American Israel Public Affairs Committee (AIPAC), which influences American foreign policy. Such groups claim to represent a particular interest and in fact are dedicated to doing so. When a lobby group hides its true purpose and support base, it is known as a front group. Moreover, governments may also lobby public relations firms in order to sway public opinion. A well illustrated example of this is the way civil war in Yugoslavia was portrayed. Governments of newly succeeded republics of Croatia and Bosnia invested heavily with American public relations firms, so that they would give them a positive war image in the USA.

Spin

In public relations, spin is sometimes a pejorative term signifying a heavily biased portrayal in specific favour of an event or situation. While traditional public relations may also rely on creative presentation of the facts, spin often, though not always, implies disingenuous, deceptive and/or highly manipulative tactics. Politicians are often accused of spin by commentators and political opponents when they produce a counterargument or position. The techniques of spin include selectively presenting facts and quotes that support ideal positions (cherry picking), the so-called "non-denial denial", phrasing that in a way presumes unproven truths, euphemisms for drawing attention away from items considered distasteful, and ambiguity in public statements. Another spin technique involves careful choice of timing in the release of certain news so it can take advantage of prominent events in the news. A famous reference to this practice occurred when British Government press officer Jo Moore used the phrase "It's now a very good day to get out anything we want to bury", (widely paraphrased or misquoted as "It's a good day to bury bad news"), in an email sent on the day of the September 11, 2001 attacks. The furor caused when this email was reported in the press eventually caused her to resign.

Spin Doctors

Skilled practitioners of spin are sometimes called "spin doctors", despite the negative connotation associated with the term. Perhaps the best-known person in the UK often described as a "spin doctor" is Alastair Campbell, who was involved with Tony Blair's public relations between 1994 and 2003, and also played a controversial role as press relations officer to the British and Irish Lions rugby union side during their 2005 tour of New Zealand. State-run media in many countries also engage in spin by selectively allowing news stories that are favorable to the government while censoring anything that could be considered critical. They may also use propaganda to indoctrinate or actively influence citizens' opinions. Privately run media may also use the same techniques of "issue" versus "non-issue" to spin its particular political viewpoints.

Other

- Publicity events, pseudo-events, photo ops or publicity stunts
- Talk show circuit: a public relations spokesperson, or the client, "does the circuit" by being interviewed on television and radio talk shows with audiences that the client wishes to reach
- Books and other writings
- Blogs
- After a public relations practitioner has been working in the field for a while, he or she accumulates a list of contacts in the media and elsewhere in the public affairs sphere. This "Rolodex" becomes a prized asset, and job announcements sometimes even ask for candidates with an existing Rolodex, especially those in the media relations area of public relations.

- Direct communication (carrying messages directly to constituents, rather than through the mass media) with, e.g., newsletters – in print and e-letters
- Collateral literature, traditionally in print and now predominantly as web sites
- Speeches to constituent groups and professional organizations; receptions; seminars, and other events; personal appearances
- The slang term for a public relations practitioner or publicist is a "flack" (sometimes spelled "flak")
- A desk visit is where the public relations person literally takes their product to the desk of the journalist in order to show them emerging promotions
- Astroturfing is the act of public relations agencies placing blog and online forum messages for their clients, in the guise of a normal "grassroots" user or comment (an illegal practice across the larger practice areas such as the European Union)
- Online social media and Internet mediated public relations practices.

Politics and Civil Society

Defining the Opponent

In the USA, but not in the larger public relations markets, the tactic known as "defining one's opponent" is used in political campaigns. Opponents can be candidates, organizations and other groups of people.

In the 2004 US presidential campaign, Howard Dean defined John Kerry as a "flip-flopper," which was widely reported and repeated by the media, particularly the conservative media. Similarly, George H.W. Bush characterized Michael Dukakis as weak on crime (the Willie Horton ad) and hopelessly liberal ("a card-carrying member of the ACLU"). In 1996, President Bill Clinton seized upon opponent Bob Dole's promise to take America back to a simpler time, promising in contrast to "build a bridge to the 21st century." This painted Dole as a person who was somehow opposed to progress.

In the debate over abortion, self-titled pro-choice groups, by virtue of their name, defined their opponents as "anti-choice", while self-titled pro-life groups refer to their opponents as "pro-abortion" or "anti-life".

Managing Language

If, in the USA, a politician or organization can use an apt phrase in relation to an issue in interviews or news releases, the news media will often repeat it verbatim, without questioning its aptness. This perpetuates both the message and whatever preconceptions might underlie it. Often, something that sounds innocuous can stand in for something greater; a "culture of life" sounds like general goodwill to most people, but will evoke opposition to abortion for many pro-life advocates. The phrase "States' rights" was used as a code for anti-civil rights legislation in the United States in the 1960s, and allegedly in the 1970s and 1980s.

Conveying the Message

The means by which a message is communicated can be as important as the message itself. Direct mail, robocalling, advertising and public speaking are commonly used depending upon the intended audience and the message that is conveyed. Press releases are also used, but since many newspapers are folding in the USA, they have become a less reliable way of communicating for American practitioners, and other methods have become more popular. In the USA and India, news organizations have begun to rely more on their own websites and have developed a variety of unique approaches to publicity and public relations, on and off the web.

Long after many initiatives across the world by more advanced nations; the use of online communication by al-Qaida dating back to 2001, the country of Israel has employed a series of Web 2.0 initiatives and are indicative of how a small nation can use internet mediated communication. Israel's initiative in 2008 included a blog, MySpace page, YouTube channel, Facebook page and a political blog to reach different audiences. The Israeli Ministry of Foreign Affairs started the country's video blog as well as its political blog. The Foreign Ministry held the first microblogging press conference via Twitter about its war with Hamas, with Consul David Saranga answering live questions from a worldwide public in common text-messaging abbreviations. The questions and answers were later posted on IsraelPolitik, the country's official political blog.

Front Groups

One of the most controversial practices in public relations is the use of front groups, organizations that purport to serve a public cause while actually serving the interests of a client whose sponsorship may be obscured or concealed.

Critics of the public relations industry, such as PR Watch, contend that some public relations firms involve a "multi-billion dollar propaganda-for-hire industry" that "concocts and spins the news, organizes phony grassroots front groups, spies on citizens, and conspires with lobbyists and politicians to thwart democracy."

Instances with the use of front groups as a public relations technique have been documented in many industries. Coal mining corporations have created "environmental groups" that contend that increased carbon dioxide emissions and global warming will contribute to plant growth and will be beneficial, trade groups for bars have created and funded citizens' groups to attack anti-alcohol groups, tobacco companies have created and funded citizens' groups to advocate for tort reform and to attack personal injury lawyers, while trial lawyers have created "consumer advocacy" front groups to oppose tort reform.

Industrial Bureaucracy

Industrial bureaucracy is the hierarchical arrangement of managements seen in the industrial world. Industrial bureaucracy represents complete control of the management, and this control may suppress the needs of the individual for the benefit of everyone. An industrial bureaucracy is run by rules and regulations.

The functions it performs are clear and concise, and are performed in a mechanistic way. The owner of the organization may not necessarily be the highest ranking official; leadership depends upon the qualifications of the person.

Organizational Structure

An organizational structure is a description of the types of coordination used to organize the actions of individuals and departments that contribute to achieving a common aim. Many organizations have hierarchical structures, but not all.

Organizations are a variant of clustered entities. An organization can be structured in many different ways, depending on their objectives. The structure of an organization will determine the modes in which it operates and performs.

Organizational structure allows the expressed allocation of responsibilities for different functions and processes to different entities such as the branch, department, workgroup and individual. Individuals in an organizational structure are normally hired under time-limited work contracts or work orders, or under permanent employment contracts or program orders.

Operational Organizations and Informal Organizations

The set organizational structure may not coincide with facts, evolving in operational action. Such divergence decreases performance, when growing. E.g. a wrong organizational structure may hamper cooperation and thus hinder the completion of orders in due time and within limits of resources and budgets. Organizational structures shall be adaptive to process requirements, aiming to optimize the ratio of effort and input to output.

An effective organizational structure shall facilitate working relationships between various entities in the organization and may improve the working efficiency within the organizational units. Organization shall retain a set order and control to enable monitoring the processes. Organization shall support command for coping with a mix of orders and a change of conditions while performing work. Organization shall allow for application of individual skills to enable high flexibility and apply creativity. When a business expands, the chain of command will lengthen and the spans of control will widen. When an organization comes to age, the flexibility will decrease and the creativity will fatigue. Therefore organizational structures shall be altered from time to time to enable recovery. If such alteration is prevented internally, the final escape is to turn down the organization to prepare for a re-launch in an entirely new set up.

Success Factors

Common success criteria for organizational structures are:

- Decentralized reporting
- Flat hierarchy
- High transient speed
- High transparency
- Low residual mass
- Permanent monitoring
- Rapid response
- Shared reliability
- Matrix hierarchy.

History

Organizational structures developed from the ancient times of hunters and collectors in tribal organizations through highly royal and clerical power structures to industrial structures and today's post-industrial structures.

Organizational Structure Types

Pre-bureaucratic Structures

Pre-bureaucratic (entrepreneurial) structures lack standardization of tasks. This structure is most common in smaller organizations and is best used to solve simple tasks. The structure is totally centralized. The strategic leader makes all key decisions and most communication is done by one on one conversations. It is particularly useful for new (entrepreneurial) business as it enables the founder to control growth and development. They are usually based on traditional domination or charismatic domination in the sense of Max Weber's tripartite classification of authority.

Bureaucratic Structures

Bureaucratic structures have a certain degree of standardization. They are better suited for more complex or larger scale organizations. They usually adopt a tall structure. Then tension between bureaucratic structures and non-bureaucratic is echoed in Burns and Stalker distinction between mechanistic and organic structures. It is not the entire thing about bureaucratic structure. It is very much complex and useful for hierarchical structures organization, mostly in tall organizations.

Post-bureaucratic

The term of post bureaucratic is used in two senses in the organizational literature: one generic and one much more specific. In the generic sense the term post bureaucratic is often used to describe a range of ideas developed since the 1980s that specifically contrast themselves with Weber's ideal type bureaucracy. This may include total quality management, culture management and matrix management, amongst others. None of these however has left behind the core tenets of Bureaucracy. Hierarchies still exist, authority is still Weber's rational, legal type, and the organization is still rule bound. Heckscher, arguing along these lines, describes them as cleaned up bureaucracies, rather than a fundamental shift away from bureaucracy. Gideon Kunda, in his classic study of culture management at 'Tech' argued that 'the essence of bureaucratic control-the formalisation, codification and enforcement of rules and regulations-does not change in principle.....it shifts focus from organizational structure to the organization's culture'. Another smaller group of theorists have developed the theory of the Post-Bureaucratic Organization., provide a detailed discussion which attempts to describe an organization that is fundamentally not bureaucratic.

Charles Heckscher has developed an ideal type, the post-bureaucratic organization, in which decisions are based on dialogue and consensus rather than authority and command, the organization is a network rather than a hierarchy, open at the boundaries (in direct contrast to culture management); there is an emphasis on meta-decision making rules rather than decision making rules. This sort of horizontal decision making by consensus model is often used in housing cooperatives, other cooperatives and when running a non-profit or community organization. It is used in order to encourage participation and help to empower people who normally experience oppression in groups. Still other theorists are developing a resurgence of interest in complexity theory and organizations, and have focused on how simple structures can be used to engender organizational adaptations. For instance, Miner *et al.* (2000) studied how simple structures could be used to generate improvisational outcomes in product development. Their study makes links to simple structures and improviseal learning. Other scholars such as Jan Rivkin and Sigglekow, and Nelson Repenning revive an older interest in how structure and strategy relate in dynamic environments.

Functional Structure

Employees within the functional divisions of an organization tend to perform a specialized set of tasks, for instance the engineering department would be staffed only with software engineers. This leads to operational efficiencies within that group. However it could also lead to a lack of communication between the functional groups within an organization, making the organization slow and inflexible.

As a whole, a functional organization is best suited as a producer of standardized goods and services at large volume and low cost. Coordination and specialization of tasks are centralized in a functional structure, which makes producing a limited amount of products or services efficient and predictable. Moreover, efficiencies can further be realized as functional organizations integrate their activities vertically so that products are sold and distributed quickly and at low cost. For instance, a small business could start making the components it requires for production of its products instead of procuring it from an external organization.But not only beneficial for organization but also for employees faiths.

Divisional Structure

Also called a "product structure", the divisional structure groups each organizational function into a division. Each division within a divisional structure contains all the necessary resources and functions within it.

Divisions can be categorized from different points of view. There can be made a distinction on geographical basis (a US division and an EU division) or on product/service basis (different products for different customers: households or companies). Another example, an automobile company with a divisional structure might have one division for SUVs, another division for subcompact cars, and another division for sedans. Each division would have its own sales, engineering and marketing departments.

Matrix Structure

The matrix structure groups employees by both function and product. This structure can combine the best of both separate structures. A matrix organization frequently uses teams of employees to accomplish work, in order to take advantage of the strengths, as well as make up for the weaknesses, of functional and decentralized forms. An example would be a company that produces two products, "product a" and "product b". Using the matrix structure, this company would organize functions within the company as follows: "product a" sales department, "product a" customer service department, "product a" accounting, "product b" sales department, "product b" customer service department, "product b" accounting department. Matrix structure is amongst the purest of organizational structures, a simple lattice emulating order and regularity demonstrated in nature.

- Weak/Functional Matrix: A project manager with only limited authority is assigned to oversee the cross-functional aspects of the project. The functional managers maintain control over their resources and project areas.
- Balanced/Functional Matrix: A project manager is assigned to oversee the project. Power is shared equally between the project manager and the functional managers. It brings the best aspects of functional and projectized organizations. However, this is the most difficult system to maintain as the sharing power is delicate proposition.
- Strong/Project Matrix: A project manager is primarily responsible for the project. Functional managers provide technical expertise and assign resources as needed.

Among these matrixes, there is no best format; implementation success always depends on organization's purpose and function.

Organizational Circle: Moving back to Flat

The flat structure is common in enterprenerial start-ups, university spin offs or small companies in general. As the company grows, however, it becomes more complex and hierarchical, which leads to an expanded structure, with more levels and departments.

Often, it would result in bureaucracy, the most prevalent structure in the past. It is still, however, relevant in former Soviet Republics and China, as well as in most governmental organizations all over the world. Shell Group used to represent the typical bureaucracy: top-heavy and hierarchical. It featured multiple levels of command and duplicate service companies existing in different regions. All this made Shell apprehensive to market changes, leading to its incapacity to grow and develop further. The failure of this structure became the main reason for the company restructuring into a matrix.

Starbucks is one of the numerous large organizations that successfully developed the matrix structure supporting their focused strategy. Its design combines functional and product based divisions, with employees reporting to two heads. Creating a team spirit, the company empowers employees to make their own decisions and train them to develop both hard and soft skills. That makes Starbucks one of the best at customer service.

Some experts also mention the multinational design, common in global companies, such as Procter & Gamble, Toyota and Unilever. This structure can be seen as a complex form of the matrix, as it maintains coordination among products, functions and geographic areas. In general, over the last decade, it has become increasingly clear that through the forces of globalization, competition and more demanding customers, the structure of many companies has become flatter, less hierarchical, more fluid and even virtual.

Team

One of the newest organizational structures developed in the 20th century is *team*. In small businesses, the team structure can define the entire organization. Teams can be both horizontal and vertical. While an organization is constituted as a set of people who synergize individual competencies to achieve newer dimensions, the quality of organizational structure revolves around the competencies of teams in totality. For example, every one of the Whole Foods Market stores, the largest natural-foods grocer in the US developing a focused strategy, is an autonomous profit centre composed of an average of 10 self-managed teams, while team leaders in each store and each region are also a team. Larger bureaucratic organizations can benefit from the flexibility of teams as well. Xerox, Motorola, and DaimlerChrysler are all among the companies that actively use teams to perform tasks.

Network

Another modern structure is network. While business giants risk becoming *too clumsy to proact (such as), act and react efficiently*, the new network organizations contract out any business function, that can be done better or more cheaply. In essence, managers in network structures spend most of their time coordinating and controlling external relations, usually by electronic means. H&M is outsourcing its clothing to a network of 700 suppliers, more than two-thirds of which are based in low-cost Asian countries. Not owning any factories, H&M can be more flexible than many other retailers in lowering its costs, which aligns with its low-cost strategy. The potential management opportunities offered by recent advances in complex networks theory have been demonstrated including applications to product design and development, and innovation problem in markets and industries.

Virtual

A special form of boundaryless organization is *virtual*. It works in a network of external alliances, using the Internet. This means while the core of the organization can be small but still the company can operate globally be a market leader in its niche. According to Anderson, because of the unlimited shelf space of the Web, the cost of reaching niche goods is falling dramatically. Although none sell in huge numbers, there are so many niche products that collectively they make a significant profit, and that is what made highly innovative Amazon.com so successful.

2

Counterproductive Work Behaviour

Counterproductive work behaviour (CWB) is employee behaviour that goes against the goals of an organization. These behaviours can be intentional or unintentional and result from a wide range of underlying causes and motivations. It has been proposed that a person-by-environment interaction can be utilized to explain a variety of counter-productive behaviours. For instance, an employee who steals from the company may do so because of lax supervision (environment) and underlying psychopathology (person) that work in concert to result in the counterproductive behaviour.

Counterproductive work behaviour is a topic of research in industrial and organizational psychologyý.

Forms of Counterproductive Work Behaviour

The forms of counterproductive work behaviour with the most empirical examination are ineffective job performance, absenteeism, job turnover, theft, and accidents. Less common but potentially more detrimental forms of counterproductive behaviour have also been investigated including theft, violence, substance use, and sexual harassment.

Within organizations, ineffective job performance is often difficult to detect, diagnose the cause of, prevent, or resolve. This is because most performance measurement systems only assess the impact of various employee behaviours rather than the behaviours themselves. Performance data is the most common method of evaluating ineffective job performance and often includes personnel data, production data, subjective evaluations, and electronic performance monitoring.

The causes of ineffective job performance have been evaluated from different theoretical approaches including: attribution theory that links performance to employee characteristics, selection errors that evaluate mistakes of hiring the wrong employees, and inadequate socialization/ training that evaluate the social environment and structured training employees receive.

Employers need to be careful to avoid the fundamental attribution error whereby performance is linked to characteristics of the employee rather than the environment.

Absenteeism is typically measured by time lost measures and frequency measures. It is weakly linked to affective predictors such as job satisfaction and commitment. Research has found that women are more likely to be absent than men, and that the absence control policies and culture of an organization will predict absenteeism.

Research on employee job turnover has attempted to understand the causes of individual decisions to leave an organization. It has been found that lower performance, lack of reward contingencies for performance, and better external job opportunities. Accidents are a serious and costly form of counterproductive behaviour. Most research on this topic has attempted to evaluate characteristics of the work-place environment that lead to accidents and determination of ways to avoid accidents. There has also been some research on the characteristics of accident-prone employees has found they are typically younger, more distractible, and less socially adjusted than other employees.

Strike

Strike action, often simply called a strike, is a work stoppage caused by the mass refusal of employees to work. A strike usually takes place in response to employee grievances. Strikes became important during the industrial revolution, when mass labour became important in factories and mines. In most countries, they were quickly made illegal, as factory owners had far more political power than workers. Most western countries partially legalized striking in the late 19th or early 20th centuries.

Strikes are sometimes used to put pressure on governments to change policies. Occasionally, strikes destabilise the rule of a particular political party. A notable example is the Gdañsk Shipyard strike led by Lech Wa^{3}êsa. This strike was significant in the struggle for political change in Poland, and was an important mobilised effort that contributed to the fall of the Iron Curtain.

History

The strike tactic has a very long history. Towards the end of the 20th dynasty, under Pharaoh Ramses III in ancient Egypt on 14 November 1152 BC, the artisans of the Royal Necropolis at Deir el-Medina organized the first known strike or workers' uprising in recorded history.

The event was reported in detail on a papyrus at the time, which has been preserved, and is currently located in Turin. The strike is narrated by John Romer in *Ancient Lives: The story of the Pharaohs' Tombmakers* The strike so terrified the Egyptian authorities, as such rebellion was virtually unheard of, that they gave in and raised their wages.

The use of the English word "strike" first appeared in 1768, when sailors, in support of demonstrations in London, "struck" or removed the topgallant sails of merchant ships at port, thus crippling the ships. Official publications have typically used the more neutral words "work stoppage" or "industrial dispute".

In 1917, the Mexican Constitution was the first national constitution that constitutionally guaranteed the right to strike.

In 1937 there were 4,740 strikes in the United States. This was the greatest strike wave in American history. This outburst of strikes occurred during a period of deep depression and massive unemployment.

A list of strikes of historic significance may be found here.

Categories of Strikes

Most strikes are undertaken by labour unions during collective bargaining. The object of collective bargaining is to obtain a contract (an agreement between the union and the company) which may include a no-strike clause which prevents strikes, or penalizes the union and/or the workers if they walk out while the contract is in force. The strike is typically reserved as a threat of last resort during negotiations between the company and the union, which may occur just before, or immediately after, the contract expires.

Sometimes a union will strike rather than sign an agreement with a no-strike clause. Such an action was documented in *Harlan County, USA*, a video about a United Mine Workers strike.

In some industrial unions, the no-strike clause is considered controversial.

Generally, strikes are rare: according to the News Media Guild, 98% of union contracts in the United States are settled each year without a strike. Occasionally, workers decide to strike without the sanction of a labour union, either because the union refuses to endorse such a tactic, or because the workers concerned are not unionized. Such strikes are often described as *unofficial*. Strikes without formal union authorization are also known as wildcat strikes.

In many countries, wildcat strikes do not enjoy the same legal protections as recognized union strikes, and may result in penalties for the union members who participate or their union. The same often applies in the case of strikes conducted without an official ballot of the union membership, as is required in some countries such as the United Kingdom.

A strike may consist of workers refusing to attend work or picketing outside the workplace to prevent or dissuade people from working in their place or conducting business with their employer. Less frequently workers may occupy the workplace, but refuse either to do their jobs or to leave. This is known as a sit-down strike (also known as an *Italian strike*, in Italian *Sciopero bianco*). A similar tactic is the work-in, where employees occupy the workplace but still continue work, often without pay, which to attempts to show they are still useful, or that worker self-management can be successful. This occurred for instance with factory occupations in the *Bienno Rossi* strikes-the "two red years" of Italy from 1919-1920.

Another unconventional tactic is work-to-rule, in which workers perform their tasks exactly as they are required to but no better. For example, workers might follow all safety regulations in such a way that it impedes their productivity or they might refuse to work overtime. Such strikes may in some cases be a form of "partial strike" or "slowdown".

During the development boom of the 1970s in Australia, the Green ban was developed by certain more socially conscious unions. This is a form of strike action taken by a trade union or other organised labour group for environmentalist or conservationist purposes. This developed from the black ban, strike action taken against a particular job or employer in order to protect the economic interests of the strikers.

United States labour law also draws a distinction, in the case of private sector employers covered by the National Labour Relations Act, between "economic" and "unfair labour practice" strikes. An employer may not fire, but may permanently replace, workers who engage in a strike over economic issues. On the other hand, employers who commit unfair labour practices (ULPs) may not replace employees who strike over ULPs, and must fire any strikebreakers they have hired as replacements in order to reinstate the striking workers.

Strikes may be specific to a particular workplace, employer, or unit within a workplace, or they may encompass an entire industry, or every worker within a city or country. Strikes that involve all workers, or a number of large and important groups of workers, in a particular community or region are known as general strikes. Under some circumstances, strikes may take place in order to put pressure on the State or other authorities or may be a response to unsafe conditions in the workplace.

A sympathy strike is, in a way, a small scale version of a general strike in which one group of workers refuses to cross a picket line established by another as a means of supporting the striking workers. Sympathy strikes, once the norm in the construction industry in the United States, have been made much more difficult to conduct due to decisions of the National Labour Relations Board permitting employers to establish separate or "reserved" gates for particular trades, making it an unlawful secondary boycott for a union to establish a picket line at any gate other than the one reserved for the employer it is picketing. Sympathy strikes may be undertaken by a union as an organization or by individual union members choosing not to cross a picket line. A jurisdictional strike in United States labour law refers to a concerted refusal to work undertaken by a union to assert its members' right to particular job assignments and to protest the assignment of disputed work to members of another union or to unorganized workers.

A student strike has the students (sometimes supported by faculty) not attending schools. In some cases, the strike is intended to draw media attention to the institution so that the grievances that are causing the students to "strike" can be aired before the public; this usually damages the institution's (or government's) public image. In other cases, especially in government-supported institutions, the student strike can cause a budgetary imbalance and have actual economic repercussions for the institution.

A hunger strike is a deliberate refusal to eat. Hunger strikes are often used in prisons as a form of political protest. Like student strikes, a hunger strike aims to worsen the public image of the target.

A "sickout", or (especially by uniformed police officers) "blue flu", is a type of strike action in which the strikers call in sick. This is used in cases where laws prohibit certain employees from declaring a strike. Police, firefighters, and air traffic controllers are among the groups commonly barred from striking: usually by state and federal laws meant to ensure the safety and/or security of the general public. So are teachers in some U.S. states. Workers have sometimes circumvented these restrictions by falsely claiming inability to work due to illness.

Newspaper writers may withhold their names from their stories as a way to protest actions of their employer.

Legal Prohibitions on Strikes

In the People's Republic of China and the Former Soviet Union

In some "Marxist-Leninist" regimes, such as the former USSR or the People's Republic of China, striking is illegal and viewed as counter-revolutionary see Trade unions in the Soviet Union, All-China Federation of Trade Unions. Since the government in such systems claims to represent the working class, it has been argued that unions and strikes were not necessary. In 1976, China signed the International Covenant on Economic, Social and Cultural Rights, which guaranteed the right to unions and striking, but Chinese officials declared that they had no interest in allowing these liberties. (In June 2008, however, the municipal government in Shenzhen in southern China introduced draft labour regulations, which labour rights advocacy groups say would, if implemented, virtually restore Chinese workers' right to strike.). Trade unions in the Soviet Union served in part as a means to educate workers about the country's economic system. Lenin referred to trade unions as "Schools of Communism." They were essentially state propaganda and control organs to regulate the workforce, also providing them with social activities.

In France

A "minimum service" during strikes in public transport was a promise of Nicolas Sarkozy during his campaign for the French presidential election. A law "on social dialogue and continuity of public service in regular terrestrial transports of passengers" was adopted on August 12, 2007, and it took effect on 1 January 2008.

This law, amongst other measures, forces certain categories of public transport workers (such as train and bus drivers) to declare to their employer 48 hours in advance if they intend to go on strike. Should they go on strike without having declared their intention to do so beforehand, they leave themselves open to sanctions.

The unions did and still do oppose this law and argue these 48 hours are used not only to pressure the workers but also to keep files on the more militant workers, who will more easily be undermined in their careers by the employers. Most importantly, they argue this law prevents the more hesitant workers from making the decision to join the strike the day before, once they've been convinced to do so by their colleagues and more particularly the union militants, who maximise their efforts in building the strike (by handing out leaflets, organising meetings, discussing the demands with their colleagues) in the last few days preceding the strike. This law makes it also more difficult for the strike to spread rapidly to other workers, as they are required to wait at least 48 hours before joining the strike.

This law also makes it easier for the employers to organise the production as it may use its human resources more effectively, knowing beforehand who is going to be at work and not, thus undermining, albeit not that much, the effects of the strike. However, this law has not had much effect as strikes in public transports still occur in France and at times, the workers refuse to comply by the rules of this law. The public transport industry-public or privately owned-remains very militant in France and keen on taking strike action when their interests are threatened by the employers or the government.

The public transport workers in France, in particular the "Cheminots" (employees of the national French railway company) are often seen as the most radical "vanguard" of the French working class. This law has not, in the eyes of many, changed this fact.

In the United Kingdom

The Industrial Relations Act 1971 was repealed through the Trade Union and Labour Relations Act 1974, sections of which were repealed by the Employment Act 1982.

The Code of Practice on Industrial Action Ballots and Notices, and sections 22 and 25 of the Employment Relations Act 2004, which concern industrial action notices, commenced on 1 October 2005.

Legislation was enacted in the aftermath of the 1919 police strikes, forbidding British police from both taking industrial action, and discussing the possibility with colleagues. The Police Federation which was created at the time to deal with employment grievances, and provide representation to police officers, has increasingly put pressure on the government, and repeatedly threatened strike action.

In the United States

The Railway Labour Act bans strikes by United States airline and railroad employees except in narrowly defined circumstances. The National Labour Relations Act generally permits strikes, but provides a mechanism to enjoin strikes in industries in which a strike would create a national emergency. The federal government most recently invoked these statutory provisions to obtain an injunction requiring the International Longshore and Warehouse Union return to work in 2002 after having been locked out by the employer group, the Pacific Maritime Association. Some jurisdictions prohibit all strikes by public employees, under laws such as the "Taylor Law" in New York. Other jurisdictions impose strike bans only on certain categories of workers, particularly those regarded as critical to society: police and firefighters are among the groups commonly barred from striking in these jurisdictions. Some states, such as Michigan, Iowa or Florida, do not allow teachers in public schools to strike. Workers have sometimes circumvented these restrictions by falsely claiming inability to work due to illness— this is sometimes called a "sickout" or "blue flu", the latter receiving its name from the uniforms worn by police officers, who are traditionally prohibited from striking. The term "red flu" has sometimes been used to describe this action when undertaken by firefighters.

Postal workers involved in 1978 wildcat strikes in Jersey City, Kearny, New Jersey, San Francisco, and Washington, D.C. were fired under the presidency of Jimmy Carter, and President Ronald Reagan fired air traffic controllers and the PATCO union after the air traffic controllers' strike of 1981.

Strikebreakers

A *strikebreaker* is someone who continues to work during strike action by trade unionists or temporary and permanent replacement workers hired to take the place of those on strike. Strikebreakers are commonly given derogatory terms like *scab* and *blackleg*. The act of working during a strike – whether by strikebreakers, management personnel, non-unionized employees or members of other unions not on strike – is known as *crossing the picket line*, regardless of whether it involves actually physically crossing a line of picketing strikers. Crossing a picket line can result in passive and/or active retaliation against that working person.

The classic example from United Kingdom industrial history is that of the miners from Nottinghamshire, who during the 1984-85 miners' strike did not support strike action by fellow mineworkers in other parts of the country. Those who supported the strike claimed that this was because they enjoyed more favourable mining conditions and thus better wages. However, the Nottinghamshire miners argued that they did not participate because the law required a ballot for a national strike and their area vote had seen around 75% vote against a strike.

Irwin, Jones, McGovern (2008) believe that the term 'scab' is part of a larger metaphor involving strikes. They argue that the picket line is symbolic of a wound and those who break its borders to return to work are the scabs who bond that wound. Others have argued that the word is not a part of a larger metaphor but, rather, originates from the old-fashioned English insult, "scab." The OED gives the etymology of 'scab' in this sense as a term of abuse or depreciation derived from the MDu. *schabbe*, applied to women with the senses 'slut' and 'scold' and 'scurvy'.

"Blackleg" is an older word and is found in the late-nineteenth/ early-twentieth century folk song from Northumberland, *Blackleg Miner*. The term does not necessarily owe its origins to this tune of unknown origin. The song is, however, notable for its lyrics that encourage violent acts against strikebreakers.

Union Strikebreaking

The concept of *union strikebreaking* or *union scabbing* refers to any circumstance in which union workers, who normally might be expected to honor picket lines established by fellow working folk during a strike, are inclined or compelled to cross those picket lines or, in some manner, otherwise engage in workplace activity which may prove injurious to the strike.

Unionized workers are sometimes required to cross the picket lines established by other unions due to their organizations having signed contracts which include no-strike clauses. The no-strike clause typically requires that members of the union not conduct any strike action for the duration of the contract; such actions are called *sympathy* or *secondary strikes*. Members who honor the picket line in spite of the contract frequently face discipline, for their action may be viewed as a violation of provisions of the contract. Therefore, any union conducting a strike action typically seeks to include a provision of amnesty for all who honored the picket line in the agreement that settles the strike.

No-strike clauses may also prevent unionized workers from engaging in solidarity actions for other workers even when no picket line is crossed. For example, striking workers in manufacturing or mining produce a product which must be transported. In a situation where the factory or mine owners have replaced the strikers, unionized transport workers may feel inclined to refuse to haul any product that is produced by strikebreakers, yet their own contract obligates them to do so.

Historically the practice of union strikebreaking has been a contentious issue in the union movement, and a point of contention between adherents of different union philosophies. For example, supporters of industrial unions, which have sought to organize entire workplaces without regard to individual skills, have criticized craft unions for organizing workplaces into separate unions according to skill, a circumstance that makes union strikebreaking more common. Union strikebreaking is not, however, unique to craft unions.

Methods used by Employers to Deal with Strikes

Most strikes called by unions are somewhat predictable; they typically occur after the contract has expired. However, not all strikes are called by union organizations — some strikes have been called in an effort to pressure employers to recognize unions. Other strikes may be spontaneous actions by working people. Spontaneous strikes are sometimes called "wildcat strikes"; they were the key fighting point in May '68; most commonly, they are responses to serious (often life-threatening) safety hazards in the workplace rather than wage or hour disputes, etc.

Whatever the cause of the strike, employers are generally motivated to take measures to prevent them, mitigate the impact, or to undermine strikes when they do occur.

Strike Preparation

Companies which produce products for sale will frequently increase inventories prior to a strike. Salaried employees may be called upon to take the place of strikers, which may entail advance training. If the company has multiple locations, personnel may be redeployed to meet the needs of reduced staff.

Companies may also take out *strike insurance* prior to an anticipated strike, to help offset the losses which the strike would cause.

Strike Breaking

Some companies negotiate with the union during a strike; other companies may see a strike as an opportunity to eliminate the union.

This is sometimes accomplished by the importation of replacement workers, strikebreakers or "scabs". Historically, strike breaking has often coincided with union busting. It was also called 'Black legging' in the early 20th century, during the Russian socialist movement.

Union Busting

One method of inhibiting a strike is elimination of the union that may launch it, which is sometimes accomplished through union busting. Union busting campaigns may be orchestrated by labour relations consultants, and may utilize the services of labour spies, or asset protection services. Similar services may be engaged during attempts to defeat organizing drives. A modern example of a union buster is The Burke Group.

Lockout

Another counter to a strike is a lockout, the form of work stoppage in which an employer refuses to allow employees to work. Two of the three employers involved in the Caravan park grocery workers strike of 2003-2004 locked out their employees in response to a strike against the third member of the employer bargaining group. Lockouts are, with certain exceptions, lawful under United States labour law.

Violence

Historically, some employers have attempted to break union strikes by force. One of the most famous examples of this occurred during the Homestead Strike of 1892. Industrialist Henry Clay Frick sent private security agents from the Pinkerton National Detective Agency to break the Amalgamated Association of Iron and Steel Workers strike at a Homestead, Pennsylvania steel mill. Two strikers were killed, twelve wounded, along with two Pinkertons killed and eleven wounded. In the aftermath, Frick was shot in the neck and then stabbed by Alexander Berkman, surviving the attack, while Berkman was sentenced to 22 years in prison.

Salary

A salary is a form of periodic payment from an employer to an employee, which may be specified in an employment contract. It is contrasted with piece wages, where each job, hour or other unit is paid separately, rather than on a periodic basis. From the point of a business, salary can also be viewed as the cost of acquiring human resources for running operations, and is then termed personnel expense or salary expense. In accounting, salaries are recorded in payroll accounts.

History

First Paid Salary

While there is no first pay stub for the first work-for-pay exchange, the first salaried work would have required a human society advanced enough to have a barter system to allow work to be exchanged for goods or other work. More significantly, it presupposes the existence of organized employers—perhaps a government or a religious body—that would facilitate work-for-hire exchanges on a regular enough basis to constitute salaried work. From this, most infer that the first salary would have been paid in a village or city during the Neolithic Revolution, sometime between 10,000 BC and 6,000 BC.

By the time of the Hebrew Book of Ezra (550 BC to 450 BC), accepting salt from a person was synonymous with drawing sustenance, taking pay, or being in that person's service. At that time salt production was strictly controlled by the monarchy or ruling elite. Depending on the translation of Ezra 4:14, the servants of King Artaxerxes I of Persia explain their loyalty variously as "because we are salted with the salt of the palace" or "because we have maintenance from the king" or "because we are responsible to the king."

The Roman Word Salarium

Similarly, the Roman word *salarium* linked employment, salt and soldiers, but the exact link is unclear. The least common theory is that the word soldier itself comes from the Latin *sal dare* (to give salt). Alternatively, the Roman historian Pliny the Elder stated as an aside in his Natural History's discussion of sea water, that "[I]n Rome...the soldier's pay was originally salt and the word salary derives from it..." *Plinius Naturalis Historia XXXI*. Others note that *soldier* more likely derives from the gold solidus, with which soldiers were known to have been paid, and maintain instead that the *salarium* was either an allowance for the purchase of salt or the price of having soldiers conquer salt supplies and guard the Salt Roads (*Via Salarium*) that led to Rome.

Payment in the Roman Empire and Medieval and Pre-industrial Europe

Regardless of the exact connection, the *salarium* paid to Roman soldiers has defined a form of work-for-hire ever since in the Western world, and gave rise to such expressions as "being worth one's salt." Yet within the Roman Empire or (later) medieval and pre-industrial Europe and its mercantile colonies, salaried employment appears to have been relatively rare and mostly limited to servants and higher status roles, especially in government service. Such roles were largely remunerated by the provision of lodging and food, and livery clothes, but cash was also paid. Many courtiers, such as valets de chambre in late medieval courts were paid annual amounts, sometimes supplemented by large if unpredictable extra payments. At the other end of the social scale, those in many forms of employment either received no pay, as with slavery (though many slaves were paid some money at least), serfdom, and indentured servitude, or received only a fraction of what was produced, as with sharecropping. Other common alternative models of work included self-or co-operative employment, as with masters in artisan guilds, who often had salaried assistants, or corporate work and ownership, as with medieval universities and monasteries.

Payment During the Commercial Revolution

Even many of the jobs initially created by the Commercial Revolution in the years from 1520 to 1650 and later during Industrialisation in the 18th and 19th centuries would not have been salaried, but, to the extent they were paid as employees, probably paid an hourly or daily wage or paid per unit produced (also called piece work).

Share in Earnings as Payment

In corporations of this time, such as the several East India Companies, many managers would have been remunerated as owner-shareholders. Such a remuneration scheme is still common today in accounting, investment, and law firm partnerships where the leading professionals are equity partners, and do not technically receive a salary, but rather make a periodic "draw" against their share of annual earnings.

The Second Industrial Revolution and Salaried Payment

From 1870 to 1930, the Second Industrial Revolution gave rise to the modern business corporation powered by railroads, electricity and the telegraph and telephone. This era saw the widespread emergence of a class of salaried executives and administrators who served the new, large-scale enterprises being created.

New managerial jobs lent themselves to salaried employment, in part because the effort and output of "office work" were hard to measure hourly or piecewise, and in part because they did not necessarily draw remuneration from share ownership.

As Japan rapidly industrialized in the 20th century, the idea of office work was novel enough that a new Japanese word (salaryman), was coined to describe those who performed it, and their remuneration.

Salaried Employment in the 20th Century

In the 20th century, the rise of the service economy made salaried employment even more common in developed countries, where the relative share of industrial production jobs declined, and the share of executive, administrative, computer, marketing, and creative jobs—all of which tended to be salaried—increased.

Salary and other Forms of Payment Today

Today, the idea of a salary continues to evolve as part of a system of all the combined rewards that employers offer to employees. Salary is coming to be seen as part of a "total rewards" system which includes bonuses, incentive pay, and commissions), benefits and perquisites (or perks), and various other tools which help employers link rewards to an employee's measured performance.

Salaries in the U.S.

In the United States, the distinction between periodic salaries (which are normally paid regardless of hours worked) and hourly wages (meeting a minimum wage test and providing for overtime) was first codified by the Fair Labour Standards Act of 1938. At that time, five categories were identified as being "exempt" from minimum wage and overtime protections, and therefore salariable. In 1991, some computer workers were added as a sixth category but effective August 23, 2004 the categories were revised and reduced back down to five (Executive, Administrative, Professional, Computer, and Outside Sales Employees). Salary is generally set on a yearly basis.

"The FLSA requires that most employees in the United States be paid at least the federal minimum wage for all hours worked and overtime pay at time and one-half the regular rate of pay for all hours worked over 40 hours in a workweek.

However, Section 13(a)(1) of the FLSA provides an exemption from both minimum wage and overtime pay for employees employed as bona fide executive, administrative, professional and outside sales employees. Section 13(a)(1) and Section 13(a)(17) also exempt certain computer employees. To qualify for exemption, employees generally must meet certain tests regarding their job duties *and* be paid on a salary basis at not less than $455 per week."

Of these five categories only Computer Employees has an hourly wage-based exemption ($27.63 per hour) while Outside Sales Employee is the only main category not to have the minimum salary ($455 per week) test though some sub categories under Professional (like teachers and practitioners of law or medicine) also do not have the minimum salary test.

A general rule for comparing periodic salaries to hourly wages is based on a standard 40 hour work week with 50 weeks per year (minus two weeks for vacation). (Example: $40,000/year periodic salary divided by 50 weeks equals $800/week. Divide $800/week by 40 standard hours equals $20/hour). Real median household income in the United States climbed 1.3 percent between 2006 and 2007, reaching $50,233 according to a report released by the U.S. census bureau. This is the third annual increase in real median household income.

Salaries in Japan

In Japan, owners would notify employees of salary increases through "jirei". The concept still exists and has been replaced with an electronic form, or email in larger companies.

Salaries in India

In India, Salaries are generally paid on the 7th of every month. The minimum wages in India are governed by the Minimum Wages Act, 1948.

Training

The term *training* refers to the acquisition of knowledge, skills, and competencies as a result of the teaching of vocational or practical skills and knowledge that relate to specific useful competencies. It forms the core of apprenticeships and provides the backbone of content at institutes of technology (also known as technical colleges or polytechnics). In addition to the basic training required for a trade, occupation or profession, observers of the labour-market recognize today the need to continue training beyond initial qualifications: to maintain, upgrade and update skills throughout working life. People within many professions and occupations may refer to this sort of training as professional development.

Some commentators use a similar term for workplace learning to improve performance: training and development. One can generally categorize such training as *on-the-job* or *off-the-job*:

- On-the-job training takes place in a normal working situation, using the actual tools, equipment, documents or materials that trainees will use when fully trained. On-the-job training has a general reputation as most effective for vocational work.

- Off-the-job training takes place away from normal work situations — implying that the employee does not count as a directly productive worker while such training takes place. Off-the-job training has the advantage that it allows people to get away from work and concentrate more thoroughly on the training itself. This type of training has proven more effective in inculcating concepts and ideas.

Training differs from exercise in that people may dabble in exercise as an occasional activity for fun. Training has specific goals of improving one's capability, capacity, and performance.

Compare:

- Education
- Learning.

Types of Training

Physical Training

Physical training concentrates on mechanistic goals: training-programs in this area develop specific skills or muscles, often with a view to peaking at a particular time. Some physical training programs focus on raising overall physical fitness.

In military use, training means gaining the physical ability to perform and survive in combat, and learning the many skills needed in a time of war. These include how to use a variety of weapons, outdoor survival skills, and how to survive capture by the enemy, among others.

For psychological or physiological reasons, people who believe it may be beneficial to them can choose to practice relaxation training, or autogenic training, in an attempt to increase their ability to relax or deal with stress. While some studies have indicated relaxation training is useful for some medical conditions, autogenic training has limited results or has been the result of few studies.

Religion and Spirituality

In religious and spiritual use, training may refer to the purification of the mind, heart, understanding and actions to obtain a variety of spiritual goals such as closeness to God or freedom from suffering. Note for example the institutionalized spiritual training of Threefold Training in Buddhism, or discipleship in Christianity.

Artificial-intelligence Feedback

Researchers have developed training-methods for artificial-intelligence devices as well. Evolutionary algorithms, including genetic programming and other methods of machine learning, use a system of feedback based on "fitness functions" to allow computer programs to determine how well an entity performs a task. The methods construct a series of programs, known as a "population" of programs, and then automatically test them for "fitness", observing how well they perform the intended task. The system automatically generates new programs based on members of the population that perform the best. These new members replace programs that perform the worst. The procedure repeats until the achievement of optimum performance. In robotics, such a system can continue to run in real-time after initial training, allowing robots to adapt to new situations and to changes in themselves, for example, due to wear or damage. Researchers have also developed robots that can appear to mimic simple human behaviour as a starting point for training.

Apprenticeship

Apprenticeship is a system of training a new generation of practitioners of a skill. Apprentices (or in early modern usage "prentices") or protégés build their careers from apprenticeships. Most of their training is done on the job while working for an employer who helps the apprentices learn their trade, in exchange for their continuing labour for an agreed period after they become skilled. Theoretical education may also be involved, informally via the workplace and/or by attending vocational schools while still being paid by the employer.

Development

The system of apprenticeship first developed in the later Middle Ages and came to be supervised by craft guilds and town governments. A master craftsman was entitled to employ young people as an inexpensive form of labour in exchange for providing food, lodging and formal training in the craft.

Most apprentices were males, but female apprentices were found in crafts such as seamstress, tailor, cordwainer, baker and stationer. Apprentices usually began at ten to fifteen years of age, and would live in the master craftsman's household. Most apprentices aspired to becoming master craftsmen themselves on completion of their contract (usually a term of seven years), but some would spend time as a journeyman and a significant proportion would never acquire their own workshop. Subsequently governmental regulation and the licensing of polytechnics and vocational education formalized and bureaucratized the details of apprenticeship.

Analogs at Universities and Professional Development

The modern concept of an internship is similar to an apprenticeship. Universities still use apprenticeship schemes in their production of scholars: bachelors are promoted to masters and then produce a thesis under the oversight of a supervisor before the corporate body of the university recognises the achievement of the standard of a doctorate. Another view of this system is of graduate students in the role of apprentices, post-docs as journeymen, and professors as masters.

Also similar to apprenticeships are the professional development arrangements for new graduates in the professions of accountancy and the law. A British example was training contracts known as 'articles of clerkship'. The learning curve in modern professional service firms, such as law firms or accountancies, generally resembles the traditional master-apprentice model: the newcomer to the firm is assigned to one or several more experienced colleagues (ideally partners in the firm) and learns his skills on the job.

Australia

Australian Apprenticeships is the new name for the scheme formerly known as 'New Apprenticeships'. Under the scheme, involving 400,000 people in 500 occupations, the Australian Government incentives and personal benefits programme are still the same. Australian Apprenticeships still encompass all apprenticeships and traineeships. They combine time at work with training and can be full-time, part-time or school-based. Youth can become apprentices starting as early as age 14 if there are willing employers.

As part of its policy paper-Skilling Australia for the Future, the Australian Government announced that it will expand the role of existing Australian Apprenticeships Centres to establish the Skills and Training Information Centres (STICs), providing information and advice skills & training.

Australian Apprenticeships is the generic term for apprentices and trainees. The distinction between the two lies mainly around traditional trades and the time it takes to gain a qualification. The Australian government uses Australian Apprenticeships Centres such as BUSY At Work or MEGT (Australia) to administer and facilitate the Australian Apprenticeships so that funding can be disseminated to eligible businesses and apprentices and trainees and to support the whole process as it underpins the future skills of Australian industry. Australia also has a fairly unique safety net in place for businesses and Australian Apprentices with its Group Training scheme. This is where businesses that are not able to employ the Australian Apprentice for the full period until they qualify, are able to lease or hire the Australian Apprentice from a Group Training Organisation. It's a safety net because the Group Training Organisation is the employer and provides continuity of employment and training for the Australian Apprentice.

Austria

Apprenticeship Training in Austria is organized in a Dual education system: company-based training of apprentices is complemented by compulsory attendance of a part-time vocational school for apprentices (Berufsschule). It lasts two to four years-the duration varies between the 250 different legally recognized apprenticeship trades.

About 40 percent of all Austrian teenagers enter apprenticeship training upon completion of compulsory education (at age 15). This number has been stable since the 1950s.

The five most popular trades are: Retail Salesperson (5,000 people complete this apprenticeship per year), Clerk (3,500/year), Car Mechanic (2,000/year), Hairdresser (1,700/year), Cook (1,600/year). There are many smaller trades with small numbers of apprentices, like "EDV-Systemtechniker" (Sysadmin) which is completed by less than 100 people a year.

The Apprenticeship Leave Certificate provides the apprentice with access to two different vocational careers. On the one hand, it is a prerequisite for the admission to the Master Craftsman Exam and for qualification tests, and on the other hand it gives access to higher education via the TVE-Exam or the Higher Education Entrance Exam which are prerequisites for taking up studies at colleges, universities, "Fachhochschulen", post-secondary courses and post-secondary colleges.

The person responsible for overseeing the training inside the company is called "Lehrherr" or "Ausbilder". An Ausbilder must prove he has the professional qualifications needed to educate another person. The "Ausbilder" must also prove he does not have a criminal record and is an otherwise respectable person. According to the laws: *the person wanting to educate a young apprentice must prove that he has an ethical way of living and the civic qualities of a good citizen.*

France

In France, apprenticeships also developed between the ninth and thirteenth centuries, with guilds structured around apprentices, journeymen and master craftsmen, continuing in this way until 1791, when the guilds were suppressed.

In 1851 the first law on apprenticeships came into force because people would kill other people. From 1919, young people had to take 150 hours of theory and general lessons in their subject a year. This minimum training time rose to 360 hours a year in 1961, then 400 in 1986.

The first training centres for apprentices (*centres de formation d'apprentis*, CFAs) appeared in 1961, and in 1971 apprenticeships were legally made part of professional training. In 1986 the age limit for beginning an apprenticeship was raised from 20 to 25. From 1987 the range of qualifications achieveable through an apprenticeship was widened to include the *brevet professionnel* (certificate of vocational aptitude), the *bac professionnel* (vocational baccalaureate diploma), the *brevet de technicien supérieur*(advanced technician's certificate), engineering diplomas, masters degree and more.

On January 18, 2005, President Jacques Chirac announced the introduction of a law on a programme for social cohesion comprising the three pillars of employment, housing and equal opportunities. The French government pledged to further develop apprenticeship as a path to success at school and to employment, based on its success: in 2005, 80% of young French people who had completed an apprenticeship entered employment. In France, the term apprenticeship often denotes manual labour but it also include other jobs like secretary, manager, engineer, shop assistant... The plan aimed to raise the number of apprentices from 365,000 in 2005 to 500,000 in 2009. To achieve this aim, the government is, for example, granting tax relief for companies when they take on apprentices. (Since 1925 a tax has been levied to pay for apprenticeships.) The minister in charge of the campaign, Jean-Louis Borloo, also hoped to improve the image of apprenticeships with an information campaign, as they are often connected with academic failure at school and an ability to grasp only practical skills and not theory. After the civil unrest end of 2005, the government, led by prime minister Dominique de Villepin, announced a new law. Dubbed "law on equality of chances", it created the First Employment Contract as well as manual apprenticeship from as early as 14 years of age. From this age, students are allowed to quit the compulsory school system in order to quickly learn a vocation. This measure has long been a policy of conservative French political parties, and was met by tough opposition from trade unions and students.

Germany

Apprenticeships are part of Germany's dual education system, and as such form an integral part of many people's working life. Finding employment without having completed an apprenticeship is almost impossible. For some particular technical university professions, such as food technology, a completed apprenticeship is often recommended; for some, such as marine engineering it may even be mandatory.

In Germany, there are 342 recognized trades (*Ausbildungsberufe*) where an apprenticeship can be completed. They include for example doctor's assistant, banker, dispensing optician, plumber or oven builder. The dual system means that apprentices spend about 50-70% of their time in companies and the rest in formal education. Depending on the profession, they may work for three to four days a week in the company and then spend one or two days at a vocational school (*Berufsschule*). This is usually the case for trade and craftspeople. For other professions, usually which require more theoretical learning, the working and school times take place blockwise e.g. in a 12–18 weeks interval. These *Berufsschulen* have been part of the education system since the 19th century.

In 2001, two thirds of young people aged under 22 began an apprenticeship, and 78% of them completed it, meaning that approximately 51% of all young people under 22 have completed an apprenticeship. One in three companies offered apprenticeships in 2003, in 2004 the government signed a pledge with industrial unions that all companies except very small ones must take on apprentices.

The latent decrease of the German population due to low birth rates is now causing a lack of young people available to start an apprenticeship.

Apprenticeship after General Education

After graduation from school at the age of fifteen to nineteen (depending on type of school), students start an apprenticeship in their chosen professions. Realschule and Gymnasium graduates usually have better chances for being accepted as an apprentice for sophisticated craft professions or apprenticeships in white-collar jobs in finance or administration.

An apprenticeship takes between 2,5 and 3,5 years. Originally, at the beginning of the 20th century, less than 1% of German students attended the Gymnasium (the 8-9 year university-preparatory school) to obtain the Abitur graduation which was the only way to university back then. In the 1950 still only 5% of German youngsters entered university and in 1960 only 6% did. Due to the risen social wealth and the increased demand for academic professionals in Germany, about 24% of the youngsters entered college/university in 2000. Of those, who did not enter university many started an apprenticeship. The apprenticeships usually end a person's education by age 18-20, but also older apprentices are accepted by the employers under certain conditions. This is frequently the case for immigrants from countries without an compatible professional training system. In the U.S. apprenticeships could occur at any age.

History

In 1969, a law (the *Berufsbildungsgesetz*) was passed which regulated and unified the vocational training system and codified the shared responsibility of the state, the unions, associations and the chambers of trade and industry. The dual system was successful in both parts of the divided Germany. In the GDR, three quarters of the working population had completed apprenticeships.

Business and Administrative Professions

The precise skills and theory taught on German apprenticeships are strictly regulated. The employer is responsible for the entire education programme coordinated by the german chamber of commerce. Apprentices obtain a special apprenticeship contract until the end of the education programme.

During the programme it is not allowed to assign the apprentice to a regularly employment and he is well protected from abrupt dismissal until the programme ends. The defined content and skillset of the apprentice profession must be fully provided and taught by the employer. The time taken is also regulated. Each profession takes a different time, usually between 24 and 36 months.

Thus, everyone who had e.g. completed an apprenticeship as an industrial manager (*Industriekaufmann*) has learned the same skills and has attended the same courses in procurement and stocking up, controlling, staffing, accounting procedures, production planning, terms of trade and transport logistics and various other subjects. Someone who has not taken this apprenticeship or did not pass the final examinations at the chamber of industry and commerce is not allowed to call himself an *Industriekaufmann*. Most job titles are legally standardized and restricted. An employment in such function in any company would require this completed degree.

Trade and Craft Professions

The rules and laws for the trade and craftswork apprentices such as mechanics, bakers, joiners, etc. are as strict as and even broader than for the business professions. The involved procedures, titles and traditions still strongly reflect the medieval origin of the system. Here, the average duration is about 36 months, some specialized crafts even take up to 42 months. After completion of the dual education, e.g. a baker is allowed to call himself a bakery journeyman (*Bäckereigeselle*). After the apprenticeship the journeyman can enter the master's school (*Meisterschule*) and continue his education at evening courses for 3–4 years or full-time for about one year. The graduation from the master's school leads to the title of a master craftsman (*Meister*) of his profession, so e.g. a bakery master is entitled as *Bäckermeister*. A master is officially entered in the local trade register, the craftspeople's roll (*Handwerksrolle*). A master craftsman is allowed to employ and to train new apprentices. In some mostly safety-related professions, e.g. that of electricians only a master is allowed to found his own company.

License for Educating Apprentices

To employ and to educate apprentices requires a specific license. The AdA-*Ausbildung der Ausbilder*-"Education of the Educators" license needs to be acquired by a training at the chamber of industry and commerce.

The masters complete this license course within their own master's coursework. The training and examination of new masters is only possible for masters who have been working several years in their profession and who have been accepted by the chambers as a trainer and examiner.

Academic professionals, e.g. engineers, seeking this license need to complete the AdA during or after their university studies, usually by a one-year evening course.

The holder of the license is only allowed to train apprentices within his own field of expertise. For example a mechanical engineer would be able to educate industrial mechanics, but not e.g. laboratory assistants or civil builders.

After the Apprenticeship of Trade and Craft Professions

When the apprenticeship is ended, the former apprentice now is considered a journeyman. He may choose to go on his journeyman years-travels.

India

In India, the Apprentices Act was enacted in 1961. It regulates the programme of training of apprentices in the industry so as to conform to the syllabi, period of training etc. as laid down by the Central Apprenticeship Council and to utilise fully the facilities available in industry for imparting practical training with a view to meeting the requirements of skilled manpower for industry.

The Apprentices Act enacted in 1961 and was implemented effectively in 1962. Initially the Act envisaged training of trade apprentices. The Act was amended in 1973 to include training of graduate and diploma engineers as "Graduate" & "Technician" Apprentices. The Act was further amended in 1986 to bring within its purview the training of the 10+2 vocational stream as "Technician (Vocational)" Apprentices.

Overall responsibility is with the Directorate General of Employment & Training (DGE&T) in the Union Ministry of Labour.

DGE&T is also responsible for implementation of the Act in respect of Trade Apprentices in the Central Govt. Undertakings & Departments. This is done through six Regional Directorates of Apprenticeship Training located at Kolkata, Mumbai, Chennai, Hyderabad, Kanpur & Faridabad.

State Apprenticeship Advisers are responsible for implementation of the Act in respect of Trade Apprentices in State Government Undertakings/Departments and Private Establishments. Department of Education in the Ministry of HRD is responsible for implementation of the Act in respect of Graduate, Technician & Technician (Vocational) Apprentices. This is done through four Boards of Apprenticeship Training located at Kanpur, Kolkata, Mumbai & Chennai.

Pakistan

In Pakistan, special apprenticeship programs running to fulfill the needs of IT industry in the coming years. So, for this purpose Pakistan Software Export Board formerly PSEB has launched a very attractive program for young IT graduates.

Under the IT Industry Apprenticeship Program, PSEB offers financial subsidy for the companies to recruit graduates possessing the basic skills and knowledge in Information Technology and other related disciplines to provide IT/ITeS services.

These recruits, generally graduates with some experience rather than traditional apprentices, are hired by companies as full-time employees and put through a 12-month program, consisting of in-company training, on-the-job training and mentoring. Since its launch, the IT Industry Apprenticeship Program has been awarded to 7 companies, approved by PSEB and ICT R&D Fund's Project Committee, which will result in the creation of over 700 job opportunities in the IT industry.

Turkey

In Turkey, apprenticeship has been part of the small business culture for centuries since the time of Seljuk Turks who claimed Anatolia as their homeland in 11th century.

There are three levels of apprenticeship. First level is the apprentice, i.e. the "cirak" in Turkish. The second level is pre-master which is called, "kalfa" in Turkish. The mastery level is called as "usta" and is the highest level of achievement. An 'usta' is eligible to take in and accept new 'ciraks' to train and bring them up. The training process usually starts when the small boy is of age 10-11 and becomes a full grown master at the age of 20-25. Many years of hard work and disciplining under the authority of the master is the key to the young apprentice's education and learning process.

In Turkey today there are many vocational schools that train children to gain skills to learn a new profession. The student after graduation looks for a job at the nearest local marketplace usually under the authority of a master.

United Kingdom

Apprenticeships have a long tradition in the United Kingdom, dating back to around the 12th century and flourishing by the 14th century. The parents or guardians of a minor would agree with a Guild's Master craftsman the conditions for an apprenticeship which would bind the minor for 5–9 years. They would pay a premium to the craftsman and the contract would be recorded in an indenture. In 1563, the Statute of Artificers and Apprentices was passed to regulate and protect the apprenticeship system, forbidding anyone from practising a trade or craft without first serving a 7-year period as an apprentice to a master (though in practice Freemen's sons could negotiate shorter terms).

From 1601, 'parish' apprenticeships under the Elizabethan Poor Law came to be used as a way of providing for poor, illegitimate and orphaned children of both sexes alongside the regular system of skilled apprenticeships, which tended to provide for boys from slightly more affluent backgrounds. These parish apprenticeships, which could be created with the assent of two Justices of the Peace, supplied apprentices for occupations of lower status such as farm labouring, brickmaking and menial household service.

In the early years of the Industrial Revolution entrepreneurs began to resist the restrictions of the apprenticeship system, and a legal ruling established that the Statute of Apprentices did not apply to trades that were not in existence when it was passed in 1563, thus excluding many new 18th century industries. In 1814 compulsory apprenticeship by indenture was abolished.

In modern times, apprenticeship became less important, especially as employment in heavy industry and artisan trades declined. Traditional apprenticeships reached their lowest point in the 1970s: by that time, training programmes were rare and people who were apprentices learned mainly by example. In 1986, National Vocational Qualifications (NVQs) were introduced, in an attempt to revitalise vocational training. Still, by 1990, apprenticeship took up only two-thirds of one percent of total employment.

In 1994, the Government introduced Modern Apprenticeships (since renamed 'Apprenticeships' in England, Wales and Northern Ireland; Scotland has retained Modern Apprenticeship), based on frameworks that are now devised by Sector Skills Councils. Apprenticeship frameworks contain a number of separately-certified elements:

- a knowledge based element, typically certified through a qualification known as a 'Technical Certificate' (this component is not mandatory in the Scottish Modern Apprenticeship);
- a competence-based element, typically certified through an NVQ (in Scotland this can be through an SVQ or an alternative Competence Based Qualification); and
- Key Skills (in Scotland, Core Skills).

In Scotland, Modern Apprenticeship Frameworks are approved by the Modern Apprenticeship Group (MAG) and it, with the support of the Scottish Government, has determined that from January 2010, all Frameworks submitted to it for approval, must have the mandatory elements credit rated for the Scottish Credit and Qualifications Framework (SCQF).

As of 2009 there are over 180 apprenticeship frameworks. Unlike traditional apprenticeships, the current scheme extends beyond craft and skilled trades to parts of the service sector with no apprenticeship tradition. The Department for Children, Schools and Families has stated its intention to make apprenticeships a "mainstream" part of England's education system.

Employers who offer apprenticeship places have an employment contract with their apprentices, but off-the-job training and assessment is wholly funded by the state for apprentices aged between 16 and 18. In England, Government only contributes 50% of the cost of training for apprentices aged 19 and over.

Government funding agencies (in England, the Learning and Skills Council) contract with 'learning providers' to deliver apprenticeships, and may accredit them as a Centre of Vocational Excellence or National Skills Academy. These organisations provide off-the-job tuition and manage the bureaucratic workload associated with the apprenticeships. Providers are usually private training companies but might also be Further Education colleges, voluntary sector organisations, Chambers of Commerce or employers themselves.

United States

Apprenticeship programs in the United States are regulated by the National Apprenticeship Act, also known as the "Fitzgerald Act."

American Apprenticeship Educational Regime

In the United States, education officials and nonprofit organizations who seek to emulate the apprenticeship system in other nations have created school to work education reforms. They seek to link academic education to careers. Some programs include job shadowing, watching a real worker for a short period of time, or actually spending significant time at a job at no or reduced pay that would otherwise be spent in academic classes or working at a local business. Some legislators raised the issue of child labour laws for unpaid labour or jobs with hazards.

In the United States, school to work programs usually occur only in high school. American high schools were introduced in the early 20th century to educate students of all ability and interests in one learning community rather than prepare a small number for college. Traditionally, American students are tracked within a wide choice of courses based on ability, with vocational courses (such as auto repair and carpentry) tending to be at the lower end of academic ability and trigonometry and pre-calculus at the upper end. American education reformers have sought to end such tracking, which is seen as a barrier to opportunity. By contrast, the system studied by the NCEE actually relies much more heavily on tracking. Education officials in the U.S., based largely on school redesign proposals by NCEE and other organizations, have chosen to use criterion-referenced tests that define one high standard that must be achieved by all students to receive a uniform diploma. American education policy under the "No Child Left Behind Act" has as an official goal the elimination of the achievement gap between populations. This has often led to the need for remedial classes in college.

Many U.S. states now requiring passing a high school graduation examination to ensure that students across all ethnic, gender and income groups possess the same skills. In states such as Washington, critics have questioned whether this ensures success for all or just creates massive failure (as only half of all 10th graders have demonstrated they can meet the standards).

There is a movement in the U.S. to revive vocational education. For example, the International Union of Painters and Allied Trades (IUPAT) has opened the Finishing Trades Institute (FTI). The FTI is working towards national accreditation so that it may offer associate and bachelor degrees that integrate academics with a more traditional apprentice programs. The IUPAT has joined forces with the Professional Decorative Painters Association (PDPA) to build educational standards using a model of apprenticeship created by the PDPA.

Example of a U.S. Apprenticeship Program

Persons interested in learning to become electricians can join one of several apprenticeship programs offered jointly by the International Brotherhood of Electrical Workers and the National Electrical Contractors Association. No background in electrical work is required. A minimum age of 18 is required. There is no maximum age. Men and women are equally invited to participate. The organization in charge of the program is called the National Joint Apprenticeship and Training Committee.

Apprentice electricians work 37 to 40 hours per week at the trade under the supervision of a journeyman electrician and receive pay and benefits. They spend an additional 6 hours per week in classroom training. At the conclusion of training (five years for commercial and industrial construction, less for residential construction), apprentices become journeymen (and women). All of this is offered at no charge, except for the cost of books (which is approximately $200 per year). Persons completing this program are considered highly skilled by employers and command high pay and benefits. Other unions such as the Ironworkers, Sheet Metal Workers, Plasterers, Bricklayers and others offer similar programs.

Trade associations such as the Independent Electrical Contractors and Associated Builders and Contractors also offer a variety of apprentice training programs.

Professional Development

Professional development refers to skills and knowledge attained for both personal development and career advancement. Professional development encompasses all types of facilitated learning opportunities, ranging from college degrees to formal coursework, conferences and informal learning opportunities situated in practice. It has been described as intensive and collaborative, ideally incorporating an evaluative stage There are a variety of approaches to professional development, including consultation, coaching, communities of practice, lesson study, mentoring, reflective supervision and technical assistance.

Who Participates and Why

A wide variety of people, such as teachers, military officers and non-commissioned officers, health care professionals, lawyers, accountants and engineers engage in professional development. Individuals may participate in professional development because of an interest in lifelong learning, a sense of moral obligation, to maintain and improve professional competence, enhance career progression, keep abreast of new technology and practice, or to comply with professional regulatory organizations. Many American states have professional development requirements for school teachers. For example, Arkansas teachers must complete 60 hours of documented professional development activities annually. Professional development credits are named differently from state to state. For example, teachers: in Indiana are required to earn 90 Continuing Renewal Units (CRUs) per year; in Massachusetts, need 150 Professional Development Points (PDPs); and in Georgia, must earn 10 Professional Learning Units (PLUs). American and Canadian nurses, as well as those in the United Kingdom, are required to participate in formal and informal professional development (earning Continuing education units, or CEUs) in order to maintain professional registration. Other groups such as engineering and geoscience regulatory bodies also have mandatory professional development requirements.

Approaches to Professional Development

In a broad sense, professional development may include *formal* types of vocational education, typically post-secondary or poly-technical training leading to qualification or credential required to obtain or retain employment. Professional development may also come in the form of pre-service or in-service professional development programs. These programs may be formal, or informal, group or individualized. Individuals may pursue professional development independently, or programs may be offered by human resource departments. Professional development on the job may develop or enhance process skills, sometimes referred to as leadership skills, as well as task skills. Some examples for process skills are 'effectiveness skills', 'team functioning skills', and 'systems thinking skills'. Professional development opportunities can range from a single workshop to a semester-long academic course, to services offered by a medley of different professional development providers and varying widely with respect to the philosophy, content, and format of the learning experiences. Some examples of approaches to professional development include:

- Case Study Method-The case method is a teaching approach that consists in presenting the students with a case, putting them in the role of a decision maker facing a problem (Hammond 1976).
- Consultation-to assist an individual or group of individuals to clarify and address immediate concerns by following a systematic problem-solving process.
- Coaching-to enhance a person's competencies in a specific skill area by providing a process of observation, reflection, and action.
- Communities of Practice-to improve professional practice by engaging in shared inquiry and learning with people who have a common goal
- Lesson Study-to solve practical dilemmas related to intervention or instruction through participation with other professionals in systematically examining practice
- Mentoring-to promote an individual's awareness and refinement of his or her own professional development by providing and recommending structured opportunities for reflection and observation
- Reflective Supervision-to support, develop, and ultimately evaluate the performance of employees through a process of

inquiry that encourages their understanding and articulation of the rationale for their own practices

- Technical Assistance-to assist individuals and their organization to improve by offering resources and information, supporting networking and change efforts

Professional development is a broad term, encompassing a range of people, interests and approaches. Those who engage in professional development share a common purpose of enhancing their ability to do their work. At the heart of professional development is the individual's interest in lifelong learning and increasing their own skills and knowledge. The 21st century has seen a significant growth in online professional development. Content providers incorporate collaborative platforms such as discussion boards and wikis, thereby encouraging and facilitating interaction, and optimizing training effectiveness.

Affirmative Action

Affirmative action refers to policies that take factors including "race, color, religion, sex or national origin" into consideration in order to benefit an underrepresented group, usually as a means to counter the effects of a history of discrimination. The focus of such policies ranges from employment and education to public contracting and health programs. "Affirmative action" is action taken to increase the representation of women and minorities in areas of employment, education, and business from which they have been historically excluded.

Origins

The term "affirmative action" originated in the United States, and first appeared in President John F. Kennedy's Executive Order 10925. The term was used to refer to measures to achieve non-discrimination. In 1965, President Lyndon Johnson issued Executive Order 11246 which required federal contractors to take "affirmative action" to hire without regard to race, religion and national origin. In 1968, gender was added to the anti-discrimination list. Matching procedures in other countries are also known as reservation in India, positive discrimination in the United Kingdom and employment equity in Canada.

Purpose

Affirmative action is an attempt to promote equal opportunity. It is often instituted in government and educational settings to ensure that minority groups within a society are included in all programs.

The justification for affirmative action is to compensate for past discrimination, persecution or exploitation by the ruling class of a culture, or to address existing discrimination.

International Policies

The International Convention on the Elimination of All Forms of Racial Discrimination stipulates that affirmative action programs may be required of countries that have ratified the convention, in order to rectify systematic discrimination. It states, however, that such programs "shall in no case entail as a consequence the maintenance of unequal or separate rights for different racial groups after the objectives for which they were taken have been achieved." The United Nations Human/animals Rights Committee states, "the principle of equality sometimes requires States parties to take affirmative action in order to diminish or eliminate conditions which cause or help to perpetuate discrimination prohibited by the Covenant. For example, in a State where the general conditions of a certain part of the population prevent or impair their enjoyment of human rights, the State should take specific action to correct those conditions. Such action may involve granting for a time to the part of the population concerned certain preferential treatment in specific matters as compared with the rest of the population. However, as long as such action is needed to correct discrimination, in fact, it is a case of legitimate differentiation under the Covenant."

National Approaches

In some countries which have laws on racial equality, affirmative action is rendered illegal because it doesn't treat all races equally. This approach of equal treatment is sometimes described as being "color blind", in hopes that it is effective against discrimination without engaging in reverse discrimination.

In such countries, the focus tends to be on ensuring equal opportunity and, for example, targeted advertising campaigns to encourage ethnic minority candidates to join the police force. This is sometimes described as "positive action."

The Americas

- Brazil. Some Brazilian Universities (State and Federal) have created systems of preferred admissions (quotas) for racial minorities (blacks and native Brazilians), the poor and people with disabilities. There are already quotas of up to 20% of vacancies reserved for the disabled in the civil public services.

The Democrats party, accusing the board of directors of University of Brasília of "nazism", questioned the constitutionality of the quotas the University reserves to minorities on the Supreme Federal Court.

- Canada. The equality section of the Canadian Charter of Rights and Freedoms explicitly permits affirmative action type legislation, although the Charter does not *require* legislation that gives preferential treatment. Subsection 2 of Section 15 states that the equality provisions do "not preclude any law, program or activity that has as its object the amelioration of conditions of disadvantaged individuals or groups including those that are disadvantaged because of race, national or ethnic origin, colour, religion, sex, age or mental or physical disability." The Canadian Employment Equity Act requires employers in federally-regulated industries to give preferential treatment to four designated groups: Women, people with disabilities, aboriginal people, and visible minorities. In most Canadian Universities, people of Aboriginal background normally have lower entrance requirements and are eligible to receive exclusive scholarships. Some provinces and territories also have affirmative action-type polices. For example, in Northwest Territories in the Canadian north, aboriginal people are given preference for jobs and education and are considered to have P1 status. Non-aboriginal people who were born in the NWT or have resided half of their life there are considered a P2, as well as women and disabled people.
- United States. Affirmative action was first established in Executive Order 10925, which was signed by President John F. Kennedy on March 6, 1961 and required government contractors to "not discriminate against any employee or applicant for employment because of race, creed, color, or national origin" as well as to "take affirmative action to ensure that applicants are employed, and that employees are treated during employment, without regard to their race, creed, color, or national origin". This executive order was superseded by Executive Order 11246, which was signed by President Lyndon B. Johnson on September 24, 1965 and affirmed the Federal Government's commitment "to promote the full realization of equal employment opportunity through a positive, continuing program in each executive department and agency". It is notable that affirmative action was not extended to women until Executive Order 11375

amended Executive Order 11246 on October 13, 1967, expanding the definition to include "sex." As it currently stands, affirmative action through Executive Order 11246 applies to "race, color, religion, sex, or national origin." In the U.S., affirmative action's original purpose was to pressure institutions into compliance with the nondiscrimination mandate of the Civil Rights Act of 1964. The Civil Rights Acts do not cover veterans, people with disabilities, or people over 40. These groups are protected from discrimination under different laws. Affirmative action has been the subject of numerous court cases, and has been contested on constitutional grounds. In 2003, a Supreme Court decision concerning affirmative action in universities allowed educational institutions to consider race as a factor in admitting students, but ruled that strict point systems are unconstitutional. Conservatives say that state officials have widely disobeyed it. Alternatively, some colleges use financial criteria to attract racial groups that have typically been under represented and typically have lower living conditions. Some states such as California (California Civil Rights Initiative) and Michigan have passed constitutional amendments banning affirmative action within their respective states. A study conducted at the University of Chicago in 2003 found that people with "black-sounding" names such as Lakisha and Jamal are 50 percent less likely to be interviewed for a job compared to people with "white-sounding" names such as Emily or Greg.

South Asia

- India
- Sri Lanka: In 1971 the Standardization policy of Sri Lankan universities was introduced as an affirmative action program for students from areas which had poor educational facilities due to 200 years purposeful discrimination by British colonialists. The British had practised communal favoritism towards Christians and the minority Tamil community for the entire 200 years they had controlled Sri Lanka, as part of a policy of divide and conquer.

East Asia

- Japan: Admission to universities as well as all government positions (including teachers) are determined by the entrance exam, which is extremely competitive at the top level. It is illegal to include sex, ethnicity or other social background (but not nationality) in criteria; however, there are informal policies to provide employment and long term welfare (which is usually not available to general public) to Burakumin at municipality level.

- People's Republic of China: "Preferential policies" required some of the top positions in governments be distributed to ethnic minorities and women. Also, many universities are required by government to give preferred admissions to ethnic minorities.
- South Korea: Admission to universities is also determined by the strict entrance exam, which is extremely competitive at the top level. But most of all Korean universities at the top level are adapting some affirmative actions in cases of Chinese ethnic minority, North Korean refugees, etc. in their recruiting new students. Besides, national universities have been pressed by the Korean government, so now they are trying to meet the governmental goal which is to recruit a proportion of female professors.

South East Asia and Oceania

- Malaysia: The Malaysian New Economic Policy or NEP serves as a form of affirmative action. Malaysia is the only other country (other one being South Africa) in the world which provides affirmative action to the majority because in general, the Malays have lower income than the Chinese who have traditionally been involved businesses and industries. Malaysia is a multiethnic country, with Malays making up the majority of close to 52% of the population. About 30% of the population are Malaysians of Chinese descent, while Malaysians of Indian descent comprise about 8% of the population. Government policy provides preferential placement for ethnic Malays, and 95% of all new intakes for the army, hospital nurses, police, and other government institutions are Malays. As of 2004, only 7% of all government servants are ethnic Chinese, a drop from 30% in 1960. All eight of the directors of the national petroleum company, Petronas, are Malays, and only 3% of Petronas employees are Chinese. Additionally, 95% of all government contracts are awarded to ethnic Malays. The mean income for Malays, Chinese and Indians in 1957/58 were 134, 288 and 228 respectively. In 1967/68 it was 154, 329 and 245, and in 1970 it was 170, 390 and 300. Mean income disparity ratio for Chinese/ Malays rose from 2.1 in 1957/58 to 2.3 in 1970, whereas for

Indians/Malays the disparity ratio also rose from 1.7 to 1.8 in the same period. The Malays viewed Independence as restoring their proper place in their own country's socioeconomic order while the non-Malays were opposing government efforts to advance Malay political primacy and economic welfare. The rising tension and resentment of the Malays for the Chinese and vice versa culminated in the vicious riots of 13 May 1969.

- New Zealand: Individuals of Mâori or other Polynesian descent are often afforded improved access to university courses, or have scholarships earmarked specifically for them.

Europe

- Finland: In certain university education programs, including legal and medical education, there are quotas for Swedish-speaking applicants. The aim of the quotas is to guarantee that a sufficient number of Swedish speaking professionals are educated, thus safeguarding the linguistic rights of the Swedish-speaking Finns. The quota system has met with criticism from the Finnish speaking majority, some of whom consider the system unfair. In addition to these linguistic quotas, women may get preferential treatment in recruitment for certain public sector jobs if there is a gender imbalance in the field.
- France: No distinctions based on race, religion or sex are allowed under the 1958 French Constitution. Since the 1980s, a French version of affirmative action based on neighbourhood is in place for primary and secondary education. Some schools, in neighborhoods labeled "Prioritary Education Zones", are granted more funds than the others. Students from these schools also benefit from special policies in certain institutions (such as Sciences Po). The French Ministry of Defence tried in 1990 to give more easily higher ranks and driving licenses to young French soldiers with North-African ancestry. After a strong protest by a young French lieutenant in the Ministry of Defence newspaper ("Armées d'aujourd'hui"), this driving license and rank project was cancelled. After the Sarkozy election, a new attempt in favour of Arabian-French students was made but Sarkozy did not gain enough political support to change the French constitution. However, highly ranked French schools do implement affirmative action in that they are obligated to take a certain amount of students from impoverished families.

- Germany: Article 3 of the German basic law provides for equal rights of all people regardless of sex, race or social background. There are programs stating that if men and women have equal qualifications, women have to be preferred for a job; moreover, the handicapped should be preferred to healthy people. This is typical for all positions in state and university service as of 2007, typically using the phrase "We try to increase diversity in this line of work". In recent years, there has been a long public debate about whether to issue programs that would grant women a privileged access to jobs in order to fight discrimination. Germany's *Left Party* brought up the discussion about affirmative action in Germany's school system. According to Stefan Zillich, quotas should be "a possibility" to help working class children who did not do well in school gain access to a *Gymnasium* (University-preparatory school). Headmasters of *Gymnasien* have objected, saying that this type of policy would "be a disservice" to poor children.

In 2009 the Berlin Senate decided that Berlin's Gymnasium should no longer be allowed to handpick all of their students. It was ruled that while Gymnasien should be able to pick 70 % to 65 % of their students, the other places at the Gymnasien are to be allocated by lottery. Every child will be able to enter the lottery, no matter how he or she performed in primary school. It is hoped that this policy will increase the number of working class students attending a Gymnasium. The Left proposed that Berlin Gymnasien should no longer be allowed to expel students who perform poorly so that the students who won a Gymnasium place in the lottery have a fair chance of graduating from that school. It is not clear yet if Berlin's senate will decide in favour of The Lefts proposal. There is also a discussion going on if affirmative action should be employed to help the children and grandchildren of the so called Gastarbeiter gain better access to German universities. One prominent proponent of this was Lord Ralf Dahrendorf It is argued that the Gastarbeiter willingly came to Germany to help build the industry and this should be honored.

- Norway: In all public limited companies (PCL) boards, either gender should be represented by 40%. This affects roughly 400 companies.
- Republic of Macedonia: Minorities, most notably Albanians, are allocated quotas for access to state universities, as well as in civil public services.

- Romania: Roma people (gipsy) are allocated quotas for access to state universities.
- Slovakia: The Constitutional Court declared in October 2005 that affirmative action i.e. "providing advantages for people of an ethnic or racial minority group" as being against its Constitution.
- Sweden: Special treatments of certain groups are commonplace in Sweden. Leveraging of the opportunities of these groups is encouraged by the state. One example is the police, who give women and people from other cultural and ethnic backgrounds concessions when it comes to testing for entrance to the police academy.
- United Kingdom: In the UK, any discrimination, quotas or favouritism on the grounds of sex, race and ethnicity is generally illegal in both education and employment. Specific exceptions include:
  - The 1998 Good Friday Agreement required that the Police Service of Northern Ireland recruit equal numbers of Catholics and Protestants in order to eliminate the service's perceived bias towards Protestants.
  - The Labour Party passed the Sex Discrimination (Election Candidates) Act 2002, allowing them to use all-women shortlists to select more women as election candidates.

South Africa

The Apartheid government favoured white-owned companies and as a result, the majority of companies in South Africa were, and still are owned by white people. The aforementioned policies achieved the desired results, but in the process they marginalised and excluded black people. A notable exception is the high number of businesses owned and operated by people of Indian descent-keen business people who thrived even under Apartheid laws due to their entrepreneurship and the political difficulties faced by them. Many people of Chinese ancestry in South Africa, also classified as "black" under the Apartheid government, also thrived through owning and operating their own businesses.

When the new majority government came to power in 1994, led by the ANC, they decided to implement an affirmative action campaign to correct previous imbalances. As such, the previously disenfranchised majority and minority groups are being supported by forcing the formerly privileged white minority group to implement certain policies. These policies include quotas regarding how much of the procurement is from non-white companies, how much of the equity is owned by non-whites, how many employees are non-white and what position the non-whites have.

The Employment Equity Act and the Broad Based Black Economic Empowerment Act aim to promote and achieve equality in the workplace (in South Africa termed "equity"), by not only advancing people from designated groups but also specifically dis-advancing the others. Those specifically hindered are the white minority. By legal definition, the designated groups who are to be advanced in society include all people of color, white women, people with disabilities, and people from rural areas. The term "black economic empowerment" is somewhat of a misnomer, therefore, because the acts cover empowerment of any member of the designated groups, regardless of race. However, government's employment legislation reserves 80% of new jobs for black people and favours black-owned companies. It is quota-based, with specific required outcomes. By a relatively complex scoring system, which allows for some flexibility in the manner in which each company meets its legal commitments, each company is required to meet minimum requirements in terms of representation by previously disadvantaged groups. The matters covered include equity ownership, representation at employee and management level (up to board of director level), procurement from black-owned businesses and social investment programs, amongst others. In 2008, the High Court in South Africa has ruled that Chinese South Africans are to be reclassified as black people. As a result of this ruling, ethnically Chinese citizens will be able to benefit from government Black Economic Empowerment (BEE) policies.

There is growing discontent in South Africa that the Broad Based Black Economic Empowerment Act has only enriched a select few black people in the country, generally those who were well-connected within the ANC so as to benefit from smart BEE deals and tender awarding, often thought to border on corruption. The same black people appear further enriched in each large BEE deal made in South Africa.

3

Industrial Leadership

Leadership has been described as the "process of social influence in which one person can enlist the aid and support of others in the accomplishment of a common task." Definitions more inclusive of followers have also emerged. Alan Keith stated that, "Leadership is ultimately about creating a way for people to contribute to making something extraordinary happen." Tom DeMarco says that leadership needs to be distinguished from posturing.

The following sections discuss several important aspects of leadership including a description of what leadership is and a description of several popular theories and styles of leadership. This article also discusses topics such as the role of emotions and vision, as well as leadership effectiveness and performance, leadership in different contexts, how it may differ from related concepts (i.e., management), and some critiques of leadership as generally conceived.

Leadership is "organizing a group of people to achieve a common goal." The leader may or may not have any formal authority. Students of leadership have produced theories involving traits, situational interaction, function, behaviour, power, vision and values, charisma, and intelligence among others.

Early History

The search for the characteristics or traits of leaders has been ongoing for centuries. History's greatest philosophical writings from Plato's *Republic* to Plutarch's *Lives* have explored the question of "What qualities distinguish an individual as a leader?" Underlying this search was the early recognition of the importance of leadership and the assumption that leadership is rooted in the characteristics that certain individuals possess. This idea that leadership is based on individual attributes is known as the "trait theory of leadership."

This view of leadership, the trait theory, was explored at length in a number of works in the previous century. Most notable are the writings of Thomas Carlyle and Francis Galton, whose works have prompted decades of research. In *Heroes and Hero Worship* (1841), Carlyle identified the talents, skills, and physical characteristics of men who rose to power. In Galton's (1869) *Hereditary Genius*, he examined leadership qualities in the families of powerful men. After showing that the numbers of eminent relatives dropped off when moving from first degree to second degree relatives, Galton concluded that leadership was inherited. In other words, leaders were born, not developed. Both of these notable works lent great initial support for the notion that leadership is rooted in characteristics of the leader.

For decades, this trait-based perspective dominated empirical and theoretical work in leadership. Using early research techniques, researchers conducted over a hundred studies proposing a number of characteristics that distinguished leaders from nonleaders: intelligence, dominance, adaptability, persistence, integrity, socioeconomic status, and self-confidence just to name a few.

Rise of Alternative Theories

In the late 1940s and early 1950s, however, a series of qualitative reviews of these studies prompted researchers to take a drastically different view of the driving forces behind leadership. In reviewing the extant literature, Stogdill and Mann found that while some traits were common across a number of studies, the overall evidence suggested that persons who are leaders in one situation may not necessarily be leaders in other situations. Subsequently, leadership was no longer characterized as an enduring individual trait, as situational approaches posited that individuals can be effective in certain situations, but not others. This approach dominated much of the leadership theory and research for the next few decades.

Reemergence of Trait Theory

New methods and measurements were developed after these influential reviews that would ultimately reestablish the trait theory as a viable approach to the study of leadership. For example, improvements in researchers' use of the round robin research design methodology allowed researchers to see that individuals can and do emerge as leaders across a variety of situations and tasks. Additionally, during the 1980s statistical advances allowed researchers to conduct meta-analyses, in which they could quantitatively analyse and summarize the findings from a wide array of studies. This advent allowed trait theorists to create a comprehensive and parsimonious picture of previous leadership research rather than rely on the qualitative reviews of the past. Equipped with new methods, leadership researchers revealed the following:

- Individuals can and do emerge as leaders across a variety of situations and tasks
- Significant relationships exist between leadership and such individual traits as:
- intelligence
- adjustment
- extraversion
- conscientiousness
- openness to experience
- general self-efficacy.

While the trait theory of leadership has certainly regained popularity, its reemergence has not been accompanied by a corresponding increase in sophisticated conceptual frameworks.

Specifically, Zaccaro (2007) noted that trait theories still:

1. Focus on a small set of individual attributes such as Big Five personality traits, to the neglect of cognitive abilities, motives, values, social skills, expertise, and problem-solving skills
2. Fail to consider patterns or integrations of multiple attributes
3. Do not distinguish between those leader attributes that are generally not malleable over time and those that are shaped by, and bound to, situational influences
4. Do not consider how stable leader attributes account for the behavioural diversity necessary for effective leadership.

Attribute Pattern Approach

Considering the criticisms of the trait theory outlined above, several researchers have begun to adopt a different perspective of leader individual differences-the leader attribute pattern approach. In contrast to the traditional approach, the leader attribute pattern approach is based on theorists' arguments that the influence of individual characteristics on outcomes is best understood by considering the person as an integrated totality rather than a summation of individual variables. In other words, the leader attribute pattern approach argues that integrated constellations or combinations of individual differences may explain substantial variance in both leader emergence and leader effectiveness beyond that explained by single attributes, or by additive combinations of multiple attributes.

Behavioural and Style Theories

In response to the early criticisms of the trait approach, theorists began to research leadership as a set of behaviours, evaluating the behaviour of 'successful' leaders, determining a behaviour taxonomy and identifying broad leadership styles. David McClelland, for example, Leadership takes a strong personality with a well developed positive ego. Not so much as a pattern of motives, but a set of traits is crucial.

Kurt Lewin, Ronald Lipitt, and Ralph White developed in 1939 the seminal work on the influence of leadership styles and performance. The researchers evaluated the performance of groups of eleven-year-old boys under different types of work climate. In each, the leader exercised his influence regarding the type of group decision making, praise and criticism and the management of the group tasks (project management) according to three styles: (1) authoritarian, (2) democratic and (3) laissez-faire. *Authoritarian climates* were characterized by leaders who make decisions alone, demand strict compliance to his orders, and dictate each step taken; future steps were uncertain to a large degree.

The leader is not necessarily hostile but is aloof from participation in work and commonly offers personal praise and criticism for the work done. *Democratic climates* were characterized by collective decision processes, assisted by the leader. Before accomplishing tasks, perspectives are gained from group discussion and technical advice from a leader. Members are given choices and collectively decide the division of labour. Praise and criticism in such an environment are objective, fact minded and given by a group member without necessarily having participated extensively in the actual work. *Laissez faire climates* gave freedom to the group for policy determination without any participation from the leader. The leader remains uninvolved in work decisions unless asked, does not participate in the division of labour, and very infrequently gives praise. The results seemed to confirm that the democratic climate was preferred.

The managerial grid model is also based on a behavioural theory. The model was developed by Robert Blake and Jane Mouton in 1964 and suggests five different leadership styles, based on the leaders' concern for people and their concern for goal achievement.

B.F. Skinner is the father of Behaviour Modification and developed the concept of positive reinforcement. Positive reinforcement occurs when a positive stimulus is presented in response to a behaviour, increasing the likelihood of that behaviour in the future. The following is an example of how positive reinforcement can be used in a business setting. Assume praise is a positive reinforcer for a particular employee. This employee does not show up to work on time every day. The manager of this employee decides to praise the employee for showing up on time every day the employee actually shows up to work on time. As a result, the employee comes to work on time more often because the employee likes to be praised. In this example, praise (i.e. stimulus) is a positive reinforcer for this employee because the employee arrives (i.e. behaviour) to work on time more frequently after being praised for showing up to work on time.

The use of positive reinforcement is a successful and growing technique used by leaders to motivate and attain desired behaviours from subordinates. Organizations such as Frito-Lay, 3M, Goodrich, Michigan Bell, and Emery Air Freight have all used reinforcement to increase productivity. Empirical research covering the last 20 years suggests that reinforcement theory has a 17 percent increase in performance. Additionally, many reinforcement techniques such as the use of praise are inexpensive, providing higher performance for lower costs.

Situational and Contingency Theories

Situational theory also appeared as a reaction to the trait theory of leadership. Social scientists argued that history was more than the result of intervention of great men as Carlyle suggested. Herbert Spencer (1884) said that the times produce the person and not the other way around. This theory assumes that different situations call for different characteristics; according to this group of theories, no single optimal psychographic profile of a leader exists. According to the theory, "what an individual actually does when acting as a leader is in large part dependent upon characteristics of the situation in which he functions."

Some theorists started to synthesize the trait and situational approaches. Building upon the research of Lewin et al., academics began to normatize the descriptive models of leadership climates, defining three leadership styles and identifying which situations each style works better in. The *authoritarian leadership style*, for example, is approved in periods of crisis but fails to win the "hearts and minds" of their followers in the day-to-day management; the *democratic leadership style* is more adequate in situations that require consensus building; finally, the *laissez faire leadership style* is appreciated by the degree of freedom it provides, but as the leader does not "take charge", he can be perceived as a failure in protracted or thorny organizational problems. Thus, theorists defined the style of leadership as contingent to the situation, which is sometimes classified as contingency theory. Four contingency leadership theories appear more prominently in the recent years: Fiedler contingency model, Vroom-Yetton decision model, the path-goal theory, and the Hersey-Blanchard situational theory.

The Fiedler contingency model bases the leader's effectiveness on what Fred Fiedler called *situational contingency*. This results from the interaction of leadership style and situational favorableness (later called "situational control"). The theory defined two types of leader: those who tend to accomplish the task by developing good-relationships with the group (*relationship-oriented*), and those who have as their prime concern carrying out the task itself (*task-oriented*). According to Fiedler, there is no ideal leader. Both task-oriented and relationship-oriented leaders can be effective if their leadership orientation fits the situation. When there is a good leader-member relation, a highly structured task, and high leader position power, the situation is considered a "favorable situation". Fiedler found that task-oriented leaders are more effective in extremely favourable or unfavourable situations, whereas relationship-oriented leaders perform best in situations with intermediate favourability.

Victor Vroom, in collaboration with Phillip Yetton (1973) and later with Arthur Jago (1988), developed a taxonomy for describing leadership situations, taxonomy that was used in a normative decision model where leadership styles were connected to situational variables, defining which approach was more suitable to which situation. This approach was novel because it supported the idea that the same manager could rely on different group decision making approaches depending on the attributes of each situation. This model was later referred as situational contingency theory.

The path-goal theory of leadership was developed by Robert House (1971) and was based on the expectancy theory of Victor Vroom. According to House, the essence of the theory is "the meta proposition that leaders, to be effective, engage in behaviours that complement subordinates' environments and abilities in a manner that compensates for deficiencies and is instrumental to subordinate satisfaction and individual and work unit performance.

The theory identifies four leader behaviours, *achievement-oriented*, *directive*, *participative*, and *supportive*, that are contingent to the environment factors and follower characteristics. In contrast to the Fiedler contingency model, the path-goal model states that the four leadership behaviours are fluid, and that leaders can adopt any of the four depending on what the situation demands. The path-goal model can be classified both as a contingency theory, as it depends on the circumstances, but also as a transactional leadership theory, as the theory emphasizes the reciprocity behaviour between the leader and the followers.

The situational leadership model proposed by Hersey and Blanchard suggests four leadership-styles and four levels of follower-development. For effectiveness, the model posits that the leadership-style must match the appropriate level of followership-development. In this model, leadership behaviour becomes a function not only of the characteristics of the leader, but of the characteristics of followers as well.

Functional Theory

Functional leadership theory is a particularly useful theory for addressing specific leader behaviours expected to contribute to organizational or unit effectiveness. This theory argues that the leader's main job is to see that whatever is necessary to group needs is taken care of; thus, a leader can be said to have done their job well when they have contributed to group effectiveness and cohesion. While functional leadership theory has most often been applied to team leadership it has also been effectively applied to broader organizational leadership as well. In summarizing literature on functional leadership, Klein, Zeigert, Knight, and Xiao (2006) observed five broad functions a leader performs when promoting organisation's effectiveness. These functions include: (1) environmental monitoring, (2) organizing subordinate activities, (3) teaching and coaching subordinates, (4) motivating others, and (5) intervening actively in the group's work.

A variety of leadership behaviours are expected to facilitate these functions. In initial work identifying leader behaviour, Fleishman (1953) observed that subordinates perceived their supervisors' behaviour in terms of two broad categories referred to as consideration and initiating structure. Consideration includes behaviour involved in fostering effective relationships. Examples of such behaviour would include showing concern for a subordinate or acting in a supportive manner towards others. Initiating structure involves the actions of the leader focused specifically on task accomplishment. This could include role clarification, setting performance standards, and holding subordinates accountable to those standards.

Transactional and Transformational Theories

The transactional leader is given power to perform certain tasks and reward or punish for the team's performance. It gives the opportunity to the manager to lead the group and the group agrees to follow his lead to accomplish a predetermined goal in exchange for something else. Power is given to the leader to evaluate, correct and train subordinates when productivity is not up to the desired level and reward effectiveness when expected outcome is reached.

The transformational leader motivates its team to be effective and efficient. Communication is the base for goal achievement focusing the group on the final desired outcome or goal attainment. This leader is highly visible and uses chain of command to get the job done. Transformational leaders focus on the big picture, needing to be surrounded by people who take care of the details. The leader is always looking for ideas that move the organization to reach the company's vision.

Emotions

Leadership can be perceived as a particularly emotion-laden process, with emotions entwined with the social influence process. In an organization, the leader's mood has some effects on his/her group. These effects can be described in 3 levels:

1. The mood of individual group members. Group members with leaders in a positive mood experience more positive mood than do group members with leaders in a negative mood. The leaders transmit their moods to other group members through the mechanism of emotional contagion. Mood contagion may be one of the psychological mechanisms by which charismatic leaders influence followers.
2. The affective tone of the group. Group affective tone represents the consistent or homogeneous affective reactions within a group. Group affective tone is an aggregate of the moods of the individual members of the group and refers to mood at the group level of analysis. Groups with leaders in a positive mood have a

more positive affective tone than do groups with leaders in a negative mood.

3. Group processes like coordination, effort expenditure, and task strategy. Public expressions of mood impact how group members think and act. When people experience and express mood, they send signals to others. Leaders signal their goals, intentions, and attitudes through their expressions of moods. For example, expressions of positive moods by leaders signal that leaders deem progress toward goals to be good. The group members respond to those signals cognitively and behaviourally in ways that are reflected in the group processes.

In research about client service, it was found that expressions of positive mood by the leader improve the performance of the group, although in other sectors there were other findings.

Beyond the leader's mood, her/his behaviour is a source for employee positive and negative emotions at work. The leader creates situations and events that lead to emotional response. Certain leader behaviours displayed during interactions with their employees are the sources of these affective events. Leaders shape workplace affective events. Examples – feedback giving, allocating tasks, resource distribution. Since employee behaviour and productivity are directly affected by their emotional states, it is imperative to consider employee emotional responses to organizational leaders. Emotional intelligence, the ability to understand and manage moods and emotions in the self and others, contributes to effective leadership in organizations. Leadership is about being responsible.

Neo-emergent Theory

The Neo-emergent leadership theory (from the Oxford school of leadership) espouses that leadership is created through the emergence of information by the leader or other stakeholders, not through the true actions of the leader himself. In other words, the reproduction of information or stories form the basis of the perception of leadership by the majority. It is well known that the great naval hero Lord Nelson often wrote his own versions of battles he was involved in, so that when he arrived home in England he would receive a true hero's welcome. In modern society, the press, blogs and other sources report their own views of a leader, which may be based on reality, but may also be based on a political command, a payment, or an inherent interest of the author, media or leader. Therefore, it can be contended that the perception of all leaders is created and in fact does not reflect their true leadership qualities at all.

Environmental Leadership Theory

The Environmental leadership model (Carmazzi) describes leadership from a Group dynamics perspective incorporating group psychology and self awareness to nurture "Environments" that promote self sustaining group leadership based on personal emotional gratification from the activities of the group. The Environmental Leader creates the psychological structure by which employees can find and attain this gratification through work or activity.

It stems from the idea that each individual has various environments that bring out different facets from their own Identity, and each facet is driven by emotionally charged perceptions within each environment... The Environmental Leader creates a platform through education and awareness where individuals fill each others emotional needs and become more conscious of when, and how they affect personal and team emotional gratifications. This is accomplished by knowing why people "react" to their environment instead of act intelligently.

"Environmental Leadership is not about changing the mindset of the group or individual, but in the cultivation of an environment that brings out the best and inspires the individuals in that group. It is not the ability to influence others to do something they are not committed to, but rather to nurture a culture that motivates and even excites individuals to do what is required for the benefit of all. It is not carrying others to the end result, but setting the surrounding for developing qualities in them to so they may carry each other."

Carmazzi

The role of an Environmental Leader is to instill passion and direction to a group and the dynamics of that group. This leader implements a psychological support system within a group that fills the emotional and developmental needs of the group.

Styles

Leadership style refers to a leader's behaviour. It is the result of the philosophy, personality and experience of the leader.

Kurt Lewin

Kurt Lewin and colleagues identified different styles of leadership:

- Autocratic
- Participative
- Laissez-Faire.

Autocratic or Authoritarian Style

Under the autocratic leadership style, all decision-making powers are centralized in the leader, as with dictator leaders.

They do not entertain any suggestions or initiatives from subordinates. The autocratic management has been successful as it provides strong motivation to the manager. It permits quick decision-making, as only one person decides for the whole group and keeps each decision to himself until he feels it is needed to be shared with the rest of the group.

Participative or Democratic Style

The democratic leadership style favors decision-making by the group as shown, such as leader gives instruction after consulting the group. They can win the co-operation of their group and can motivate them effectively and positively. The decisions of the democratic leader are not unilateral as with the autocrat because they arise from consultation with the group members and participation by them.

Laissez-faire or Free Rein Style

A free rein leader does not lead, but leaves the group entirely to itself as shown; such a leader allows maximum freedom to subordinates, i.e., they are given a free hand in deciding their own policies and methods.

Different situations call for different leadership styles. In an emergency when there is little time to converge on an agreement and where a designated authority has significantly more experience or expertise than the rest of the team, an autocratic leadership style may be most effective; however, in a highly motivated and aligned team with a homogeneous level of expertise, a more democratic or laissez-faire style may be more effective. The style adopted should be the one that most effectively achieves the objectives of the group while balancing the interests of its individual members.

Performance

In the past, some researchers have argued that the actual influence of leaders on organizational outcomes is overrated and romanticized as a result of biased attributions about leaders. Despite these assertions however, it is largely recognized and accepted by practitioners and researchers that leadership is important, and research supports the notion that leaders do contribute to key organizational outcomes. To facilitate successful performance it is important to understand and accurately measure leadership performance. Job performance generally refers to behaviour that is expected to contribute to organizational success. Campbell identified a number of specific types of performance dimensions; leadership was one of the dimensions that he identified. There is no consistent, overall definition of leadership performance (Yukl, 2006). Many distinct conceptualizations are often lumped together under the umbrella of leadership performance, including outcomes such as leader effectiveness, leader advancement, and leader emergence. For instance, leadership performance may be used to refer to the career success of the individual leader, performance of the group or organization, or even leader emergence. Each of these measures can be considered conceptually distinct. While these aspects may be related, they are different outcomes and their inclusion should depend on the applied/research focus.

Contexts—Organizations

An organization that is established as an instrument or means for achieving defined objectives has been referred to as a formal organization. Its design specifies how goals are subdivided and reflected in subdivisions of the organization. Divisions, departments, sections, positions, jobs, and tasks make up this work structure. Thus, the formal organization is expected to behave impersonally in regard to relationships with clients or with its members. According to Weber's definition, entry and subsequent advancement is by merit or seniority. Each employee receives a salary and enjoys a degree of tenure that safeguards her/him from the arbitrary influence of superiors or of powerful clients. The higher his position in the hierarchy, the greater his presumed expertise in adjudicating problems that may arise in the course of the work carried out at lower levels of the organization. It is this bureaucratic structure that forms the basis for the appointment of heads or chiefs of administrative subdivisions in the organization and endows them with the authority attached to their position.

In contrast to the appointed head or chief of an administrative unit, a leader emerges within the context of the informal organization that underlies the formal structure. The informal organization expresses the personal objectives and goals of the individual membership. Their objectives and goals may or may not coincide with those of the formal organization. The informal organization represents an extension of the social structures that generally characterize human life — the spontaneous emergence of groups and organizations as ends in themselves.

In prehistoric times, humanity was preoccupied with personal security, maintenance, protection, and survival. Now humanity spends a major portion of waking hours working for organizations. Her/His need to identify with a community that provides security, protection, maintenance, and a feeling of belonging continues unchanged from prehistoric times. This need is met by the informal organization and its emergent, or unofficial, leaders.

Leaders emerge from within the structure of the informal organization. Their personal qualities, the demands of the situation, or a combination of these and other factors attract followers who accept their leadership within one or several overlay structures. Instead of the authority of position held by an appointed head or chief, the emergent leader wields influence or power. Influence is the ability of a person to gain co-operation from others by means of persuasion or control over rewards. Power is a stronger form of influence because it reflects a person's ability to enforce action through the control of a means of punishment.

A leader is a person who influences a group of people towards a specific result. It is not dependent on title or formal authority. (elevos, paraphrased from Leaders, Bennis, and Leadership Presence, Halpern & Lubar). Leaders are recognized by their capacity for caring for others, clear communication, and a commitment to persist. An individual who is appointed to a managerial position has the right to command and enforce obedience by virtue of the authority of his position. However, she or he must possess adequate personal attributes to match his authority, because authority is only potentially available to him. In the absence of sufficient personal competence, a manager may be confronted by an emergent leader who can challenge her/his role in the organization and reduce it to that of a figurehead. However, only authority of position has the backing of formal sanctions. It follows that whoever wields personal influence and power can legitimize this only by gaining a formal position in the hierarchy, with commensurate authority. Leadership can be defined as one's ability to get others to willingly follow. Every organization needs leaders at every level.

Management

Over the years the philosophical terminology of "management" and "leadership" have, in the organisational context, been used both as synonyms and with clearly differentiated meanings. Debate is fairly common about whether the use of these terms should be restricted, and generally reflects an awareness of the distinction made by Burns

(1978) between "transactional" leadership (characterised by e.g. emphasis on procedures, contingent reward, management by exception) and "transformational" leadership (characterised by e.g. charisma, personal relationships, creativity).

Group Leadership

In contrast to individual leadership, some organizations have adopted group leadership. In this situation, more than one person provides direction to the group as a whole. Some organizations have taken this approach in hopes of increasing creativity, reducing costs, or downsizing. Others may see the traditional leadership of a boss as costing too much in team performance. In some situations, the maintenance of the boss becomes too expensive-either by draining the resources of the group as a whole, or by impeding the creativity within the team, even unintentionally.

A common example of group leadership involves cross-functional teams. A team of people with diverse skills and from all parts of an organization assembles to lead a project. A team structure can involve sharing power equally on all issues, but more commonly uses *rotating leadership*. The team member(s) best able to handle any given phase of the project become(s) the temporary leader(s). Additionally, as each team member has the opportunity to experience the elevated level of empowerment, it energizes staff and feeds the cycle of success. Leaders who demonstrate persistence, tenacity, determination and synergistic communication skills will bring out the same qualities in their groups. Good leaders use their own inner mentors to energize their team and organizations and lead a team to achieve success.

According to the National School Boards Association (USA): These Group Leadership or Leadership Teams have specific characteristics:

Characteristics of a Team

- There must be an awareness of unity on the part of all its members.
- There must be interpersonal relationship. Members must have a chance to contribute, learn from and work with others.
- The member must have the ability to act together toward a common goal.

Ten characteristics of well-functioning teams:

- Purpose: Members proudly share a sense of why the team exists and are invested in accomplishing its mission and goals.

- Priorities: Members know what needs to be done next, by whom, and by when to achieve team goals.
- Roles: Members know their roles in getting tasks done and when to allow a more skilful member to do a certain task.
- Decisions: Authority and decision-making lines are clearly understood.
- Conflict: Conflict is dealt with openly and is considered important to decision-making and personal growth.
- Personal traits: members feel their unique personalities are appreciated and well utilized.
- Norms: Group norms for working together are set and seen as standards for every one in the groups.
- Effectiveness: Members find team meetings efficient and productive and look forward to this time together.
- Success: Members know clearly when the team has met with success and share in this equally and proudly.
- Training: Opportunities for feedback and updating skills are provided and taken advantage of by team members.

Primates

Richard Wrangham and Dale Peterson, in *Demonic Males: Apes and the Origins of Human Violence* present evidence that only humans and chimpanzees, among all the animals living on earth, share a similar tendency for a cluster of behaviours: violence, territoriality, and competition for uniting behind the one chief male of the land. This position is contentious. Many animals beyond apes are territorial, compete, exhibit violence, and have a social structure controlled by a dominant male (lions, wolves, etc.), suggesting Wrangham and Peterson's evidence is not empirical. However, we must examine other species as well, including elephants (which are matriarchal and follow an alpha female), meerkats (who are likewise matriarchal), and many others.

It would be beneficial, to examine that most accounts of leadership over the past few millennia (since the creation of Christian religions) are through the perspective of a patriarchal society, founded on Christian literature. If one looks before these times, it is noticed that Pagan and Earth-based tribes in fact had female leaders. It is important also to note that the peculiarities of one tribe cannot necessarily be ascribed to another, as even our modern-day customs differ. The current day patrilineal custom is only a recent invention in human history and our original method of familial practices were matrilineal (Dr. Christopher Shelley and Bianca Rus, UBC). The fundamental assumption that has been built into 90% of the world's countries is that patriarchy is the 'natural' biological predisposition of homo sapiens. Unfortunately, this belief has led to the widespread oppression of women in all of those countries, but in varying degrees. (Whole Earth Review, Winter, 1995 by Thomas Laird, Michael Victor). The Iroquoian First Nations tribes are an example of a matrilineal tribe, along with Mayan tribes, and also the society of Meghalaya, India. (Laird and Victor,).

By comparison, bonobos, the second-closest species-relatives of man, do *not* unite behind the chief male of the land. The bonobos show deference to an alpha or top-ranking female that, with the support of her coalition of other females, can prove as strong as the strongest male in the land. Thus, if leadership amounts to getting the greatest number of followers, then among the bonobos, a female almost always exerts the strongest and most effective leadership. However, not all scientists agree on the allegedly "peaceful" nature of the bonobo or its reputation as a "hippie chimp".

Historical Views

Sanskrit literature identifies ten types of leaders. Defining characteristics of the ten types of leaders are explained with examples from history and mythology.

Aristocratic thinkers have postulated that leadership depends on one's blue blood or genes: monarchy takes an extreme view of the same idea, and may prop up its assertions against the claims of mere aristocrats by invoking divine sanction: see the divine right of kings. Contrariwise, more democratically-inclined theorists have pointed to examples of meritocratic leaders, such as the Napoleonic marshals profiting from careers open to talent.

In the autocratic/paternalistic strain of thought, traditionalists recall the role of leadership of the Roman *pater familias*. Feminist thinking, on the other hand, may object to such models as patriarchal and posit against them emotionally-attuned, responsive, and consensual empathetic guidance, which is sometimes associated with matriarchies.

Comparable to the Roman tradition, the views of Confucianism on "right living" relate very much to the ideal of the (male) scholar-leader and his benevolent rule, buttressed by a tradition of filial piety.

Leadership is a matter of intelligence, trustworthiness, humaneness, courage, and discipline... Reliance on intelligence alone results in rebelliousness. Exercise of humaneness alone results in weakness. Fixation on trust results in folly. Dependence on the strength of courage results in violence. Excessive discipline and sternness in command result in cruelty. When one has all five virtues together, each appropriate to its function, then one can be a leader. — Sun Tzu

In the 19th century, the elaboration of anarchist thought called the whole concept of leadership into question. (Note that the *Oxford English Dictionary* traces the word "leadership" in English only as far back as the 19th century.) One response to this denial of élitism came with Leninism, which demanded an élite group of disciplined cadres to act as the vanguard of a socialist revolution, bringing into existence the dictatorship of the proletariat.

Other historical views of leadership have addressed the seeming contrasts between secular and religious leadership. The doctrines of Caesaro-papism have recurred and had their detractors over several centuries. Christian thinking on leadership has often emphasized stewardship of divinely-provided resources-human and material-and their deployment in accordance with a Divine plan. Compare servant leadership.

Action Oriented Environments

This is a unique approach to team leadership that is aimed at action oriented environments where effective functional leadership is required to achieve critical or reactive tasks by small teams deployed into the field. In other words leadership of small groups often created to respond to a situation or critical incident.

In most cases these teams are tasked to operate in remote and changeable environments with limited support or backup (action environments). Leadership of people in these environments requires a different set of skills to that of front line management. These leaders must effectively operate remotely and negotiate both the needs of the individual, team and task within a changeable environment. This has been termed Action Oriented Leadership. Some example action oriented leadership is demonstrated in the following ways: extinguishing a rural fire, locating a missing person, leading a team on an outdoor expedition or rescuing a person from a potentially hazardous environment.

Titles Emphasizing Authority

At certain stages in their development, the hierarchies of social ranks implied different degrees or ranks of leadership in society. Thus a knight led fewer men in general than did a duke; a baronet might in theory control less land than an earl. In the course of the 18th and 20th centuries, several political operators took non-traditional paths to become dominant in their societies. They or their systems often expressed a belief in strong individual leadership, but existing titles and labels ("King", "Emperor", "President" and so on) often seemed inappropriate, insufficient or downright inaccurate in some circumstances. The formal or informal titles or descriptions they or their flunkies employ express and foster a general veneration for leadership of the inspired and autocratic variety. The definite article when used as part of the title (in languages that use definite articles) emphasizes the existence of a sole "true" leader.

Critical Thought

Noam Chomsky and others have brought critical thinking to the very concept of leadership and have provided an analysis that asserts that people abrogate their responsibility to think and will actions for themselves.

While the conventional view of leadership is rather satisfying to people who "want to be told what to do", these critics say that one should question why they are being subjected to a will or intellect other than their own if the leader is not a Subject Matter Expert (SME).

The fundamentally anti-democratic nature of the leadership principle is challenged by the introduction of concepts such as autogestion, employeeship, common civic virtue, etc., which stress individual responsibility and/or group authority in the work place and elsewhere by focusing on the skills and attitudes that a person needs in general rather than separating out leadership as the basis of a special class of individuals.

Similarly, various historical calamities are attributed to a misplaced reliance on the principle of leadership.

Varieties of Individual Power

According to Patrick J. Montana and Bruce H. Charnov, the ability to attain these unique powers is what enables leadership to influence subordinates and peers by controlling organizational resources. The successful leader effectively uses these power(s) to influence employees, and it is important for the leader to understand the uses of power to strengthen the leadership functioning.

The authors distinguish the following types of organizational power:

- Legitimate Power refers to the different types of professional positions within an organization structure that inherent such power. E.g. Manager, Vice President, Director, Supervisor, et cetera. These levels of power commands to the hierarchical executive levels within the organization itself. The higher position such as President of the company has a higher power than the rest of professional positions in the hierarchical executive levels.
- Reward Power given the power to managers that attain administrative power over a range of rewards. Employees whom work for managers desire the reward from the manager, they will be influenced by receiving them as the product of work performance. The rewards may be the obvious—pay raise or promotions.
- Coercive Power given the manager's ability to punish an employee whom did not follow the company policy, loss of profit, et cetera. Punishment can be determined range of mild to serious punishment... a mild punishment is a suspension and serious punishment is actual termination.
- Expert Power an expert power attained by the manager by their own talents such as skills, knowledge, abilities, or previous experience. Any of these manager has the power within the organization will be very valuable and important manager in the company.
- Charisma Power a manager has a charisma that will positively influence on workers, and admired manager that creates the opportunity for interpersonal influence. A person has charisma, and this will confer great power as a manager.
- Referent Power a power that gained by association. This person with whom he or she is associated or has a relationship, often referred to assistant or deputy.
- Information Power a person who has possession of important information at a important time when such information is needed to organizational functioning. Someone who has this information knowledge has genuine power. Manager's secretary would be in a powerful position if a secretary has information power.

Human Resource Management

Human resource management (HRM) is the strategic and coherent approach to the management of an organization's most valued assets-the people working there who individually and collectively contribute to the achievement of the objectives of the business. The terms "human resource management" and "human resources" (HR) have largely replaced the term "personnel management" as a description of the processes involved in managing people in organizations. In simple words, HRM means employing people, developing their capacities, utilizing, maintaining and compensating their services in tune with the job and organizational requirement.

Features

Its features include:

- Organizational management
- Personnel administration
- Manpower management
- Industrial management.

But these traditional expressions are becoming less common for the theoretical discipline. Sometimes even employee and industrial relations are confusingly listed as synonyms, although these normally refer to the relationship between management and workers and the behaviour of workers in companies. The theoretical discipline is based primarily on the assumption that employees are individuals with varying goals and needs, and as such should not be thought of as basic business resources, such as trucks and filing cabinets.

The field takes a positive view of workers, assuming that virtually all wish to contribute to the enterprise productively, and that the main obstacles to their endeavors are lack of knowledge, insufficient training, and failures of process.

Human Resource Management (HRM) is seen by practitioners in the field as a more innovative view of workplace management than the traditional approach. Its techniques force the managers of an enterprise to express their goals with specificity so that they can be understood and undertaken by the workforce, and to provide the resources needed for them to successfully accomplish their assignments. As such, HRM techniques, when properly practiced, are expressive of the goals and operating practices of the enterprise overall. HRM is also seen by many to have a key role in risk reduction within organisations.

Synonyms such as *personnel management* are often used in a more restricted sense to describe activities that are necessary in the recruiting of a workforce, providing its members with payroll and benefits, and administrating their work-life needs. So if we move to actual definitions, Torrington and Hall (1987) define personnel management as being:

> *"a series of activities which: first enable working people and their employing organisations to agree about the objectives and nature of their working relationship and, secondly, ensures that the agreement is fulfilled".*

While Miller (1987) suggests that HRM relates to:

> *".......those decisions and actions which concern the management of employees at all levels in the business and which are related to the implementation of strategies directed towards creating and sustaining competitive advantage".*

Academic Theory

Research in the area of HRM has much to contribute to the organisational practice of HRM. For the last 20 years, empirical work has paid particular attention to the link between the practice of HRM and organisational performance, evident in improved employee commitment, lower levels of absenteeism and turnover, higher levels of skills and therefore higher productivity, enhanced quality and efficiency. This area of work is sometimes referred to as 'Strategic HRM' or SHRM. The notion of best practice-sometimes called 'high commitment' HRM-proposes that the adoption of certain best practices in HRM will result in better organisational performance. Perhaps the most popular work in this area is that of Pfeffer who argued that there were seven best practices for achieving competitive advantage through people and 'building profits by putting people first'. These practices included: providing employment security, selective hiring, extensive training, sharing information, self-managed teams, high pay based on company performance and the reduction of status differentials.

Best fit, or the contingency approach to HRM, argues that HRM improves performance where there is a close vertical fit between the HRM practices and the company's strategy. This link ensures close coherence between the HR people processes and policies and the external market or business strategy. There are a range of theories about the nature of this vertical integration. For example, a set of 'lifecycle' models argue that HR policies and practices can be mapped onto the stage of an organisation's development or lifecycle. Competitive advantage models take Porter's (1985) ideas about strategic choice and map a range of HR practices onto the organisation's choice of competitive strategy. Finally 'configurational models' provide a more sophisticated approach which advocates a close examination of the organisation's strategy in order to determine the appropriate HR policies and practices. However, this approach assumes that the strategy of the organisation can be identified-many organisations exist in a state of flux and development.

The Resource Based View (RBV), argued by some to be at the foundation of modern HRM, focusses on the internal resources of the organisation and how they contribute to competitive advantage. The uniqueness of these resources is preferred to homogeneity and HRM has a central role in developing human resources that are valuable, rare, difficult to copy or substitute and that are effectively organised. Overall, the theory of HRM argues that the goal of human resource management is to help an organization to meet strategic goals by attracting, and maintaining employees and also to manage them effectively. The key word here perhaps is "fit", i.e. a HRM approach seeks to ensure a fit between the management of an organisation's employees, and the overall strategic direction of the company (Miller, 1989). The basic premise of the academic theory of HRM is that humans are not machines, therefore we need to have an interdisciplinary examination of people in the workplace. Fields such as psychology, industrial relations, industrial engineering, sociology, economics, and critical theories: postmodernism, post-structuralism play a major role. Many colleges and universities offer bachelor and master degrees in Human Resources Management or in Human Resources and Industrial Relations. One widely used scheme to describe the role of HRM, developed by Dave Ulrich, defines 4 fields for the HRM function:

- Strategic business partner
- Change management
- Employee champion
- Administration.

However, many HR functions these days struggle to get beyond the roles of administration and employee champion, and are seen as reactive rather than strategically proactive partners for the top management. In addition, HR organisations also have difficulty in proving how their activities and processes add value to the company. Only in recent years have HR scholars and professionals focused on developing models that can measure the value added by HR.

Business Practice

Human resources management involves several processes. Together they are supposed to achieve the above mentioned goal. These processes can be performed in an HR department, but some tasks can also be outsourced or performed by line-managers or other departments. When effectively integrated they provide significant economic benefit to the company.

- Workforce planning
- Recruitment (sometimes separated into attraction and selection)
- Induction, Orientation and Onboarding
- Skills management
- Training and development
- Personnel administration
- Compensation in wage or salary
- Time management
- Travel management (sometimes assigned to accounting rather than HRM)
- Payroll (sometimes assigned to accounting rather than HRM)
- Employee benefits administration
- Personnel cost planning
- Performance appraisal
- Labour relations.

HRM Strategy

An HRM strategy pertains to the means as to how to implement the specific functions of HRM. An organization's HR function may possess recruitment and selection policies, disciplinary procedures, reward/recognition policies, an HR plan, or learning and development policies, however all of these functional areas of HRM need to be aligned and correlated, in order to correspond with the overall business strategy. An HRM strategy thus is an overall plan, concerning the implementation of specific HRM functional areas.

An HRM strategy typically consists of the following factors:

- "Best fit" and "best practice"-meaning that there is correlation between the HRM strategy and the overall corporate strategy. As HRM as a field seeks to manage human resources in order to achieve properly organizational goals, an organization's HRM strategy seeks to accomplish such management by applying a firm's personnel needs with the goals/objectives of the organisation. As an example, a firm selling cars could have a corporate strategy of increasing car sales by 10% over a five year period. Accordingly, the HRM strategy would seek to facilitate how exactly to manage personnel in order to achieve the 10% figure. Specific HRM functions, such as recruitment and selection, reward/recognition, an HR plan, or learning and development policies, would be tailored to achieve the corporate objectives.

- Close co-operation (at least in theory) between HR and the top/ senior management, in the development of the corporate strategy. Theoretically, a senior HR representative should be present when an organization's corporate objectives are devised. This is so, since it is a firm's personnel who actually construct a good, or provide a service. The personnel's proper management is vital in the firm being successful, or even existing as a going concern. Thus, HR can be seen as one of the critical departments within the functional area of an organization.
- Continual monitoring of the strategy, via employee feedback, surveys, etc.

The implementation of an HR strategy is not always required, and may depend on a number of factors, namely the size of the firm, the organizational culture within the firm or the industry that the firm operates in and also the people in the firm.

An HRM strategy can be divided, in general, into two facets-the people strategy and the HR functional strategy. The people strategy pertains to the point listed in the first paragraph, namely the careful correlation of HRM policies/actions to attain the goals laid down in the corporate strategy. The HR functional strategy relates to the policies employed within the HR functional area itself, regarding the management of persons internal to it, to ensure its own departmental goals are met.

Functions

The Human Resources Management (HRM) function includes a variety of activities, and key among them is deciding what staffing needs you have and whether to use independent contractors or hire employees to fill these needs, recruiting and training the best employees, ensuring they are high performers, dealing with performance issues, and ensuring your personnel and management practices conform to various regulations. Activities also include managing your approach to employee benefits and compensation, employee records and personnel policies. Usually small businesses (for-profit or nonprofit) have to carry out these activities themselves because they can't yet afford part-or full-time help. However, they should always ensure that employees have—and are aware of—personnel policies which conform to current regulations. These policies are often in the form of employee manuals, which all employees have.

Note that some people distinguish a difference between HRM (a major management activity) and HRD (Human Resource Development, a profession). Those people might include HRM in HRD, explaining that HRD includes the broader range of activities to develop personnel inside of organizations, including, e.g., career development, training, organization development, etc.

There is a long-standing argument about where HR-related functions should be organized into large organizations, e.g., "should HR be in the Organization Development department or the other way around?"

The HRM function and HRD profession have undergone major changes over the past 20–30 years. Many years ago, large organizations looked to the "Personnel Department," mostly to manage the paperwork around hiring and paying people. More recently, organizations consider the "HR Department" as playing an important role in staffing, training and helping to manage people so that people and the organization are performing at maximum capability in a highly fulfilling manner.

Professional Industrial Management in India

India has a people and leadership crisis despite its huge population. Corporates whine that the Indian education system does not produce 'employable human resources.' Engineers need to be re-skilled before they can write software and face clients confidently. Graduates need extensive training before they can turn call specialists, sales staff or store managers. B-school graduates go through companies as management trainees to become functional managers...

In the midst of a high growth era, where Indian companies have been consumed by the challenge of base level hiring, have enough and competent leaders been groomed? Most Indian companies, I suspect, have been woefully myopic on that count. Thus, one sees expatriates being hired at astronomical salaries or 'the good line manager' from a well-regarded breeding ground bagging a leadership position.

Neither of the two approaches can yield results. The expatriate is hamstrung by the lack of experience with a diverse population: India, as a country, is arguably more diverse than Europe is, as a continent. The good line manager — newly crowned and eager to flag his/her arrival — is unable to come to terms right away with his/her newfound power. Most attempt to run away like racing stock and fail to understand that putting together ambitious yet happy teams is the sustainable way to build businesses.

There is no short cut to building one's own leadership. Besides business skills, leadership needs to be steeped in the culture of the company and aligned to its goals. To my mind, this is India Inc's biggest challenge, in its march forward. If one looks at the dominance of the American corporate on the world stage, one can single out leadership as the most important factor. To cite an example, GE had groomed three strong leaders to take over from Jack Welch. Within days of Jeffrey Immelt being appointed as the successor, 3M and Home Depot snapped up the other two incumbents James McNerney and Robert Nardelli, respectively. GE filled three top positions from within its ranks. With ease. Here are a few haves in leadership, in the Indian context:

Importance of Continuity and Assertiveness

Successive, strong leadership can alone produce good results in India, with all its diversity (read, myriad opinions and fractured consensus). To illustrate the point: Good leadership in the past has intermittently elevated the offices of the President, the Chief Justice of India, the Central Vigilance Commissioner and the Sebi chairman. However, when leadership has had some continuity and strength of character, the results have been better than good. The office of the Chief Election Commissioner and the relative fairness in the electoral system today versus that which prevailed a couple of decades ago is a case in point. Similarly, compare the fortunes of a Reliance or a Wipro today vis a vis the heavyweight business groups that dotted the Indian corporate world as more than their equals in 1991.

Cultural and Class Inclusiveness

In a nation as diverse as ours, it pays to build culturally inclusive leadership. A lot of Indian corporates, including the so-called professional ones, have relied on family, friends and community to build the circle of leadership. For example, one software company is grappling with the situation of having close to 60 vice presidents from a single community. How did it happen? What does it portend for the hundreds of employees the company has? Such situations abound in India. And, unfortunately, it does not build an environment of trust. Nor does a situation where young men and women from elitist backgrounds filled up the management and top rungs of an organisation. Some large MNCs in India (regarded as breeding grounds) are guilty of having fostered an environment of 'thinking Brahmanism.'

But that was in the last millennium. That is dead. Here is a new India that is emerging as much from its vibrant, small towns as from its growing cities.

4

Market Analysis and Competitor Analysis

Market Definition

In competition law the Relevant market defines the market in which one or more goods compete. Therefore, the Relevant market defines whether two or more products can be considered substitute goods and whether they constitute a particular and separate market for competition analysis.

The relevant market combines the product market and the geographic market, defined as follows:

1. A relevant product market comprises all those products and/or services which are regarded as interchangeable or substitutable by the consumer by reason of the products' characteristics, their prices and their intended use;
2. A relevant geographic market comprises the area in which the firms concerned are involved in the supply of products or services and in which the conditions of competition are sufficiently homogeneous.

Definition and Use

The notion of relevant market is used in order to identify the products and undertakings which are directly competing in a business. Therefore, the relevant market is the market where the competition takes place. The enforcement of the provisions of Competition law would be not possible without referring to the market where competition takes place. The extent to which firms are able to increase their prices above normal competition levels depends on the possibility for consumers to buy substitute goods and the ability for other firms to supply those products. The fewer the substitute products and/or the more difficult it is for other firms to begin to supply those products, the less elastic the demand curve is and the more probable is to find higher prices. For all these reasons it is necessary to define the relevant markets for the different cases which fall under the Law.

The Relevant market contains all those substitute products and regions which provide a significant competitive constraint on the products and regions of interest. An interesting guiding principle provided by Bishop and Darcey (1995) states that a relevant market is something worth monopolising, in the sense that the relevant market includes all the substitute products and therefore control of that market would allow the monopoliser to profitably increase the prices of the products to the monopoly level. This can only be possible if the products in this "market" are not subject to significant competitive constraints by products outside that market.

A relevant market comprises a product or group of products and the geographic area in which these products are produced and/or traded. Therefore, the relevant market has two components: the product market and the geographic market.

Product Market

The relevant product market is determined according to three criteria:

1. Demand-side substitution.
2. Supply-side substitution.
3. Potential competition.

Demand-side Substitution

Demand-side substitution takes place when consumers switch from one product to another in response to a change in the relative prices of the products. If consumers are in a position to switch to available substitute products or to begin sourcing their requirements from suppliers located in other areas, then it is unlikely that price increases will be profitable. Therefore, it is necessary to progressively include in the Relevant market the products to which consumers would most likely switch in response to a relative price rise, repeating the exercise at each stage until a collection of products is reached that is worth monopolising.

When examining the likely responses of consumers, it is the response of the *marginal consumer*, not the *average consumer* which is important. Therefore, a small but significant number of consumers (generally 5 to 10 percent) switching to another product when there is a price increase is considered a sufficient condition for both goods to be defined as forming part of the same relevant market. Therefore, the existence of a group of consumers who would never switch in response to a relative price increase is not by itself sufficient to conclude that the relevant market should be defined narrowly. Determining both the likely extent of demand-side substitution, and the level of substitution which would imply that monopolisation was not worthwhile, requires an assessment of the price-elasticity of demand. This is generally done using the SSNIP-test.

Supply-side Substitution

Sometimes consumers may be unable to react to a price increase, nevertheless, producers may be able to do so by for example, increasing their supply to satisfy the demand of these consumers. If other producers respond to an increase in the relative price of the products supplied by the single supplier by switching production facilities to producing the monopolised collection of products, the increased level of supply may render any attempted price increase unprofitable. In this case, those producers with the ability for supply-side substitution should be included in the Relevant market.

Geographic Market

The geographic market is an area in which the conditions of competition applying to the product concerned are the same for all traders. The same factors used in delineating relevant product markets should be used to define the relevant geographic market. The elements to be taken into consideration when defining the relevant geographic market include the nature and characteristics of the concerned products, the existence of entry barriers, consumer preferences, differences among the market shares of undertakings in the neighbouring geographic areas, as well as significant differences between suppliers' prices and transport costs level. An interesting aspect to which competition authorities look at are transport costs, given that high transport costs may explain why trade between two regions is economically infeasible.

Market Size

A market is any one of a variety of systems, institutions, procedures, social relations and infrastructures whereby businesses sell their goods, services and labor to people in exchange for money. Goods and services are sold using a legal tender such as fiat money. This activity forms part of the economy. It is an arrangement that allows buyers and sellers to exchange goods. Competition is essential in markets, and separates market from trade. Two people may trade, but it takes at least three persons to have a market, so that there is competition on at least one of its two sides. Markets vary in size, range, geographic scale, location, types and variety of human communities, as well as the types of goods and services traded. Some examples include local farmers' markets held in town squares or parking lots, shopping centres and shopping malls, international currency and commodity markets, legally created markets such as for pollution permits, and illegal markets such as the market for illicit drugs.

In mainstream economics, the concept of a market is any structure that allows buyers and sellers to exchange any type of goods, services and information. The exchange of goods or services for money is a transaction. Market participants consist of all the buyers and sellers of a good who influence its price. This influence is a major study of economics and has given rise to several theories and models concerning the basic market forces of supply and demand. There are two roles in markets, buyers and sellers. The market facilitates trade and enables the distribution and allocation of resources in a society. Markets allow any tradable item to be evaluated and priced. A market emerges more or less spontaneously or is constructed deliberately by human interaction in order to enable the exchange of rights (cf. ownership) of services and goods.

Historically, markets originated in physical marketplaces which would often develop into — or from — small communities, towns and cities.

Types of Markets

Although many markets exist in the traditional sense — such as a marketplace — there are various other types of markets and various organizational structures to assist their functions. The nature of business transactions could define markets.

Financial Markets

Financial markets facilitate the exchange of liquid assets. Most investors prefer investing in two markets, the stock markets and the bond markets. NYSE, AMEX, and the NASDAQ are the most common stock markets in the US. Futures markets, where contracts are exchanged regarding the future delivery of goods are often an outgrowth of general commodity markets. Currency markets are used to trade one currency for another, and are often used for speculation on currency exchange rates.

The money market is the name for the global market for lending and borrowing.

Prediction Markets

Prediction markets are a type of speculative market in which the goods exchanged are futures on the occurrence of certain events. They apply the market dynamics to facilitate information aggregation.

Organization of Markets

A market can be organized as an auction, as a private electronic market, as a commodity wholesale market, as a shopping center, as a complex institution such as a stock market, and as an informal discussion between two individuals. Markets of varying types can spontaneously arise whenever a party has interest in a good or service that some other party can provide. Hence there can be a market for cigarettes in correctional facilities, another for chewing gum in a playground, and yet another for contracts for the future delivery of a commodity. There can be black markets, where a good is exchanged illegally and virtual markets, such as eBay, in which buyers and sellers do not physically interact during negotiation. There can also be markets for goods under a command economy despite pressure to repress them.

Mechanisms of Markets

In economics, a market that runs under laissez-faire policies is a free market. It is "free" in the sense that the government makes no attempt to intervene through taxes, subsidies, minimum wages, price ceilings, etc. Market prices may be distorted by a seller or sellers with monopoly power, or a buyer with monopsony power. Such price distortions can have an adverse effect on market participant's welfare and reduce the efficiency of market outcomes. Also, the relative level of organization and negotiating power of buyers and sellers markedly affects the functioning of the market. Markets where price negotiations meet equilibrium though still do not arrive at desired outcomes for both sides are said to experience market failure.

Study of Markets

The study of actual existing markets made up of persons interacting in space and place in diverse ways is widely seen as an antidote to abstract and all-encompassing concepts of "the market" and has historical precedent in the works of Fernand Braudel and Karl Polanyi. The latter term is now generally used in two ways. First, to denote the abstract mechanisms whereby supply and demand confront each other and deals are made. In its place, reference to markets reflects ordinary experience and the places, processes and institutions in which exchanges occurs. Second, the market is often used to signify an integrated, all-encompassing and cohesive capitalist world economy. A widespread trend in economic history and sociology is skeptical of the idea that it is possible to develop a theory to capture an essence or unifying thread to markets. For economic geographers, reference to regional, local, or commodity specific markets can serve to undermine assumptions of global integration, and highlight geographic variations in the structures, institutions, histories, path dependencies, forms of interaction and modes of self-understanding of agents in different spheres of market exchange. Reference to actual markets can show capitalism not as a totalizing force or completely encompassing mode of economic activity, but rather as "a set of economic practices scattered over a landscape, rather than a systemic concentration of power".

C. B. Macpherson identifies an underlying model of the market underlying Anglo-American liberal-democratic political economy and philosophy in the seventeenth and eighteenth centuries: Persons are cast as self-interested individuals, who enter into contractual relations with other such individuals, concerning the exchange of goods or personal capacities cast as commodities, with the motive of maximizing pecuniary interest. The state and its governance systems are cast as outside of this framework. This model came to dominant economic thinking in the later nineteenth century, as economists such as Ricardo, Mill, Jevons, Walras and later neo-classical economics shifted from reference to geographically located marketplaces to an abstract "market". This tradition is continued in contemporary neoliberalism, where the market is held up as optimal for wealth creation and human freedom, and the states' role imagined as minimal, reduced to that of upholding and keeping stable property rights, contract, and money supply. This allowed for boilerplate economic and institutional restructuring under structural adjustment and post-Communist reconstruction.

Similar formalism occurs in a wide variety of social democratic and Marxist discourses that situate political action as antagonistic to the market. In particular, commodification theorists such as Georg Lukacs insist that market relations necessarily lead to undue exploitation of labour and so need to be opposed in toto. Pierre Bourdieu has suggested the market model is becoming self-realizing, in virtue of its wide acceptance in national and international institutions through the 1990s. The formalist conception faces a number of insuperable difficulties, concerning the putatively global scope of the market to cover the entire Earth, in terms of penetration of particular economies, and in terms of whether particular claims about the subjects (individuals with pecuniary interest), objects (commodities), and modes of exchange (transactions) apply to any actually existing markets.

A central theme of empirical analyses is the variation and proliferation of types of markets since the rise of capitalism and global scale economies. The Regulation School stresses the ways in which developed capitalist countries have implemented varying degrees and types of environmental, economic, and social regulation, taxation and public spending, fiscal policy and government provisioning of goods, all of which have transformed markets in uneven and geographical varied ways and created a variety of mixed economies. Drawing on concepts of institutional variance and path dependency, varieties of capitalism theorists (such as Hall and Soskice) identify two dominant modes of economic ordering in the developed capitalist countries, "coordinated market economies" such as Germany and Japan, and an Anglo-American "liberal market economies". However, such approaches imply that the Anglo-American liberal market economies in fact operate in a matter close to the abstract notion of "the market". While Anglo-American countries have seen increasing introduction of neo-liberal forms of economic ordering, this has not lead to simple convergence, but rather a variety of hybrid institutional orderings. Rather, a variety of new markets have emerged, such as for carbon trading or rights to pollute. In some cases, such as emerging markets for water, different forms of privatization of different aspects of previously state run infrastructure have created hybrid private-public formations and graded degrees of commodification, commercialization and privatization.

Problematic for market formalism is the relationship between formal capitalist economic processes and a variety of alternative forms, ranging from semi-feudal and peasant economies widely operative in many developing economies, to informal markets, barter systems, worker cooperatives, or illegal trades that occur in most developed countries. Practices of incorporation of non-Western peoples into global markets in the nineteenth and twentieth century did not merely result in the quashing of former social economic institutions. Rather, various modes of articulation arose between transformed and hybridized local traditions and social practices and the emergence world economy. So called capitalist markets in fact include and depend on a wide range of geographically situated economic practices that do not follow the market model. Economies are thus hybrids of market and non-market elements.

Helpful here is J. K. Gibson-Graham's complex topology of the diversity of contemporary market economies describing different types of transactions, labour, and economic agents. Transactions can occur in underground markets (such as for marijuana) or be artificially protected (such as for patents). They can cover the sale of public goods under privatization schemes to co-operative exchanges and occur under varying degrees of monopoly power and state regulation. Likewise, there are a wide variety of economic agents, which engage in different types of transactions on different terms: One cannot assume the practices of a religious kindergarten, multinational corporation, state enterprise, or community-based cooperative can be subsumed under the same logic of calculability. This emphasis on proliferation can also be contrasted with continuing scholarly attempts to show underlying cohesive and structural similarities to different markets. A prominent entry point for challenging the market model's applicability concerns exchange transactions and the homo economicus assumption of self-interest maximization.

There are now a number of streams of economic sociological analysis of markets focusing on the role of the social in transactions, and the ways transactions involve social networks and relations of trust, cooperation and other bonds. Economic geographers in turn draw attention to the ways in exchange transactions occur against the backdrop of institutional, social and geographic processes, including class relations, uneven development, and historically contingent path dependencies. A useful schema is provided by Michel Callon's concept of framing: Each economic act or transaction occurs against, incorporates and also re-performs a geographically and cultural specific complex of social histories, institutional arrangements, rules and connections.

These network relations are simultaneously bracketed, so that persons and transactions may be disentangled from thick social bonds. The character of calculability is imposed upon agents as they come to work in markets and are "formatted" as calculative agencies. Market exchanges contain a history of struggle and contestation that produced actors predisposed to exchange under c An emerging theme worthy of further study is the interrelationship, interpenetrability and variations of concepts of persons, commodities, and modes of exchange under particular market formations. This is most pronounced in recent movement towards post-structuralist theorizing that draws on Foucault and Actor Network Theory and stress relational aspects of personhood, and dependence and integration into networks and practical systems. Commodity network approaches further both deconstruct and show alternatives to the market models concept of commodities. Here, both researchers and market actors are understood as reframing commodities in terms of processes and social and ecological relationships. Rather than a mere objectification of things traded, the complex network relationships of exchange in different markets calls on agents to alternatively deconstruct or "get with" the fetish of commodities. Gibson-Graham thus read a variety of alternative markets, for fair trade and organic foods, or those using Local Exchange Trading Systems as not only contributing to proliferation, but also forging new modes of ethical exchange and economic subjectivities.

Most markets are regulated by state wide laws and regulations. While barter markets exist, most markets use currency or some other form of money. Any investments made in markets should be carefully analysed and read through before investing if the market crashes value of stock may go down leading to heavy losses.

Size Parameters

Market size can be given in terms of the number of buyers and sellers in a particular market or in terms of the total exchange of money in the market, generally annually (per year). When given in terms of money, market size is often termed market value, but in a distinguished sense than the market value of individual products. For one and the same goods, there may be different (and generally increasing) market values at the production level, the wholesale level and the retail level. For example, the value of the global illicit drug market for the year 2003 was estimated by the United Nations to be US$13 billion at the production level, $94 billion at the wholesale level (taking seizures into account), and US$322 billion at the retail level (based on retail prices and taking seizures and other losses into account).

Agricultural Marketing

Agricultural marketing covers the services involved in moving an agricultural product from the farm to the consumer. Numerous interconnected activities are involved in doing this, such as planning production, growing and harvesting, grading, packing, transport, storage, agro-and food processing, distribution, and sale. Such activities cannot take place without the exchange of information and are often heavily dependent on the availability of suitable finance.

Marketing systems are dynamic; they are competitive and involve continuous change and improvement. Businesses that have lower costs, are more efficient, and can deliver quality products, are those that prosper. Those that have high costs, fail to adapt to changes in market demand, and provide poorer quality, are often forced out of business. Marketing has to be customer-oriented and has to provide the farmer, transporter, trader, processor, etc. with a profit. This requires those involved in marketing chains to understand buyer requirements, both in terms of product and business conditions.

Support to developing countries with agricultural marketing development is carried out by various donor organizations. Activities include market information development, marketing extension, training in marketing and infrastructure development. Since the 1990s trends have seen the growing importance of supermarkets and a growing interest in contract farming, both of which impact significantly on the way in which marketing takes place.

Agricultural Marketing in Developing Countries

Improvement of marketing systems necessitates a strong private sector backed up by appropriate policy and legislative frameworks and effective government support services. Such services can include provision of market infrastructure, supply of market information, and agricultural extension services able to advise farmers on marketing. Training in marketing at all levels is also needed. One of many problems faced in agricultural marketing in developing countries is the latent hostility to the private sector and the lack of understanding of the role of the intermediary. For this reason "middleman" has become very much a pejorative word.

Several organizations provide support to developing countries to develop their agricultural marketing systems, including FAO's agricultural marketing unit and various donor organizations. There has also recently been considerable interest by NGOs to carry out activities to link farmers to markets.

Agricultural Advisory Services and the Market

Promoting market orientation in agricultural advisory services aims to provide for the sustainable enhancement of the capabilities of the rural poor to enable them to benefit from agricultural markets and help them to adapt to factors which impact upon these. As a study by the Overseas Development Institute demonstrates, a value chain approach to advisory services indicates that the range of clients serviced should go beyond farmers to include input providers, producers, producer organisations and processors and traders.

Market Infrastructure

Efficient marketing infrastructure such as wholesale, retail and assembly markets and storage facilities is essential for cost-effective marketing, to minimise post-harvest losses and to reduce health risks. Markets play an important role in rural development, income generation, food security, developing rural-market linkages and gender issues. Planners need to be aware of how to design markets that meet a community's social and economic needs and how to choose a suitable site for a new market. In many cases sites are chosen that are inappropriate and result in under-use or even no use of the infrastructure constructed. It is also not sufficient just to build a market: attention needs to be paid to how that market will be managed, operated and maintained. In most cases, where market improvements were only aimed at infrastructure upgrading and did not guarantee maintenance and management, most failed within a few years.

Rural assembly markets are located in production areas and primarily serve as places where farmers can meet with traders to sell their products. These may be occasional (perhaps weekly) markets, such as haat bazaars in India and Nepal, or permanent. Terminal wholesale markets are located in major metropolitan areas, where produce is finally channelled to consumers through trade between wholesalers and retailers, caterers, etc. The characteristics of wholesale markets have changed considerably as retailing changes in response to urban growth, the increasing role of supermarkets and increased consumer spending capacity. These changes require responses in the way in which traditional wholesale markets are organized and managed.

Retail marketing systems in western countries have broadly evolved from traditional street markets through to the modern hypermarket or out-of-town shopping centre. Despite the growth of supermarkets there remains considerable scope to improve agricultural marketing in developing countries by constructing new retail markets. However, there is little point in undertaking market development improvements unless they result in a positive socio-economic impact. Effective regulation of markets is essential. Inside the market, both hygiene rules and revenue collection activities have to be enforced. Of equal importance, however, is the maintenance of order outside the market. Licensed traders in a market will not be willing to cooperate in raising standards if they face competition from unlicensed operators outside who do not pay any of the costs involved in providing a proper service.

Market Information

Efficient market information can be shown to have positive benefits for farmers and traders. Up-to-date information on prices and other market factors enables farmers to negotiate with traders and also facilitates spatial distribution of products from rural areas to towns and between markets. Most governments in developing countries have tried to provide market information services to farmers, but these have tended to experience problems of sustainability. Moreover, even when they function, the service provided is often insufficient to allow commercial decisions to be made because of time lags between data collection and dissemination. Modern communications technologies open up the possibility for market information services to improve information delivery through SMS on cell phones and the rapid growth of FM radio stations in many developing countries offers the possibility of more localised information services. In the longer run, the internet may become an effective way of delivering information to farmers. However, problems associated with the cost and accuracy of data collection still remain to be addressed. Even when they have access to market information, farmers often require assistance in interpreting that information. For example, the market price quoted on the radio may refer to a wholesale selling price and farmers may have difficulty in translating this into a realistic price at their local assembly market. Various attempts have been made in developing countries to introduce commercial market information services but these have largely been targeted at traders, commercial farmers or exporters. It is not easy to see how small, poor farmers can generate sufficient income for a commercial service to be profitable although in India a new service introduced by Thompson Reuters was reportedly used by over 100,000 farmers in its first year of operation. Esoko in West Africa attempts to subsidize the cost of such services to farmers by charging access to a more advanced feature set of mobile-based tools to businesses.

Marketing Training

Farmers frequently consider marketing as being their major problem. However, while they are able to identify such problems as poor prices, lack of transport and high post-harvest losses, they are often poorly equipped to identify potential solutions. Successful marketing requires learning new skills, new techniques and new ways of obtaining information. Extension officers working with ministries of agriculture or NGOs are often well-trained in horticultural production techniques but usually lack knowledge of marketing or post-harvest handling. Ways of helping them develop their knowledge of these areas, in order to be better able to advise farmers about market-oriented horticulture, need to be explored. While there is a range of generic guides and other training materials available from FAO and others, these should ideally be tailored to national circumstances to have maximum effect.

Enabling Environments

Agricultural marketing needs to be conducted within a supportive policy, legal, institutional, macro-economic, infrastructural and bureaucratic environment. Traders and others cannot make investments in a climate of arbitrary government policy changes, such as those that restrict imports and exports or internal produce movement. Those in business cannot function if their trading activities are hampered by excessive bureaucracy. Inappropriate law can distort and reduce the efficiency of the market, increase the costs of doing business and retard the development of a competitive private sector. Poor support institutions, such as agricultural extension services, municipalities that operate markets inefficiently and export promotion bodies, can be particularly damaging. Poor roads increase the cost of doing business, reduce payments to farmers and increase prices to consumers. Finally, the ever-present problem of corruption can seriously impact on agricultural marketing efficiency in many countries.

Recent Developments

New marketing linkages between agribusiness, large retailers and farmers are gradually being developed, e.g. through contract farming, group marketing and other forms of collective action. Donors and NGOs are paying increasing attention to ways of promoting direct linkages between farmers and buyers. The growth of supermarkets, particularly in Latin America and East and South East Asia, is having a significant impact on marketing channels for horticultural, dairy and livestock products Nevertheless, "spot" markets will continue to be important for many years, necessitating attention to infrastructure improvement such as for retail and wholesale markets.

Farmers' Market

Farmers Markets, sometimes called greenmarkets and green grocers, are markets, usually held outdoors, in public spaces, where farmers can sell produce to the public. Whereas these markets were commonplace before the Industrial age, they were often replaced in modernized cities with grocery stores that sell food that is usually pre-packaged and shipped from long distances. With the start of the modern environmental movement in the 1970s farmer's markets, even in inner-city environments, became economically sustainable with renewed interest in locally-grown, chemical-free and organic produce. Markets can range from a few stalls to many city blocks. In some cultures, live animals, imported delicacies unavailable locally, and personal goods are also sold.

History

Farmers market produce is renowned for being locally grown and very fresh. People argue farmers markets allow farmers to pick produce at the peak of flavour, preserve the nutritional content of fresh produce, and since locally grown produce does not travel as far to get to your table, the difference in mileage saves fossil fuels.

Farmers markets often feature produce grown naturally or organically, meats that are raised humanely on pasture, handmade farmstead cheeses, eggs and poultry from free-range fowl, as well as heirloom produce and heritage breeds of meat and fowl. In many countries with strict food safety laws, farmers markets can be one of the few places beyond the farm gate to purchase raw food, such as raw milk.

Farmers market advocates believe the markets help farmers stay in business as well as preserve natural resources. Wholesale prices farmers get for their produce are very low, often near the cost of production. Farmers who sell direct to the public without going through a middle man get a better price. It can be shown that the preservation of farmland is important for the health of the environment and water supply. According to the American Farmland Trust, sustainable and managed farms conserve soil and clean water and provide a habitat for wildlife. Moreover, modern farmers markets help maintain important social ties, linking rural and urban populations and even close neighbors in mutually rewarding exchange. Farmers markets are a traditional way of selling agricultural and home manufactured products. A weekly market day is a part of normal life in villages and town squares throughout the world. A good way for a traveller to sample local foods and learn about local culture is to attend market day, especially when it coincides with a festival, such as the fiestas in many towns in Latin America. In France and other European countries, there exist street markets, as well as covered marketplaces, where farmers and purveyors sell. Farmers markets are starting to appear online.

In the U.S. and Canada, due in part to the increased interest in healthier foods, a greater desire to preserve local types of cultivars or livestock (some of which may not be up to commercial shipping or yield standards) and an increased understanding of the importance of maintaining small, sustainable farms on the fringe of urban environments, farmers markets in the US have grown from 1,755 in 1994 to 4,385 in 2006 to 5,274 in 2009. In New York City, there are 107 farmers markets in operation. In the Los Angeles area, 88 farmers markets exist, many of which support Hispanic and Asian fare.

New markets appear regularly, and existing markets—some well over a century old—are seeing renewed growth in both North America and Europe. Since the first farmers market was established in the UK in 1997, the number has grown to over 550 nationwide.

Some markets are carefully managed, with strict rules for pricing, quality and vendor selection. Others are much more relaxed in their vendor criteria. While the usual emphasis is on locally-grown/produced food and crafts, some farmers markets allow co-ops and purveyors, or allow farmers to purchase some products to resell. Sometimes there is fraud and products are mislabeled as organic or locally grown when they are not. In some cases, fraudulent farmers markets sell regular grocery store vegetables, passing them off as organic or locally grown, to which are usually sold to unsuspecting tourists.

Some farmers markets have wholesale operations, sometimes limited to specific days or hours. One such wholesale farmers market is the South Carolina State Farmers Market, which is a major supplier of watermelons, cantaloupes, and peaches for produce buyers in the northeastern US. Farmers markets also may supply buyers from produce stands, restaurants, and garden stores with fresh fruits and vegetables, plants, seedlings and nursery stock, honey, and other agricultural products. Although this is on the decline, in part due to the growth of chain stores that desire national distribution networks and cheap wholesales prices—prices driven down by the low cost of imported produce.

Financial Market

A financial market is a mechanism that allows people to buy and sell (trade) financial securities (such as stocks and bonds), commodities (such as precious metals or agricultural goods), and other fungible items of value at low transaction costs and at prices that reflect the efficient-market hypothesis.

Both general markets (where many commodities are traded) and specialized markets (where only one commodity is traded) exist. Markets work by placing many interested buyers and sellers in one "place", thus making it easier for them to find each other. An economy which relies primarily on interactions between buyers and sellers to allocate resources is known as a market economy in contrast either to a command economy or to a non-market economy such as a gift economy.

In finance, financial markets facilitate:

- The raising of capital (in the capital markets)
- The transfer of risk (in the derivatives markets)
- International trade (in the currency markets).

And are used to match those who *want* capital to those who *have* it.

Typically a borrower issues a receipt to the lender promising to pay back the capital. These receipts are *securities* which may be freely bought or sold. In return for lending money to the borrower, the lender will expect some compensation in the form of interest or dividends.

In mathematical finance, the concept of a financial market is defined in terms of a continuous-time Brownian motion stochastic process.

Definition

In economics, typically, the term market means the aggregate of possible buyers and sellers of a certain good or service and the transactions between them. The term "market" is sometimes used for what are more strictly exchanges, organizations that facilitate the trade in financial securities, e.g., a stock exchange or commodity exchange. This may be a physical location (like the NYSE) or an electronic system (like NASDAQ). Much trading of stocks takes place on an exchange; still, corporate actions (merger, spinoff) are outside an exchange, while any two companies or people, for whatever reason, may agree to sell stock from the one to the other without using an exchange.

Trading of currencies and bonds is largely on a bilateral basis, although some bonds trade on a stock exchange, and people are building electronic systems for these as well, similar to stock exchanges.

Financial markets can be domestic or they can be international.

Types of Financial Markets

The financial markets can be divided into different subtypes:

- Capital markets which consist of:
  - Stock markets, which provide financing through the issuance of shares or common stock, and enable the subsequent trading thereof.
  - Bond markets, which provide financing through the issuance of bonds, and enable the subsequent trading thereof.
- Commodity markets, which facilitate the trading of commodities.
- Money markets, which provide short term debt financing and investment.
- Derivatives markets, which provide instruments for the management of financial risk.
- Futures markets, which provide standardized forward contracts for trading products at some future date; see also forward market.
- Insurance markets, which facilitate the redistribution of various risks.
- Foreign exchange markets, which facilitate the trading of foreign exchange.

The capital markets consist of primary markets and secondary markets. Newly formed (issued) securities are bought or sold in primary markets. Secondary markets allow investors to sell securities that they hold or buy existing securities.The transaction in primary market exist between investors and public while secondary market its between investors

Raising the Capital

To understand financial markets, let us look at what they are used for, i.e. what where firms make the capital to invest

Without financial markets, borrowers would have difficulty finding lenders themselves. Intermediaries such as banks help in this process. Banks take deposits from those who have money to save. They can then lend money from this pool of deposited money to those who seek to borrow. Banks popularly lend money in the form of loans and mortgages.

More complex transactions than a simple bank deposit require markets where lenders and their agents can meet borrowers and their agents, and where existing borrowing or lending commitments can be sold on to other parties. A good example of a financial market is a stock exchange. A company can raise money by selling shares to investors and its existing shares can be bought or sold.

Lenders

Individuals

Many individuals are not aware that they are lenders, but almost everybody does lend money in many ways. A person lends money when he or she:

- puts money in a savings account at a bank;
- contributes to a pension plan;
- pays premiums to an insurance company;
- invests in government bonds; or
- invests in company shares.

Companies

Companies tend to be borrowers of capital. When companies have surplus cash that is not needed for a short period of time, they may seek to make money from their cash surplus by lending it via short term markets called money markets.

There are a few companies that have very strong cash flows. These companies tend to be lenders rather than borrowers. Such companies may decide to return cash to lenders (e.g. via a share buyback.) Alternatively, they may seek to make more money on their cash by lending it (e.g. investing in bonds and stocks.)

Borrowers

Individuals borrow money via bankers' loans for short term needs or longer term mortgages to help finance a house purchase.

Companies borrow money to aid short term or long term cash flows. They also borrow to fund modernisation or future business expansion.

Governments often find their spending requirements exceed their tax revenues. To make up this difference, they need to borrow. Governments also borrow on behalf of nationalised industries, municipalities, local authorities and other public sector bodies. In the UK, the total borrowing requirement is often referred to as the Public sector net cash requirement (PSNCR). Governments borrow by issuing bonds. In the UK, the government also borrows from individuals by offering bank accounts and Premium Bonds. Government debt seems to be permanent. Indeed the debt seemingly expands rather than being paid off. One strategy used by governments to reduce the *value* of the debt is to influence *inflation.*

Municipalities and local authorities may borrow in their own name as well as receiving funding from national governments. In the UK, this would cover an authority like Hampshire County Council.

Public Corporations typically include nationalised industries. These may include the postal services, railway companies and utility companies.

Many borrowers have difficulty raising money locally. They need to borrow internationally with the aid of Foreign exchange markets.

Derivative Products

During the 1980s and 1990s, a major growth sector in financial markets is the trade in so called derivative products, or derivatives for short.

In the financial markets, stock prices, bond prices, currency rates, interest rates and dividends go up and down, creating risk. Derivative products are financial products which are used to control risk or paradoxically exploit risk. It is also called financial economics.

Currency Markets

Seemingly, the most obvious buyers and sellers of currency are importers and exporters of goods. While this may have been true in the distant past, when international trade created the demand for currency markets, importers and exporters now represent only 1/32 of foreign exchange dealing, according to the Bank for International Settlements.

The picture of foreign currency transactions today shows:

- Banks/Institutions
- Speculators
- Government spending (for example, military bases abroad)
- Importers/Exporters
- Tourists.

Analysis of Financial Markets

Much effort has gone into the study of financial markets and how prices vary with time. Charles Dow, one of the founders of Dow Jones & Company and The Wall Street Journal, enunciated a set of ideas on the subject which are now called Dow Theory. This is the basis of the so-called technical analysis method of attempting to predict future changes. One of the tenets of "technical analysis" is that market trends give an indication of the future, at least in the short term. The claims of the technical analysts are disputed by many academics, who claim that the evidence points rather to the random walk hypothesis, which states that the next change is not correlated to the last change.

The scale of changes in price over some unit of time is called the volatility. It was discovered by Benoit Mandelbrot that changes in prices do not follow a Gaussian distribution, but are rather modelled better by Levy stable distributions. The scale of change, or volatility, depends on the length of the time unit to a power a bit more than 1/2. Large changes up or down are more likely than what one would calculate using a Gaussian distribution with an estimated standard deviation.

A new area of concern is the proper analysis of international market effects. As connected as today's global financial markets are, it is important to realize that there are both benefits and consequences to a global financial network.

As new opportunities appear due to integration, so do the possibilities of contagion. This presents unique issues when attempting to analyse markets, as a problem can ripple through the entire connected global network very quickly. For example, a bank failure in one country can spread quickly to others, which makes proper analysis more difficult.

Financial Market Slang

- Poison pill, when a company issues more shares to prevent being bought out by another company, thereby increasing the number of outstanding shares to be bought by the hostile company making the bid to establish majority.
- Quant, a quantitative analyst skilled in the *black arts* of PhD level mathematics and statistical methods.
- Rocket scientist, a financial consultant at the zenith of mathematical and computer programming skill. They are able to invent derivatives of frightening complexity and construct sophisticated pricing models. They generally handle the most advanced computing techniques adopted by the financial markets since the early 1980s. Typically, they are physicists and engineers by training; rocket scientists do not necessarily build rockets for a living.
- White Knight, a friendly party in a takeover bid. Used to describe a party that buys the shares of one organization to

help prevent against a hostile takeover of that organization by another party.

Quantitative Behavioural Finance

Quantitative behavioural finance is a new discipline that uses mathematical and statistical methodology to understand behavioural biases in conjunction with valuation. Some of this endeavour has been led by Gunduz Caginalp (Professor of Mathematics and Editor of Journal of Behavioural Finance during 2001–2004) and collaborators including Vernon Smith (2002 Nobel Laureate in Economics), David Porter, Don Balenovich, Vladimira Ilieva, Ahmet Duran). Studies by Jeff Madura, Ray Sturm and others have demonstrated significant behavioural effects in stocks and exchange traded funds.

The research can be grouped into the following areas:

1. Empirical studies that demonstrate significant deviations from classical theories.
2. Modelling using the concepts of behavioural effects together with the non-classical assumption of the finiteness of assets.
3. Forecasting based on these methods.
4. Studies of experimental asset markets and use of models to forecast experiments.

History

The prevalent theory of financial markets during the second half of the 20th century has been the efficient market hypothesis (EMH) which states that all public information is incorporated into asset prices. Any deviation from this true price is quickly exploited by informed traders who attempt to optimize their returns and it restores the true equilibrium price. For all practical purposes, then, market prices behave as though all traders were pursuing their self-interest with complete information and rationality.

Toward the end of the 20th century, this theory was challenged in several ways. First, there were a number of large market events that cast doubt on the basic assumptions. On October 19, 1987 the Dow Jones average plunged over 20% in a single day, as many smaller stocks suffered deeper losses. The large oscillations on the ensuing days provided a graph that resembled the famous crash of 1929. The crash of 1987 provided a puzzle and challenge to most economists who had believed that such volatility should not exist in an age when information and capital flows are much more efficient than they were in the 1920s.

As the decade continued, the Japanese market soared to heights that were far from any realistic assessment of the valuations. Price-earnings ratios soared to triple digits, as Nippon Telephone and Telegraph achieved a market valuation (stock market price times the number of shares) that exceeded the entire market capitalization of West Germany. In early 1990 the Nikkei index stood at 40,000, having nearly doubled in two years. In less than a year the Nikkei dropped to nearly half its peak.

Meanwhile, in the US the growth of new technology, particularly the internet, spawned a new generation of high tech companies, some of which became publicly traded long before any profits. As in the Japanese stock market bubble a decade earlier these stocks soared to market valuations of billions of dollars sometimes before they even had revenue. The bubble continued into 2000 and the consequent bust reduced many of these stocks to a few percent of their prior market value. Even some large and profitable tech companies lost 80% of their value during the period 2000-2003. These large bubbles and crashes in the absence of significant changes in valuation cast doubt on the assumption of efficient markets that incorporate all public information accurately. In his book, "Irrational Exuberance", Robert Shiller discusses the excesses that have plagued markets, and concludes that stock prices move in excess of changes in valuation. This line of reasoning has also been confirmed in several studies (e.g., Jeffrey Pontiff), of closed-end funds which trade like stocks, but have a precise valuation that is reported frequently.

In addition to these world developments, other challenges to classical economics and EMH came from the new field of experimental economics pioneered by Vernon Smith who won the 2002 Nobel Prize in Economics. These experiments (in collaboration with Gerry Suchanek, Arlington Williams and David Porter and others) featuring participants trading an asset defined by the experimenters on a network of computers. A series of experiments involved a single asset which pays a fixed dividend during each of 15 periods and then becomes worthless. Contrary to the expectations of classical economics, trading prices often soar to levels much higher than the expected payout. Similarly, other experiments showed that many of the expected results of classical economics and game theory are not borne out in experiments. A key part of these experiments is that participants earn real money as a consequence of their trading decisions, so that the experiment is an actual market rather than a survey of opinion.

Behavioural finance (BF) is a field that has grown during the past two decades in part as a reaction to the phenomena described above. Using a variety of methods researchers have documented systematic biases (e.g., underreaction, overreaction, etc.) that occur among professional investors as well as novices. Behavioural finance researchers generally do not subscribe to EMH as a consequence of these biases. However, EMH theorists counter that while EMH makes a precise prediction about a market based upon the data, BF usually does not go beyond saying that EMH is wrong.

Research in Quantitative Behavioural Finance

The attempt to quantify basic biases and to use them in mathematical models is the subject of Quantitative Behavioural Finance. Caginalp and collaborators have used both statistical and mathematical methods on both the world market data and experimental economics data in order to make quantitative predictions. In a series of papers dating back to 1989, Caginalp and collaborators have studied asset market dynamics using differential equations that incorporate strategies and biases of investors such as the price trend and valuation within a system that has finite cash and asset. This feature is distinct from classical finance in which there is the assumption of infinite arbitrage. One of the predictions of this theory by Caginalp and Balenovich (1999) was that a larger supply of cash per share would result in a larger bubble. Experiments by Caginalp, Porter and Smith (1998) confirmed that doubling the level of cash, for example, while maintaining constant number of shares essentially doubles the magnitude of the bubble.

Using the differential equations to predict experimental markets as they evolved also proved successful, as the equations were approximately as accurate as human forecasters who had been selected as the best traders of previous experiments (Caginalp, Porter and Smith).

The challenge of using these ideas to forecast price dynamics in financial markets has been the focus of some of the recent work that has merged two different mathematical methods. The differential equations can be used in conjunction with statistical methods to provide short term forecasts.

One of the difficulties in understanding the dynamics of financial markets has been the presence of "noise" (Fischer Black). Random world events are always making changes in valuations that are difficult to extract from any deterministic forces that may be present.

Consequently, many statistical studies have only shown a negligible non-random component. For example, Poterba and Summers demonstrate a tiny trend effect in stock prices. White showed that using neural networks with 500 days of IBM stock was unsuccessful in terms of short term forecasts.

In both of these examples, the level of "noise" or changes in valuation apparently exceeds any possible behavioural effects. A methodology that avoids this pitfall has been developed during the past decade. If one can subtract out the valuation as it varies in time, one can study the remaining behavioural effects, if any. An early study along these lines (Caginalp and Greg Consantine) studied the ratio of two clone closed-end funds. Since these funds had the same portfolio but traded independently, the ratio is independent of valuation. A statistical time series study showed that this ratio was highly non-random, and that the best predictor of tomorrow's price is not today's price (as suggested by EMH) but halfway between the price and the price trend.

The subject of overreactions has also been important in behavioural finance. In his 2006 PhD thesis, Duran examined 130,000 data points of daily prices for closed-end funds in terms of their deviation from the net asset value (NAV). Funds exhibiting a large deviation from NAV were likely to behave in the opposite direction of the subsequent day. Even more interesting was the statistical observation that a large deviation in the opposite direction preceded such large deviations. These precursors may suggest that an underlying cause of these large moves—in the absence of significant change in valuation—may be due to the positioning of traders in advance of anticipated news. For example, suppose many traders are anticipating positive news and buy the stock. If the positive news does not materialize they are inclined to sell in large numbers, thereby suppressing the price significantly below the previous levels. This interpretation is inconsistent with EMH but is consistent with asset flow differential equations that incorporate behavioural concepts with the finiteness of assets. Research continues on efforts to optimize the parameters of the asset flow equations in order to forecast near term prices.

Financial Market Efficiency

In the 1970s Eugene Fama defined an efficient financial market as "*one in which prices always fully reflect available information*".

The most common type of efficiency referred to in financial markets is the allocative efficiency, or the efficiency of allocating resources.

This includes producing the right goods for the right people at the right price.

A trait of allocatively efficient financial market is that it channels funds from the ultimate lenders to the ultimate borrowers in a way that the funds are used in the most socially useful manner.

Market Efficiency Levels

Eugene Fama identified three levels of market efficiency:

1. Weak-form efficiency : Prices of the securities instantly and fully reflect all information of the past prices. This means future price movements cannot be predicted by using past prices.
2. Semi-strong efficiency : Asset prices fully reflect all of the publicly available information. Therefore, only investors with additional inside information could have advantage on the market.
3. Strong-form efficiency : Asset prices fully reflect all of the public and inside information available. Therefore, no one can have advantage on the market in predicting prices since there is no data that would provide any additional value to the investors.

Efficient Market Hypothesis (EMH)

Fama also created the Efficient Market Hypothesis (EMH) theory, which states that in any given time, the prices on the market already reflect all known information, and also change fast to reflect new information. Therefore, no one could outperform the market by using the same information that is already available to all investors, except through luck.

Random Walk Theory

Another theory related to the efficient market hypothesis created by Louis Bachelier is the "random walk" theory, which states that the prices in the financial markets evolve randomly and are not connected, they are independent of each other.

Therefore, identifying trends or patterns of price changes in a market couldn't be used to predict the future value of financial instruments.

Evidence

Evidence of Financial Market Efficiency

- Predicting future asset prices is not always accurate (represents weak efficiency form)

- Asset prices always reflect all new available information quickly (represents semi-strong efficiency form)
- Investors can't outperform on the market often (represents strong efficiency form).

Evidence of Financial Market In-Efficiency

- January effect (repeating and predictable price movements and patterns occur on the market)
- Stock market crashes
- Investors that often outperform on the market such as Warren Buffet.

Market Efficiency Types

James Tobin identified four efficiency types that could be present in a financial market:

Information Arbitrage Efficiency

Asset prices fully reflect all of the privately available information (the least demanding requirement for efficient market, since arbitrage includes realizable, risk free transactions). Arbitrage involves taking advantage of price similarities of financial instruments between 2 or more markets by trading to generate losses. It involves only risk-free transactions and the information used for trading is obtained at no cost. Therefore, the profit opportunities are not fully exploited, and it can be said that arbitrage is a result of market inefficiency.

This reflects the weak-information efficiency model.

Fundamental Valuation Efficiency

Asset prices reflect the expected past flows of payments associated with holding the assets (profit forecasts are correct, they attract investors)

Fundamental valuation involves lower risks and less profit opportunities. It refers to the accuracy of the predicted return on the investment. Financial markets are characterized by predictability and inconsistant misalignments that force the prices to always deviate from their fundamental valuations. This reflects the semi-strong information efficiency model.

Full Insurance Efficiency

It ensures the continuous delivery of goods and services in all contingencies.

Functional/Operational Efficiency

The products and services available at the financial markets are provided for the least cost and are directly useful to the participants.

Every financial market will contain a unique mixture of the identified efficiency types.

Conclusion

Financial market efficiency is an important topic in the world of Finance. While most financiers believe the markets are neither 100% efficient, nor 100% inefficient, many disagree where on the efficiency line the world's markets fall.

It can be concluded that in reality a financial market can't be considered to be extremely efficient, or completely inefficient.

The financial markets are a mixture of both, sometimes the market will provide fair returns on the investment for everyone, while at other times certain investors will generate above average returns on their investment.

Grocery Store

A grocery store is a store established primarily for the retailing of food. A grocer, the owner of a grocery store, stocks different kinds of foods from assorted places and cultures, and sells them to customers. Large grocery stores that stock products other than food, such as clothing or household items, are called supermarkets. Small grocery stores that mainly sell fruits and vegetables are known as produce markets (U.S) or greengrocers (Britain), and small grocery stores that predominantly sell snack foods and sandwiches are known as convenience stores or delicatessens.

History

U.S. grocery stores are descended from trading posts, which sold not only food but clothing, household items, tools, furniture, and other miscellaneous merchandise. These trading posts evolved into larger retail businesses known as general stores. These facilities generally dealt only in "dry" goods such as flour, dry beans, baking soda, and canned foods. Perishable foods were instead obtained from specialty markets: Fresh meat was obtained from a butcher, milk from a local dairy, eggs and vegetables were either produced by families themselves, bartered for with neighbours, or purchased at a farmers' market or a local greengrocer.

Many rural areas still contain general stores that sell goods ranging from cigars to imported napkins. Traditionally, general stores have offered credit to their customers, a system of payment that works on trust rather than modern credit cards. This allowed farm families to buy staples until their harvest could be sold.

The first self-service grocery store, Piggly Wiggly, was opened in 1916 in Memphis, Tennessee by Clarence Saunders, an inventor and entrepreneur. Prior to this innovation, customers gave orders to clerks to fill. Saunder's invention allowed a much smaller number of clerks to service the customers, proving successful (according to a 1929 Time magazine) "partly because of its novelty, partly because neat packages and large advertising appropriations have made retail grocery selling almost an automatic procedure."

The US Labor Department has calcuated that food purchased at home and in restaurants are 13 percent of household purchases, behind 32 percent for housing and 18 percent for transportation. The average US family spent $280 per month or $3,305 per year at grocery stores in 2004. The newsletter Dollar Stretcher survey found $149 a month for a single person, $257 for a couple and $396 for a family of four.

Europe

Because many European cities (Rome, for example) are already so dense in population and buildings, large supermarkets, in the American sense, may not replace the neighbourhood grocery store. However, 'Metro' stores have been appearing in town and city centres in many countries, leading to the decline of independent smaller stores, and large out of town supermarkets and hypermarkets, such as Tesco and Sainsbury's in the United Kingdom, have been steadily sapping the trade from smaller stores.

Canada and United States

American grocery stores operate in many different styles ranging from rural family-owned operations, such as IGAs, boutique chains, such as Whole Foods Market and Trader Joe's to larger supermarket chain stores. In some places food cooperatives or "co-op" markets, owned by their own shoppers, have been popular. However, there has recently been a trend to larger stores serving larger geographic areas. Very large "all-in-one" hypermarkets such as Wal-Mart and Target have recently forced consolidation of the grocery business in some areas. The global buying power of such very efficient companies has put an increased financial burden on traditional local grocery stores as well as the national supermarket chains.

When a small grocery store is in competition with large supermarkets, the grocery store often must create a niche market by selling unique, premium quality, or ethnic foods that are not easily found in supermarkets. A small grocery store may also compete by locating in a mixed commercial-residential area close to, and convenient for, its customers.

Latin America

Grocery stores in Latin America have been growing fast since the early 80s. A big percentage of food sales and other articles are done by the grocery stores today. Some examples are the Chilean chains Cencosud (Jumbo and Santa Isabel covering Chile, Argentina, Brazil and Peru), D&S (Lider and Ekono) as well as Falabella (Tottus in Chile and Peru and Supermercados San Francisco in Chile).

These three chains are subsidiaries of big retail store companies which also have other kind of business units like department stores and home improvement outlets. All three also operate its own credit cards, which is a key driver, and sell as well insurances and have travel agencies. These companies are also running some malls in many countries like Argentina, Chile, Peru and Colombia.

Two other chains started in 2008, Unimarc, which bought several small local chains and has over 20% of the grocery segment in Chile and Southern Cross, a Chilean Investment Fund that has around 8.6% of the supermarket segment, mainly oriented to the southern areas of the country.

In Puerto Rico, popular grocery stores include Pueblo Supermarkets and Amigo.

Food Waste

Many grocery stores in America donate leftover food (for example, deli foods and bread past their expiration date) to homeless shelters or charity kitchens. The USDA estimates that 27% of food is lost annually.

Cultural Impact

Some groceries specialize in the foods of a certain nationality or culture, such as Italian, oriental or Middle-Eastern. These stores are known as ethnic markets and may also serve as gathering places for immigrants. In many cases, the wide range of products carried by larger supermarkets has reduced the need for such speciality stores.

Many teenagers find their first employment in grocery stores.

Notable Grocery Stores

Some notable grocery stores include:

- A&P
- Acme Markets
- Ahold
- Albertsons LLC
- ALDI
- Asda
- Big B Grocery
- Big Y World Class Market
- Bi-Lo
- Brookshire Grocery Company
- Bruno's
- Coles Supermarkets
- Costco
- Coop (Italy)
- Co-op (Atlantic)
- Co-op (Canada)
- Copps
- Cub Foods
- Cumberland Farms
- Delhaize
- Dominick's
- Dorothy Lane Market
- Esselunga (Italy)
- Extra Foods
- Fairway Market
- Fairway Markets
- Farm Boy
- Food 4 Less
- Food Emporium
- Food City
- Food Land

- Food Lion
- Fred Meyer
- Fry's Food & Drug
- FoodLand
- Giant-Carlisle
- Giant Eagle
- Giant Food Markets
- Giant-Landover
- Grocery Outlet
- H-E-B
- Haggen
- Haldanes
- Hannaford Bros.
- Harris Teeter
- Hy-Vee
- IGA
- Jewel
- Jungle Jim's International Market
- Key Food
- Kroger
- Loblaws
- Loeb
- Lowes Foods
- New Albertsons
- Macy's
- Maxi
- Meijer
- Melia's Grocers and Tea Dealers
- Metro
- Mercadona
- Morrisons
- Nakumatt
- Nandan Megashop (Bangladesh)
- Pathmark

- Pick 'N Save
- Piggly Wiggly
- Price Chopper
- Provigo
- Publix
- QFC
- Ralphs
- Real Canadian Superstore
- Reasor's Grocery
- Redner's Markets
- Roche Bros.
- Safeway
- Save-a-Lot
- Save-On-Foods
- Schnucks
- Shaws
- Shoppers Food & Pharmacy
- Shoprite
- SM Megamall (Philippines)
- Smith's Food and Drug
- Sobeys
- Somerfield
- Soriana (Mexico)
- Spartan
- Stater Bros.
- Stewart's Shops
- Stop & Shop
- Super C
- Supervalu
- Target
- Tesco
- The Big Apple
- The Fresh Market
- Tops Markets LLC

- Trader Joe's
- Ukrop's
- Vons
- Waitrose
- Waldbaum's
- Walmart
- Wegmans
- Whole Foods Market
- WinCo
- Winn-Dixie
- Woodman's Food Market
- Woolworths supermarkets (Australia)
- Indian Opus (Grocery Store) (Australia).

Knowledge Market

A knowledge market is a mechanism for distributing knowledge resources. There are two views on knowledge and how knowledge markets can function. One view uses a legal construct of intellectual property to make knowledge a typical scarce resource, so the traditional commodity market mechanism can be applied directly to distribute it. An alternative model is based on treating knowledge as a public good and hence encouraging free sharing of knowledge. This is often referred to as attention economy. Currently there is no consensus among researchers on relative merits of these two approaches.

History

A knowledge economy include the concept of exchanging knowledge-based products and services. However, as discussed by Stewart (1996), knowledge is very different from physical products. For example, it can be in more than one place at one time, selling it does not diminish the supply, buyers only purchase it once, and once sold, it cannot be recalled. Further, knowledge begets more knowledge in a never-ending cycle. Understanding of knowledge markets is beginning to emerge. As would be expected, they are very different in form from traditional markets.

Knowledge markets have been variously described by Stewart (1996), Davenport and Prusak (1998), and Simard (2000) as a mechanism for enabling, supporting, and facilitating the mobilization, sharing, or exchange of information and knowledge among providers and users. This transactional approach assumes that knowledge-based products or services are available for distribution, that someone wants to use them, and that the primary focus of the market is to connect the two. This perspective is appropriate when the market has limited or no interest or control over either the production or use of the content being exchanged, as is the case for most traditional markets. A provider-user perspective is also appropriate for emerging social networking "ideagoras" (Tapscott and Williams, 2006), in which the primary function of the market is to match existing solutions with problems and problems with those who can find solutions.

From a production perspective, processes for creating wealth through the use of intellectual capital are explained by Nonaka (1991), Edvinsson and Malone (1997), and Leonard (1998). At the marketing end of the spectrum, a number of authors, including Bishop (1996), May (2000), and Tapscott et al. (2000) describe the architecture and processes necessary to succeed in a digital economy.

Knowledge markets may also be sequential in nature. Simard (2006) describes a cyclic end-to-end knowledge-market model comprising nine stages that embed, advance, or extract value into knowledge products and services along a knowledge services value chain. The first five stages are internal to a knowledge organization (production and transfer) while the last four stages are external (intermediaries, clients, and citizens). Because the value chain cyclic, it can be used to model either a supply (post-production evaluation) or a demand (pre-production evaluation) approach to knowledge markets.

Knowledge Services

Knowledge services is an emerging concept that integrates knowledge management, a knowledge organization, and knowledge markets. Knowledge Services are programs that provide content-based (data, information, knowledge) organizational outputs (e.g., advice, answers, facilitation), to meet external user wants or needs. Knowledge services are delivered through knowledge markets.

St. Clair and Reich (2002) describe internal knowledge services as a management approach that integrates information management, knowledge management, and strategic learning into an enterprise-wide function. Kalakota and Robinson (2003) and Thomas (2005) developed service-oriented architectures for the private sector. Their focus was to transform traditional retail businesses by developing enterprise-wide platforms that support customer services. RocSearch (2006) take a broader external view, referring to a nascent knowledge services industry that goes beyond traditional cost and time leveraging advantages of the traditional consulting sector.

Simard et al. (2007) developed a holistic systems model of knowledge services for government S&T organizations. The model begins with generating new content and ends with sector outcomes and individual benefits. The model is independent of content, issues, or organizations. It is designed at a departmental level, but is scalable both upwards and downwards. The primary driver is a department's legal mandate; a secondary driver is the needs of clients and residents. The model can function from either a supply or demand approach to knowledge markets. There are two levels of resolution-performance measurement, and classifying service-related activities.

There are four types of knowledge services: generate content, develop products, provide assistance, and share solutions. Knowledge services are modelled as a circular value chain comprising nine stages that embed, advance, or extract value from knowledge-based products and services. The stages are: generate, transform, manage, use internally, transfer, enhance, use professionally, use personally, and evaluate. (Simard, 2007) described a rich to reach service delivery spectrum that is segmented into categories of recipients, with associated levels of distribution, interactions, content complexity, and channels. The categories, from rich to reach, are: unique (once only), complex (science), technical (engineering), specialized (professional), simplified (popular), and mandatory (everyone).

From the perspective of knowledge markets, Mcgee and Prusak (1993) note that people barter for information, use it as an instrument of power, or trade it for information of greater value. Davenport and Prusak (1998) used a knowledge marketplace analogy to describe the exchange of knowledge among individuals and groups. However, Shapiro and Varian (1999) indicate that information markets will not resemble textbook competitive markets with many suppliers offering similar products but lacking the ability to influence prices. Simard (2006) described knowledge markets as a group of related circular knowledge-service value chains that function collectively as a sector, to embed, advance, and extract value to yield sector outcomes and individual benefits.

Internet-based Knowledge Markets

Fee-based knowledge markets are based on traditional market mechanisms that work well for traditional goods. So this approach treats knowledge as common goods. The buyer posts a request, normally in the form of a question and sets a price for the valid answer. Alternatively, the suppliers of knowledge (answerers) can post their bids to have the question answered.

Experts-Exchange was the first fee-based knowledge markets using a virtual currency. It provided a marketplace where buyers could offer payment to have their questions answered.

NineSigma and Innocentive are web-based open innovation marketplaces. Firms post scientific problems and a choose rewards. Google Answers was another implementation of this idea. This service allowed its users to offer bounties to expert researchers for answering their questions. The Google site was closed in 2006. Two months later, fifty former Google Answers Researchers launched paid research/Q&A site Uclue.

Mahalo Answers, a product extension of the people powered search engine Mahalo.com, launched on December 15, 2008. Mahalo Answers users may ask questions for free or provide a monetary reward, or tip, in the form of Mahalo Dollars, the site's proprietary currency.

Free knowledge markets use an alternative model treating knowledge as a public good.

Yahoo Answers, Windows Live QnA, Ask Metafilter, Wikipedia:Reference Desk, Stack Overflow, Vark.com, 3form Free Knowledge Exchange, Knowledge iN, and several other websites currently use the free knowledge exchange model. None of these offer more than an increase in reputation as payment for researchers.

ChaCha.com and Answerly.com both offer subsidized knowledge markets where researchers are paid to generate answers despite the service remaining free to the question asker. Amazon.com's NowNow previously offered a subsidized knowledge market for questions asked through mobile phones and as an experimental feature in the company's ebook reader, the Amazon Kindle. The NowNow service was discontinued November 21, 2008 after an extended private beta period.

Market Economy

A market economy is an economy based on the power of division of labor in which the prices of goods and services are determined in a free price system set by supply and demand.

This is often contrasted with a planned economy, in which a central government can distribute services using a fixed price system. Market economies are also contrasted with mixed economy where the price system is not entirely free but under some government control or heavily regulated, which is sometimes combined with state-led economic planning that is not extensive enough to constitute a planned economy.

In the real world, market economies do not exist in pure form, as societies and governments regulate them to varying degrees rather than allow self-regulation by market forces. The term *free-market economy* is sometimes used synonymously with market economy, but, as Ludwig Erhard once pointed out, this does not preclude an economy from having socialist attributes opposed to a laissez-faire system.

Different perspectives exist as to how strong a role the government should have in both guiding the market economy and addressing the inequalities the market produces. For example, there is no universal agreement on issues such as central banking, and welfare. It is also possible to envision an economic system based on independent producers, cooperative, democratic worker ownership and market allocation of final goods and services; the labour-managed market economy is one of several proposed forms of market socialism.

Systems

Although no country has ever had within its border an economy in which all markets were absolutely free, the term typically is not used in an absolute sense. Many states which are said to have a market economy have a high level of market freedom, even if it is less than some parts of the population would prefer. Thus, almost all economies in the world today are mixed economies with varying degrees of free market and planned economy traits. For example, in the United States there are more market economy traits than in the Western European countries (an exception being the UK, which is considered, even by Greenspan, to be a freer market than the US).

Capitalism

Capitalism generally refers to an economic system in which the means of production are all or mostly privately owned and operated for profit, and in which investments, distribution, income,and pricing of goods and services are determined through the operation of a market economy. It is usually considered to involve the right of individuals and groups of individuals acting as "legal persons" or corporations to trade capital goods, labor, land and money.

Capitalism has been dominant in the Western world since the end of feudalism, but most feel that the term "mixed economies" more precisely describes most contemporary economies, due to their containing both private-owned and state-owned enterprises, combining elements of capitalism and socialism, or mixing the characteristics of market economies and planned economies. In capitalism, there is no central planning authority but the prices are decided by the demand-supply scale. For example, higher demand for certain goods and services lead to higher prices and lower demand for certain goods lead to lower prices.

Laissez-faire

Laissez-faire is synonymous with what was referred to as strict capitalist free market economy during the early and mid-19th century as an ideal to achieve. It is generally understood that the necessary components for the functioning of an idealized free market include the complete absence of government regulation, subsidies, artificial price pressures and government-granted monopolies (usually classified as coercive monopoly by free market advocates) and no taxes or tariffs other than what is necessary for the government to provide protection from coercion and theft and maintaining peace, and property rights.

Milton Friedman and Friedrich Hayek stated that economic freedom is a necessary condition for the creation and sustainability of civil and political freedoms. They believed that this economic freedom can only be achieved in a market-oriented economy, specifically a free market economy. They do believe, however, that sufficient economic freedom can be achieved in economies with functioning markets through price mechanisms and private property rights. They believe that the more economic freedom that is available the more civil and political freedoms a society will enjoy.

Friedman states:

- "Economic freedom is simply a requisite for political freedom. By enabling people to cooperate with one another without coercion or central direction it reduces the area over which political power is exercised" Friedman, Milton and Rose Friedman, *Free to Choose: A Personal Statement*, Harcourt Brace Jovanovich, 1980
- "Capitalism is a necessary condition for political freedom" Capitalism and freedom.

Studies by the Canadian libertarian think tank Fraser Institute, the American conservative think tank Heritage Foundation, and the Wall Street Journal state that there is a relationship between economic freedom and political and civil freedoms to the extent claimed by Friedrich von Hayek. They agree with Hayek that those countries which restrict economic freedom ultimately restrict civil and political freedoms.

Generally market economies are bottom-up in decision-making as consumers convey information to producers through prices paid in market transactions. All states today have some form of control over the market that removes the free and unrestricted direction of resources from consumers and prices such as tariffs and corporate subsidies. Milton Friedman and many other microeconomists believe that these forms of intervention provide incentives for resources to be misused and wasted, producing products society may not value as much as a product that is valued as a result of these restrictions.

Market Socialism

Market socialism refers to various economic systems in which the government owns the economic institutions or major industries but operates them according to the rules of supply and demand. In a traditional market socialist economy, prices would be determined by a government planning ministry, and enterprises would either be state-owned or cooperatively-owned and managed by their employees. Libertarian socialists and left-anarchists often promote a form of market socialism in which enterprises are owned and managed collectively by the workers, but compete with each other in the same way private companies compete in a capitalist market.

The People's Republic of China currently has a form of market socialism referred to as the socialist market economy, in which most of the industry is state-owned, but prices are not set by the government. Within this model, the state-owned enterprises are free from excessive regulation and function more autonomously in a more decentralized fashion than in other socialist economic systems.

Social Market

The social market economic model is based upon the free market economy, combined with regulative measures from the state to prevent market failure. The theoretical fundament is build on the neoliberalism (in Germany also called ordoliberalism). This model was implemented by Ludwig Erhard after World War II in West Germany. Characteristics of social market economies are a strong competition policy and a contractionary monetary policy.

Market Information Systems

Market Information Systems (otherwise known as Market Intelligence Systems, Market Information Services or MIS, but not to be confused with Management Information Systems) are information systems used in gathering, analysing and disseminating information about prices and other information relevant to farmers, animal rearers, traders, processors and others involved in handling agricultural products. Market Information Systems play an important role in agro-industrialisation and food supply chains. With the advance of ICTs in developing countries, the income-generation opportunities offered by Market Information Systems have been sought by international development organizations, NGOs and businesses alike.

Agricultural Market Information Systems

There is a wide variety of market information systems or services. OECD countries have traditionally emphasised the importance of information provision for the agricultural sector, a notable example being the service provided by USDA. Such systems are widely used in order to increase the transparency and the volume of information flowing through the supply chains for different agricultural products. The ability of market information systems to provide a valuable service has been strengthened with the development of the Internet and the advance of electronic commerce (B2B, C2C, etc.). Industry structure, product complexity and the demanding nature of agricultural transactions are considered determining factors for the development of B2B electronic commerce in agriculture.

Agricultural Market Information in Developing Countries

In developing countries, market information initiatives are often part of broader interventions and part of the agricultural marketing and agribusiness development strategy that many governments are actively engaged in. It's commonly understood that long transaction chains, lack of transparency, lack of standards, and insufficient access to markets for products has perpetuated low incomes in predominantly agrarian economies. FAO has a unit focused on agricultural marketing support, including through development of market information. Donor organizations, such as the CTA, IICD, USAID, DFID, and the Bill and Melinda Gates Foundation are all focused on improving the efficiencies within the supply chain through greater information provision. The recent surge of mobile phone usage in developing countries has provided an opportunity for innovative projects to leverage this new distribution channel to get critical market data into the hands of farmers and traders. Several projects by Reuters,

Nokia, Esoko/TradeNet, KACE, Manobi, AgRisk and others have demonstrated the impact that such information can have. Studies in Niger and India demonstrate the impact of cell phones in reducing price variations and creating equilibrium among markets. Introduction of internet kiosks and cafes that provide wholesale price information to farmers has been shown to enhance the functioning of rural markets by increasing the competitiveness of local traders in India.

5

Marketing and Industrial Organization

Nineteen Eighty-Nine was the year in which the Zimbabwean government, in its economic policies, voluntarily turned away from its earlier profession of socialism and embarked on a policy of trade liberalization. In the longer term, therefore, the first decade of Zimbabwe's independence may prove to be anomalous — an ephemeral hiccup in its essentially 'capitalist history. From another perspective, however, the impact of labour policies during this period may prove to have more lasting effects than even the government dreamed of. The altered legal framework during the first decade of Independence has given both labour and capital practice in forms of confrontation and manipulation that are unlikely to be forgotten in a hurry by either side of this production relationship.

The politicization of work and the workplace in Zimbabwe may not easily be eradicated, even by the massive unemployment currently being experienced by youthful school-leavers, which is likely to continue irrespective of what economic policies are adopted in the future. The replacement of racial discrimination during the colonial era by the problems of class differentiation among Blacks after Independence has clearly had an important (and thus far negative) impact on production output in many enterprises. These and many other experiences of Zimbabwe's temporary flirtation with socialism can be expected to influence both her immediate adjustment to 'liberal' economic policies, which will tilt the balance once again in favour of capital and its management, and any equilibrium which may be established in the longer term.

It is important, therefore, that we understand in some detail exactly what did happen during the 1980s in Zimbabwe's industrial sector, rather than run the risk that, as political ideologies, together with what counts as legitimate history, change, these experiences will be expunged from our collective memory as being history incompatible with contemporary reality in the future. It is important to record in accessible, published form the shop-floor findings of industrial sociology during the 1980s, so that they will be available to future generations of researchers and teachers in this field.

The Enterprises Studied

Although all of the workshop participants' research interests were defined individually, their choices have, fortunately, enabled this collection to cover most of the major forms of enterprise ownership in Zimbabwe. State-owned companies are represented by 'Parastatal', a single enterprise studied successively by both Shadur and Mutizwa-Mangiza. Within the private sector, the local subsidiaries of different transnationals were investigated by Maphosa and Gaidzanwa. 'Zimcor', discussed by Cheater, straddled this divide, with a majority state shareholding and participation by both transnationals and local companies, while 'Zimtex' is an example of a wholly local company quoted on the Zimbabwe Stock Exchange, with some individual shareholders resident overseas. Our examples therefore cover a wide range of ownership variation, with the exception of the handful of recently formed cooperatives. These companies, with a minimum of 500 employees, also represent the large-firm sector of the Zimbabwean economy. They have all been made anonymous.

Given the diverse nature of the enterprises studied, the congruence of the research findings by the different authors is striking, attesting to the significance of structural processes in widely differing contexts. Their interpretations of their data, however, sometimes differ. In particular, readers may be struck by the divergent interpretations offered by Shadur and Mutizwa-Mangiza of what was happening in the management of the same enterprise. Perhaps their differences confirm Karl Mannheim's (1936) assertion that there is no 'God's-eye view' of social reality, merely a series of different perspectives, even among scientific observers who, like the social actors observed, may be differently-placed in respect of their gender, nationality and other social attributes. In this respect, though, one might note the shared interpretations of the Zimbabwean industrial scene by the four Zimbabwean contributors, irrespective of their differences of race and gender. It is, therefore, especially useful to have this shared insiders' perspective leavened by that of Shadur as an outsider.

Research Themes

The articles collected here deal with a number of substantial themes, on some of which we do not have as much hard data as we would like. For others, however, more detailed information has already been published: the bibliography on industrial sociology in Zimbabwe at the end of this collection is, we hope, comprehensive and will allow interested readers to pursue specific issues in more detail should they so wish.

Among the many issues raised in these articles, some recur in many different contexts, indicating their structural importance in the system of industrial relations in Zimbabwe. These recurrently important themes include: the changing legal framework of labour relations; the limited extent of de *facto* workers' participation in the different enterprises and the causes of these limitations; the inverse relationship between democratization and bureaucratization in the workplace, which is related to differential education; the importance of the informal structure of social relations in the workplace; the links of urban workers to the countryside; the growing impact of class differentials among Zimbabwean Blacks and their impact on production relations; the impact of its non-productive welfare functions (housing, etc.) on production relations within an enterprise; the impact of race on production relations; the role and problems of supervisors on the shop-floor; and the politicization not only of production relations but also of the relationships of workers' dependants to employing companies and of the role of the 'workers' representative'.

It may be helpful to consider, in the necessary comparative detail, at least some of these themes as they are reflected in the different articles, and to provide additional background information which the papers often assume in their own arguments.

The Legal Framework of Labour Relations

Classically, newly established socialist states have begun their transformation with new laws governing land tenure and marriage. Zimbabwe, however, gave early attention to legalizing the state control of remuneration (in the Minimum Wages Act, No. 4 of 1980) and of the relations between employer and employee (in the Employment Act, No. 13 of 1980). Contrary to popular belief, however, as reflected, for example, in Sachikonye (1990, 3-4), the Minimum Wages Act did not establish for the first time the principle of a minimum wage: for certain categories of industrial worker that principle was established by the Industrial Conciliation Act (No. 21 of 1945, section 27(1)) and the Native Labour Boards Act (No. 26 of 1947, section 21(2)) and made non-racial by the Industrial Conciliation Act (No. 29 of 1959), while its generalization to agricultural workers dates from 1979 (S. I. 917 of 1979).

The Minimum Wages and Employment Acts were 'holding operations', establishing a measure of central control while the state prepared a more coherent legal framework to restructure the triangular interface between industrial capital, labour and itself. This exercise took longer than expected: the Labour Relations Act (No. 16 of 1985) was promulgated at the very end of 1985, after extensive criticism of early draft bills by both labour and capital, and became effective at the beginning of 1986. The Labour Relations Act incorporated the core provisions of both of the earlier Acts.

There is considerable misunderstanding of the intentions of both the Industrial Conciliation and Labour Relations Acts, perhaps because both are sufficiently long (89 and 80 pages, respectively) to deter all but the most determined reader. A detailed comparison of their provisions, however, is necessary to cut through misinformed popular and state discourses on the subject of labour relations in Independent Zimbabwe. Even before such a comparison, though, one needs to note the background context — to both pieces of legislation — of the development of a new state (dating from 1890) and the strengthening of its powers.

The original Industrial Conciliation Act (No. 10 of 1934) was the first attempt by this new state to exert any measure of control over a fledgling, but growing, industrial base. Earlier statutes attempting to control labour, such as the Masters and Servants Act (No. 5 of 1901) did not apply to skilled workers. The Industrial Conciliation Act exempted certain categories of employee from its provisions: those working in agriculture, domestic service, the civil service, education (including universities) and those working free for charities.

The Labour Relations Act extended considerably the theoretical reach of the state into employment, exempting only those whose conditions of employment are provided for in the Constitution of Zimbabwe.

Before comparing the content of the Industrial Conciliation and Labour Relations Acts, one should first note their different intentions.

It is clear that the Industrial Conciliation Act assumed conflict between capital and labour (or at least between employers and employees) to be endemic, requiring a system of bureaucratized adjudication to resolve such disputes. Laying down the rules for entering into and adjudicating such conflicts was considered to be the responsibility of the state, but the ensuing negotiations and their outcome were the responsibility of the conflicting parties.

To this end, the Act established two two-tier adjudication hierarchies, one concerned with matters of registration and membership of trade unions and employers' associations (an industrial court to which decisions of industrial boards could be appealed), and the other concerned with the resolution of industrial conflict through bureaucratic procedures (industrial tribunal(s) plus industrial councils/conciliation boards, both of the latter composed of both employers and employees). The Act thus brought under the bureaucratic control of the state the recognition of both trade unions and employers' organizations as part of the system of regulating industrial conflict and its resolution. Finally, it dealt with ancillary matters, including the status of unregistered trade unions and employers' organizations, procedures of mediation and arbitration, the control of savings and other funds owned by trade unions and employers' associations, and matters of publication. The objectives of the Industrial Conciliation Act were thus very limited and based on the pattern of labour relations which had emerged in the United Kingdom, Europe and North America before the Second World War.

With two important exceptions, the colonial state regarded matters of employment and dispute resolution connected with employment as strictly private affairs. These exceptions included the state's outlawing after 1959, firstly, of the differentiation or discrimination of work or work conditions on the basis of 'race, colour or religion', and, secondly, of victimization of employees giving information to the state's industrial-conciliation machinery against their employers (section 136). For the rest, the Act specifically stated that 'This Act shall not bind the State' (section 3) and severely restricted the capacity of the Minister of Labour to intervene in industrial matters. The colonial bureaucratization of labour relations involved state control exercised through civil servants, not politicians.

The role of the Minister of Labour and Social Welfare, as it then was, under this legislation was restricted to: statutorily receiving a copy of all agreements negotiated by industrial councils or conciliation boards (section 86); declaring — at the request of the industrial council or conciliation board concerned — and publishing such agreements to be binding on all parties in a particular area or sector of industry, taking into account also the interests of consumers and 'the public as a whole' (sections 113, 114, 116); having the right to make a final determination to refuse to make an agreement binding if he considered it to be contrary to the interests of consumers or the general public, but being subject to the adjudication of the industrial tribunal if he refused to make an agreement binding on any other grounds (with the later provision that the State President could, by notice in the *Government Gazette,* declare the Minister's decision to be final: section 117(4)); being able to prevent the referral, by an industrial council or conciliation board, of a dispute to an industrial tribunal for adjudication if such action would likely result in changes to an industrial agreement during its agreed duration (section 100(1)); being able to take over and operate, in the event of industrial action which prevented its normal operations, any enterprise delivering essential services (defined as the supply of light, power, water, sanitation works, fire extinction and the mining of coal (section 142)); and consulting employers on matters affecting the interests of employers or employees (section 150(3)). In addition, only the Minister could authorize, in writing, anyone to hold office simultaneously in more than one (registered or unregistered) trade union, employers' organization, or both (sections 47(1), 67(1)).

The Minister did not constitute the final state authority in any essentially judicial matters. He could not be appealed to over recognition or registration or the operation of workers' or employers' organizations, or the termination of membership in unions or employers' bodies. He appointed members of the Industrial Court (of record) and the chairmen of industrial tribunals (which could also act as courts of inquiry), but had no statutory right to become involved in the outcome of decisions on conflict resolution made by either of these appeal divisions of the adjudication hierarchies. The essentially apolitical nature of the Industrial Conciliation Act was also reflected in its insistence that no registered or unregistered trade union or employers' organization might affiliate itself to any political party or organization, use any of its funds to further any individual or collective political interests, allow its property or facilities to be used for any political purposes, or receive financial or other assistance from political organizations of any kind (sections 49, 66). Such pretensions to apolitical labour relations parallel the separation of legislative, executive and judicial powers. Both are concerned to develop a legal-rational bureaucracy, Max Weber's (1947) acme of efficient organization, especially in industrialized societies.

But in some views, of course, both apolitical labour relations and the separation of powers are dismissed as mystifications of capital's interests.

These views argue that labour relations are, by definition, political, concerned with the power relations linking capital to labour. Any legislation that does not favour labour, therefore, by definition favours capital, and all ostensibly apolitical legislation falls into this category. Such views were espoused by Zanu(PF) (cf. ZANU[PF], 1980) and the new Zimbabwean government after Independence. Hence it is not at all surprising that the fundamental assumptions as well as the content of the Labour Relations Act are very different from those of the Industrial Conciliation Act. The Labour Relations Act explicitly takes the part of labour in the capital-labour relationship, as can be demonstrated by classifying its objectives into four divisions. Firstly, this Act declares and defines 'the fundamental rights of employees [and] unfair labour practices', and regulates 'conditions of employment and other related matters'. Specifically, worker organizations are given the right to recommend industrial action (including strike action: section 29(4)(g), and the Act indemnifies individual workers as well as workers' committees and registered (but not unregistered) trade unions against civil liability for lawful collective industrial action), while employers are not given the right to lock-outs or other collective action (sections 120-123, 29(5)). In its second category of objectives, the Labour Relations Act moves on to provide for state control over the economy in ways antithetical to the assumptions of the colonial system that employment is a private matter: 'to regulate and control collective job action [and] employment agencies; to provide for the control of wages and salaries [and] the appointment of workers' committees'. A third set of objectives of this Act includes taking over, renaming and expanding the institutional base of colonial labour relations, providing for 'the formation, registration, certification and functions of trade unions, employers' organizations, employment councils and employment boards; the establishment and functions of the Labour Relations Board and the Labour Relations Tribunal'. Finally, the Labour Relations Act reveals a Utopian view of what the future might hold, in seeking 'to provide for the prevention of trade disputes, and unfair labour practices' — a united future, without preventable conflict.

In this ideological perspective, then, the law can dissolve the inherent class antagonism between capital and labour and create industrial harmony.

It is, moreover, the duty of the state and its political functionaries to oversee the dissolution of this class antagonism. Apolitical systems must be politicized. One result of this politicization, however, appears to be the conversion of a legal-rational bureaucracy into a patrimonial bureaucracy, as controlling politicians have appropriated the state apparatus in order to achieve these goals. The Industrial Conciliation Amendment Act (No. 23 of 1981, section 5(6)) outlawed discrimination on the basis of 'tribe, etc.' as well as race, and the Labour Relations Act equally prohibits discrimination in employment 'on the grounds of race, tribe, place of origin, political opinion, colour, creed or sex' (section 5(1)). But Zimbabweans have cause to believe that their state sector now operates on the particularistic principles of tribalism, nepotism and ministerial directives on appointments. It is no longer a universalistic system, if it ever was.

It is instructive to note the sheer extent to which labour relations were politicized in the Labour Relations Act by noting what functions were vested in the Minister as final authority in contrast to the colonial situation outlined above — and I should note that this list is incomplete! The Minister currently: defines unfair labour practices (section 10); grants permission to delay or withhold wage payments (section 13(2)); allows welfare and fringe benefits to be diminished (section 16(2)(b)); makes 'regulations providing for the development, improvement, protection, regulation and control of employment and conditions of employment', which regulations 'prevail over the provisions of any other statutory instrument or of any agreement or arrangement whatsoever' (section 17(1) and (2)), including, it would appear from this wording, the law of contract.

Specifically in terms of sections 17(3), 19, 20 and 22, the Minister may regulate, among many others, minimum and maximum wages, bonuses, increments, allowances, benefits, social security, retirement and superannuation benefits, wage deductions, hours of work (including overtime), rest and meal breaks, the provision of food, leave of all kinds, holiday entitlements, the establishment of and contributions to pension schemes, medical and other insurances, the settlement of disputes, the recruitment of all types of labour, whether Zimbabwean or foreign, and the reinstatement of workers suspended or dismissed without his permission.

The Minister also exercises direct and indirect control over employment councils, employers, trade unions and workers' committees. Firstly, the Labour Relations Act sets up a deliberate monopoly system in its requirement that 'there should be no more than one certified trade union or employers' organization for each undertaking or industry' (section 45(l)(d)). Secondly, 'if the Minister has reasonable cause to believe that the property or funds of any trade union, employers' organization or federation are being misappropriated or misapplied', or that their affairs 'are being conducted in a manner that is detrimental to the interests of its members as a whole', the Minister may appoint an investigation into the organization's affairs, and may accept or reject any recommendations to withdraw its recognition by the state and for it to cease operating (section 136). For some odd reason, more control (both financial (section 61) and political) is exercised by the Minister over trade unions than over employers' organizations. 'Where the national interest so demands', the Minister may not only 'cause to be supervised... elections to any office or post in a registered or certified trade union or employers' organization' (section 55(1)).

He may also, for reasons of 'national interest', prohibit any candidate from conducting an election campaign for such office (section 55(2)(d)).

The Minister may direct employers, workers and their respective organizations to negotiate or renegotiate a collective-bargaining agreement (section 25), and that parts of such a collective-bargaining agreement (notably concerning wages) be implemented before they are ratified by the negotiating parties as required in the Act (section 83). He may also refuse to allow the registration by the state of such agreements until amended (section 84). Moreover, the Minister may: 'make such regulations as he considers necessary for the control of workers' committees' (section 26(1)); specify maximum trade union, employers' organization and employment council dues (sections 28(2), 57, 58, 64(d)), levies to support the Labour Relations Board and Tribunal (section 139), and the mode of payment of such dues (section 60); direct payment of union dues 'into a trust fund and not to the trade union concerned' (section 60(3)(b)); approve or revoke the authority of a trade union to act on behalf of non-union members, as an 'agent union' (sections 31, 32, 56); and institute accreditation enquiries into the registration of any trade union or employers' organization (sections 39, 41). The-consent of the Minister is necessary for any employer to 'threaten, recommend or engage in a lock-out' or to take punitive action in respect of continued employment, wages or benefits as a result of a lock-out (section 121), even though, as I have already indicated, employers do not in fact have the right to such collective action in the first place! Perhaps section 121 is merely making doubly sure... Such industrial action may in any case be terminated or delayed for up to 90 days by a 'show-cause order' or 'disposal order' issued by the Minister (sections 122, 123). Any party aggrieved by the issuance of, or refusal to issue, such an order may appeal directly to the Labour Relations Tribunal (section 126(1)), but such an appeal does not affect in any way the implementation of such an order, although the Minister may, during the period in which an appeal is considered, 'give such directions to, or impose such restrictions on, any of the parties as he considers fair and reasonable, taking into account the respective rights of the parties and the public interest' (section 126(2)).

Employment boards, governing conditions of employment, are appointed by and report to the Minister (sections 70-73, 77), who is required 'as far as is practicable under the circumstances' (section 72(2)), to ensure 'equality of representation' of the interests of employers and employees. He must 'pay due regard to' (but not necessarily appoint!) any persons nominated by any interested party to such an employment board (section 71), and may vary its investigative authority (to another board, or to a trade union) if he considers that the interests of the employees concerned 'would be more properly served' by such a transfer (section 78).

The Minister also appoints, and may suspend or dismiss, all members of the Labour Relations Board (sections 88, 91), which is the board of appeal against determinations made by the state's regional hearing officers. In turn, appeals against the Board's determinations are heard by the Labour Relations Tribunal, members of which are appointed, suspended and dismissed by the State President (sections 99-104). From the Tribunal, appeals must be made directly to the Supreme Court of Zimbabwe. At the first level of appeal in this hierarchy, there is explicit scope for political determination: 'The Minister may give to the Board directions of a general or specific nature, and the Board shall comply with such directions' (section 93(4)). Interestingly, an appeal may be made to the Board only with the consent either of the regional hearing officer, or of a member of the Board itself (section 113): thus the right of appeal is not automatic but instead is controlled by interested gate-keepers who are part of the determination system. Moreover, although the Board and Tribunal alike may co-opt non-voting experts to assist their deliberations (sections 93(5), 105(5)), political appointees, not experts, decide. For example, if an aggrieved party alleges unfair labour practices, the Minister may order either a labour relations officer of the state or the Labour Relations Board to investigate such allegations (section 114).

The comparison of new and old appeal structures shows quite clearly the different principles on which the Industrial Conciliation and Labour Relations Acts were constructed. Laying out the comparisons in tabular form allows us to see how much authority in respect of industrialconflict resolution has been removed from the disputing actors themselves and vested in politicians controlling the state apparatus. The authority of such politicians now extends to the lower reaches of the expanded bureaucratic hierarchy controlling both capital and labour.

As might be expected in such a structure, the Labour Relations Act provides for direct links between civil servants (notably the labour relations officers and hearing officers) and the Minister. Such civil servants must inform the Minister 'forthwith' when they order compulsory arbitration of a dispute (section 117(1)), but it is then the Minister's responsibility to refer the matter to the Labour Relations Tribunal or to appoint (at the request of the disputing parties) an independent mediator (section 117(2)). Thus a senior politician is required to communicate between state functionaries and the political appointees to higher-level decision-making organs. Whereas colonial civil servants, not politicians, had decision-making authority over industrial relations issues, in Independent Zimbabwe civil servants merely implement at the lowest level of the system political decisions taken elsewhere in the expanded and fully politicized state system. Of course, one must distinguish among different types of politicization. Zimbabwe's ruling party has been quite happy to politicize the state apparatus with its own ideology and personnel. But given its orientation to the perspectives of labour, the Labour Relations Act shows one startling similarity to its predecessor: section 35(c) prohibits the use of association funds, whether by trade unions or employers' associations, for 'electioneering' or any other unspecified 'political purposes'. Moreover, sections 39 and 40 allow for 'any interested party' (including the one concerned) to request the Registrar of Labour Relations to vary, suspend or rescind the registration or certification of any trade union or employers' organization and to supply his reasons for so doing. Legitimate reasons for such action are not defined in the Act, allowing the Registrar very wide latitude. Once an employers' organization or union loses its recognition by the state, given the accreditation provisions of the Act (sections 41-44), it could be extremely difficult to restore such recognition. It would seem, from these provisions, that an organization could lose such recognition on 'political' grounds — an irrefutable allegation that it had, indeed, used funds for some 'political' purpose.

Another aspect of politicization also merits specific attention. As I have noted earlier, one of the assumptions underlying the Labour Relations Act is that a directive state can eliminate the class conflict between capital and labour. Yet whereas the Industrial Conciliation Act had required the Minister to permit an individual to hold office in both a union and an employers' organization, the Labour Relations Act (section 45(l)(b)) requires the Registrar of Labour Relations to 'ensure compliance' with the requirements that 'a trade union shall not represent employers or managerial employees' (the latter defined as enjoying a 'confidential relationship' with an employer concerning the rights and interests of other employees), and that an employers' organization shall represent only managerial employees. There is a fundamental contradiction in a position that, on the one hand, defines the class lines ever more stringently and, on the other, avers the possibility of harmonious relations between capital and labour, for such a position explicitly prevents the development of cross-cutting ties which blur definitional boundaries through the development of mutual rather than opposing interests.

Under such circumstances, it would be naive to expect in the future that workers and managers will immediately forget the techniques they have learned over the past decade to exert political influence within this politicized system. To put it differently, can the system be depoliticized?

Certainly at this point there is no indication that government intends to depoliticize the constitution or operation of its own institutions. In its attempt to cut down the bureaucratic delays that have frustrated retrenchment since 1985, the independent state has used its 'traditional' operating principles in formulating the Labour Relations (Retrenchment) Regulations (S. 1.404 of 1990), which provide for the Minister to appoint seven members (three civil servants, two employers' representatives and two workers' representatives) to the new Retrenchment Committee. This committee must decide on applications referred to it within two weeks and make recommendations to the Minister, which he may accept or reject. If the Retrenchment Committee fails to make such recommendations, the Minister will decide anyway! Both Minister and Committee are bound by two basic principles: that retrenchment should be avoided and that its consequences should be mitigated (section 7). It is true that various researchers (Cheater, 1986; Gaidzanwa. this volume) have reported dissatisfaction among workers with the practical implementation of these worker-oriented legal provisions, and that both politicians and civil servants (especially those supposed to implement the Labour Relations Act) have tended to develop class interests consonant with, rather than opposed to, those of capital. Nonetheless, the political rhetoric of national unity requires that government be seen to be on the side of the workers (and peasants). It is thus unlikely that the law will alter its form of discourse and highly probable that an even larger gap will develop in the era of trade liberalization between the law and its practical implementation. In government as in industry, informal social relations and connections are therefore likely to become increasingly important.

Formal Bureaucratic and Informal Production Relations

Larger enterprises in the Zimbabwean economy are becoming increasingly bureaucratic in their mode of operation, whether these bureaucratic procedures and relationships grow out of managerial conflict at the shopfloor level or are imposed from above (for example, in standardized practices devolved from head office in the case of subsidiaries of transnational corporations). Perhaps the most obvious index of such bureaucratization is the current popularity of the Paterson Method of job classification, which emphasizes the decision-making content of jobs in grading them as unskilled, semi-skilled or skilled and has many local variants in Zimbabwean enterprises. As Shadur (1989, 235) notes: 'There are grounds for concluding that the Paterson Method has been adopted on a major scale in Zimbabwe as a result of the weak labour movement which has not had the expertise and strength to resist this method', but personnel departments all over Zimbabwe have over the past decade been involved in job-regrading on this basis. However, Gaidzanwa indicates that standardized practices at 'Gold Mine' were very difficult to enforce, and Cheater deals with the responses of both workers and management to increasing bureaucratization more generally. Both papers, together with that of Mutizwa-Mangiza, describe some of the specific difficulties of supervisors in a situation of ongoing bureaucratization.

Supervisors have structural difficulties in all systems, of course, especially when they have been promoted from the shop-floor, and most of these difficulties centre on the differing informal social relationships between workmates and between unequals. These difficulties may be further complicated when, as Maphosa indicates, the supervisor's promotion has resulted from his initial election to workers' representative and/or to party political office. But there are particular difficulties for supervisors in negotiating informally with their subordinates about regular as well as overtime work when these subordinates have access to other productive resources.

Gaidzanwa notes, for example, that locals from the communal land surrounding Gold Mine, having their agricultural interests tended by their wives, were less tractable than 'foreigners' working at the mine to supervisory 'discipline' at work. Yet even while they regarded their mine wages as supplementary to their total productive resources, the local workers were also particularly threatened by any failure of this wage source, given the inadequacy of agriculture as a sole source of income under local environmental conditions. Local workers, therefore, had to confront at closer range the trade-offs available to them from (migratory or commuter) wage employment and agriculture in ways that, perhaps, workers without such options may have envied.

As what Maphosa calls 'bureaucratic logic' tightens its grip on the organization of production, and the 'chain of command' lengthens inexorably (best exemplified in Parastatal), so informal social relations become more, not less, important to ordinary workers. As Maphosa and Mutizwa-Mangiza point out, even those workers elected to represent others on the workers' committees do not have the necessary education or skills to manipulate the bureaucratic order: they must, therefore, manipulate people in order to get what they want. This falling-back by workers on personal relationships in the work-place exacerbates the politicization of ostensibly bureaucratic relations, diverting them into patrimonial forms and contradicting the original intention of state policy-makers to quash especially racial discrimination by legal-rational means.

Race and Class

The Industrial Conciliation Act was and is widely and wrongly thought to have disadvantaged workers mainly on the basis of race. In fact, as I indicated earlier, this Act explicitly outlawed differentiation or discrimination, including in industrial agreements, on the basis of 'race, tribe, colour or creed' in respect of work, though it did permit such discrimination on the basis of age, sex, experience, length of employment and type of premises (sections 36(2), 78(2)). The Act did not permit the Industrial Registrar to register any trade union or employers' organization formed 'for the purpose of furthering the interests of its members on a basis of race, colour or religion' (section 40(l)(e) and required him to enquire publicly, for 'reasonable cause', into unions and organizations believed to be functioning so as to further the interests of their members on the basis of 'race, colour or religion' and to cancel the registration of offending bodies 'unless cause [was] shown to the contrary' (section 57(l)(h)). The onus was thus on such organizations to prove to the state that they were not operating in a racist manner.

But the real problem in colonial Rhodesia was not legalized, structural racism of the kind characteristic of South Africa: it was *de Facto,* practical discrimination in everyday life, and that problem has by no means yet been resolved, eleven years after Independence. In the early 1980s, such practical discrimination was responsible for considerable industrial unrest in individual enterprises. Some of the papers here address this issue in the context of removing the colonial overlap between race and class. Maphosa broadly indicates the background problems inherited from colonialism. Shadur deals with these continuing problems after Independence. Cheater shows how government policy rapidly Africanized enterprise management, while exacerbating the class divide between workers and executive management. In yet more detail, Gaidzanwa shows how the response of Black managerial staff to perceived racism in promotions at Gold Mine was politicized in various ways: by calling in the local Member of Parliament and mobilizing workers' wives in a public demonstration.

Democratization and The Politicization of Production Relations

Politicization may be a strategy of last resort, used by managers and workers alike. Gaidzanwa, for example, notes that in contexts not involving accusations of racism, the ZANU(PF) Women's League at Gold Mine was mobilized to demonstrate against managerial employees with whom workers were dissatisfied. Maphosa observes that such politicization, especially by members of workers' committees, was particularly likely to occur in mining enterprises operating in relatively isolated areas. In an earlier publication, Cheater (1986, 93) described the Zimtex supervisors' 'takeover' of the local Zanu(PF) apparatus in order to reduce their post-Independence supervisory problems at work, which had been caused by after-hours political action against them in the workers' village.

These examples of the politicization of work relations, whether by supervisors, managers or workers, are perhaps related to the high but unfulfilled expectations of workplace democratization found by Maphosa immediately after Independence. These expectations far exceeded the level of democratization that the state (never mind management) was prepared to allow, as both Maphosa and Mutizwa-Mangiza detail in their articles. It could be argued that the workers were deliberately misled on the subject of worker participation by political rhetoric (for example, in the Zanu(PF) Election Manifestos of 1980 and 1985 (see ZANU[PF], 1980 and 1985)), and that their subsequent politicization of work relations represents a backlash against their continuing subordination, now to bureaucratic rather than racial control.

Such bureaucratic control is especially clear in the case of the parastatal enterprises, with their extraordinarily long chains of command culminating in the Cabinet as final decision-making manager, and in the Labour Relations Act itself. The question for the structurally-adjusted future must then become: how will previously politicized workplaces be controlled, and by whom? Industrial organization is a field of economics that studies the strategic behaviour of firms, the structure of markets and their interactions. The study of industrial organization adds to the perfectly competitive model real-world frictions such as limited information, transaction cost, of adjusting prices, government actions, and barriers to entry by new firms into a market. It then considers how firms are organized and how they compete. Perhaps a most appropriate term is the "Economics of Imperfect Competition". The development of industrial organization as a separate field owed much to Edward Chamberlin, Edward S. Mason and Joe S. Bain.

There are two major approaches to the study of industrial organization: the first approach is primarily descriptive and provides an overview of industrial organization. The second, price theory, uses microeconomic models to explain firm behaviour and market structure.

Structure, Conduct, Performance

According to the structure-conduct-performance approach, an industry's performance (the success of an industry in producing benefits for the consumer) depends on the conduct of its firms, which then depends on the structure (factors that determine the competitiveness of the market). The structure of the industry then depends on basic conditions, such as technology and demand for a product. For example: in an industry with technology that the average cost of production falls as output increases, the industry tends to have one firm, or possibly a small number of firms.

Components that make up the structure, conduct, and performance model for industrial organization.

- Basic Conditions: Consumer Demand, Production, Elasticity of Demand, Technology, Substitutes, Raw Materials, Seasonality,

Unionization, Rate of Growth, Product durability, Location, Lumpiness of orders, Scale of economies, Method of purchase, Scope economies

- Structure: Number of Buyers and Sellers, Barriers to entry of new firms, product differentiation, Vertical integration, Diversification
- Conduct: Advertising, Research and Development, Pricing behaviour, Plant Investment, Legal Tactics, Product choice, Collusion, Merger and Contracts
- Performance: Price, Production Efficiency, Allocative Efficiency, Equity, Product Quality, Technical Progress, Profits
- Government Policy: Regulation, Antitrust, Barriers to Entry, Taxes and Subsidies, Investment Incentives, Employment Incentives, Macroeconomic Policies.

Market Structures

The common market structures studied in this field are the following:

- Perfect competition
- Monopolistic competition
- Oligopoly
- Oligopsony
- Monopoly
- Monopsony.

Areas of Study

Industrial organization investigates the outcomes of these market structures in environments with

- Price discrimination
- Product differentiation
- Durable goods
- Experience goods
- Secondary markets or second-hand markets, which can affect the behaviour of firms in primary markets.
- Collusion
- Signaling, such as warranties and advertising.
- Mergers and acquisitions
- Entry and Exit.

A competitive market structure has the performance outcome of lower costs and lower prices, (Shepherd, W: 1997:4).

The subject has a theoretical side and a practical side. According to one text book: "On one plane the field is abstract, a set of analytical concepts about competition and monopoly. On a second plane the topic is about real markets, teeming with the excitement and drama of struggles among real firms" (Shepherd, W.; 1985; 1).

The extensive use of game theory in industrial economics has led to the export of this tool to other branches of microeconomics, such as behavioural economics and corporate finance. Industrial organization has also had significant practical impacts on antitrust law and competition policy.

Input-Output Model

In economics, an input-output model uses a matrix representation of a nation's (or a region's) economy to predict the effect of changes in one industry on others and by consumers, government, and foreign suppliers on the economy. Wassily Leontief (1905-1999) is credited with the development of this analysis. Francois Quesnay developed a cruder version of this technique called Tableau economique. Leontief won the Nobel Memorial Prize in Economic Sciences for his development of this model. And, in essence, Léon Walras's work *Elements of Pure Economics* on general equilibrium theory is both a forerunner and generalization of Leontief's seminal concept.

Leontief's contribution was that he was able to simplify Walras's piece so that it could be implemented empirically. The International Input-Output Association is dedicated to advance knowledge in the field input-output study, which includes "improvements in basic data, theoretical insights and modelling, and applications, both traditional and novel, of input output techniques."

Input-output depicts inter-industry relations of an economy. It shows how the output of one industry is an input to each other industry. Leontief put forward the display of this information in the form of a matrix. A given input is typically enumerated in the column of an industry and its outputs are enumerated in its corresponding row. This format, therefore, shows how dependent each industry is on all others in the economy both as customer of their outputs and as supplier of their inputs.

Each column of the input-output matrix reports the monetary value of an industry's inputs and each row represents the value of an industry's outputs. Suppose there are three industries. Column 1 reports the value of inputs to Industry 1 from Industries 1, 2, and 3. Columns 2 and 3 do the same for those industries. Row 1 reports the value of outputs from Industry 1 to Industries 1, 2, and 3. Rows 2 and 3 do the same for the other industries.

While most uses of the input-output analysis focuses on the matrix set of inter-industry exchanges, the actual focus of the analysis from the perspective of most national statistical agencies, which produce the tables, is the benchmarking of gross domestic product. Input-output tables therefore are an instrumental part of national accounts. As suggested above, the core input-output table reports only intermediate goods and services that are exchanged among industries. But an array of row vectors, typically aligned below this matrix, record non-industrial inputs by industry like payments for labour; indirect business taxes; dividends, interest, and rents; capital consumption allowances (depreciation); other property-type income (like profits); and purchases from foreign suppliers (imports).

At a national level, although excluding the imports, when summed this is called "gross product originating" or "gross domestic product by industry." Another array of column vectors is called "final demand" or "gross product consumed."

This displays columns of spending by households, governments, changes in industry stocks, and industries on investment, as well as net exports. In any case, by employing the results of an economic census which asks for the sales, payrolls, and material/equipment/service input of each establishment, statistical agencies back into estimates of industry-level profits and investments using the input-output matrix as a sort of double-accounting framework.

The mathematics of input-output economics is straightforward, but the data requirements are enormous because the expenditures and revenues of each branch of economic activity has to be represented. As a result, not all countries collect the required data and data quality varies, even though a set of standards for the data's collection has been set out by the United Nations through its System of National Accounts (SNA): the replacement for the current 1993 SNA standard is pending. Because the data collection and preparation process for the input-output accounts is necessarily labour and computer intensive, input-output tables are often published long after the year data was collected—typically as much as 5-7 years after.

Moreover, the economic "snapshot" the benchmark version of the tables provide of the economy's cross-section are taken only once every few years, at best. Although many developed countries estimate input-output accounts annually and with much greater recency.

Usefulness

In addition to studying the structure of national economies, input-output economics has been used to study regional economies within a nation, and as a tool for national and regional economic planning. Indeed a main use of input-output analysis is for measuring the economic impacts of events as well as public investments or programs as shown by IMPLAN and RIMS-II. But it is also used to identify economically related industry clusters and also so-called "key" or "target" industries—industries that are most likely to enhance the internal coherence of a specified economy. By linking industrial output to satellite accounts articulating energy use, effluent production, space needs, and so on, input-output analysts have extended the approaches application to a wide variety of uses.

Economic base Analysis

Economic base analysis was developed by Robert Murray Haig in his work on the Regional Plan of New York in 1928. Briefly, activities in an area divide into two categories – basic and non-basic. Basic industries are those exporting from the region; non-basic (or service) industries support basic industries. Because of data problems, it is not practical to study industry output and trade flows to and from a region. As an alternative, basic and non-basic concepts are operationalized using employment data. The basic industries of the region are identified by comparing employment in the region to national norms. If the national norm for employment in, e.g. Egyptian woodwind manufacturing is five percent and the region's employment is eight percent, then three percent of the region's woodwind employment is basic. Once basic employment is identified, the outlook for basic employment is investigated sector by sector and projections made sector by sector. In turn, this permits the projection of total employment in the region. Typically the basic/non-basic employment ratio is about 1:1. Extending by manipulation of data and comparisons, conjectures may be made about population and income. This is a rough, serviceable procedure and it continues in use today. It has the advantage of being readily operationalized, fiddled with, and understandable. The formula for computing location quotients can be written as:

$$LQ = \frac{e_i / e}{E_i / E}$$

Where:

e_i = Local employment in industry i

e = Total local employment

E_i = Reference area employment in industry i

E = Total reference area employment

It is assumed that the base year is identical in all of the above variables.

Economic base ideas are easy to understand as are measures made of employment. For instance, it's common knowledge that the economy of Seattle, Washington is tied to aircraft manufacturing, Detroit, Michigan to automobiles, and Silicon Valley to high tech manufacturing. When the newspapers discuss the closing of military bases, they will say some thing like: "5,000 jobs at the base will be lost. That's going to hit the economy hard because it means a loss of 10,000 jobs in the community."

To forecast, what's mainly done is to compare the region with the nation and national trends. If the economic base of a region is in industries that are declining nationwide, then we have a problem. If our economic base is concentrated in sectors that are growing, then we are in good shape.

The figure showing location quotients uses data from *Compare Minnesota: Profiles of Minnesota's Economy and Population, 2002-2003*. It uses the term location quotient, a number derived by comparing percent employment in a place (Minnesota) with percent employment nationwide. Minnesota has about the same percentage of high technology employment as does the nation. It has more medical devices employment than the national average (due to companies such as Medtronic).

Methodologically, economic base analysis views the region as if it were a small nation and uses notions of relative and comparative advantage from international trade theory (Charles Tiebout 1963). In a sense the activity is macroeconomics "written small" (and it has not been of much interest to urban economists in recent years because it does not get at within-city relationships.) The analysis usually takes US growth patterns as a given. The fates of regions are determined by trends in the national economy.

Critique of the Economic base Concept

The economic base concept emerged in the 1920s, when economics focused on different industrial strengths and economic techniques were not as nuanced.

The exporting (basic) activities were manufacturing and trade activities and they could be readily identified in the data series. One could think of changes in those activities as causing growth or decline.

Today, export activities purchase many services, and the comparative advantage of an area may well lie in the services it produces. Peter Drucker (1986) imagines a world dominated by trade in ideas and designs. There is little merchandise trade because technology permits small-scale manufacturing. Such a world would change our ideas of what's basic.

The concept is that of a trading region. But in practice economic base concepts are often applied to areas that fit the concept. The Minnesota study, cited before, compared the Minnesota to the US. One can speak of the economic base of Saint Paul, Minneapolis, or Duluth, but to go on and compare such areas using economic base techniques isn't very meaningful.

Forecasting is a precursor to actions, and there is no explicit way to get from the economic base to the kinds of actions most communities are interested in.

That is, the economic base study doesn't say what to do. Leaders say they want desirable economic activities, such as high tech ones. Indeed, we have seen studies of the transport needs of high tech industries, studies done prior to investments to attract such industries (for example in Pennsylvania). Again, the economic base study doesn't say what to do.

Even if we could make what-to-do linkages, the calculus of "desirable" is not simple. We suppose that high pay, little environmental insult, upward mobility for workers, and stability or growth are among the attributes desired of new activities. The table below gives information on the pay attribute. Clearly, that attribute has to be traded off against other attributes.

Table: *Average weekly earnings of production or non-supervisory workers on private non-farm payrolls by major industry, in current dollars*

Industry (April 2003)	***Average weekly earnings***
Mining	774.58
Construction	721.58
Manufacturing	629.43
Transportation and public utilities	670.32

Contd...

Industry (April 2003)	*Average weekly earnings*
Wholesale trade	627.13
Retail trade	296.80
Finance, insurance, and real estate	611.90
Services	507.43
Total private	511.39

The NBER Industrial Organization Program

The NBER's Program on Industrial Organization (IO) celebrates its fifteenth anniversary this year. Researchers in the IO program explore a wide range of topics within the field. Rather than attempting to skim the full scope of program activity, this report highlights work in three broad areas: regulation and antitrust policy; pricing behaviour by firms; and auctions markets. Discussion of the substantial body of research on technology and technical change is deferred to reports of the Productivity Program and the NBER Project on Industrial Technology and Productivity. Those interested in learning more about the IO program may visit the NBER website for links to the full set of Industrial Organization Working Papers.

Regulatory and Antitrust Policy

When markets deviate from competitive ideals, assessing the desirability of government intervention requires a careful assessment of the costs of market failures relative to the benefits of imperfect regulation. The recognition that even imperfect markets may be preferable to regulated outcomes accompanied a dramatic transformation in the nature and extent of government intervention across a broad range of markets over the past thirty years. Many industries long subject to price and entry regulation in the United States — among them airlines, trucking, railroads, and banking — were deregulated. Telecommunications and electric utilities have been vertically disintegrated and structurally competitive segments were opened to market-based outcomes. Privatization of state-owned enterprises outside the United States has substantially increased reliance on market outcomes in many sectors, although regulators in some cases have replaced government managers in providing oversight. Where government intervention ha s been maintained, various forms of incentive-based regulation increasingly have replaced state ownership or traditional cost-of-service rate determination.

IO program members are among the leading scholars of antitrust and regulatory policy, and many have been directly involved in the design or implementation of reforms through their government service, advice to regulatory agencies, or consulting to affected firms. In the face of continuing policy debates over regulatory reform, highlighted more than a decade ago by Paul Joskow and Roger Noll in the NBER's 1994 *American Economic Policy in the 1980s*, the NBER recently sponsored a research project designed to leverage this expertise. Project participants were asked to identify key issues in economic regulation, assess the impact of regulatory reforms across a variety of industries, and evaluate significant contemporary concerns about these reforms. Two dozen scholars assembled for a September 2005 conference in Cambridge to discuss the results of this project, to be assembled in an NBER volume on "Economic Regulation and Its Reform: What Have We Learned?" This project complements a substantial body of primary research by NBER associates on regulatory and antitrust policy. A selection of research from the conference and from NBER working papers is described below.

Economic Regulation and Its Reform

Electricity Restructuring: Competition and Incentive Regulation

NBER researchers continue in the vanguard of research, market design, and implementation of electricity restructuring. Much of the empirical work to date has focused on restructured generation markets, in which prices generally are determined through a competitive bidding process. Frank Wolak describes the evolutionary nature of the restructuring process, emphasizing the tension between an imperfectly competitive market and an imperfect regulatory process in providing incentives for least-cost supply at various stages of the production process. In one of the first empirical analyses of restructuring supply-side benefits (11001), the potential for these incentives to reduce costs is highlighted: Kira Fabrizio, Catherine Wolfram, and I show that restructuring is associated with increased productivity, documenting generating-plant efficiency gains in the use of labour and materials input from replacing a regulated monopoly with market competition. As Wolak points out, though, the technical characteristics of electricity supply and demand suggest that market power may be of particular concern, limiting the benefits of restructuring. Joskow (8442) discusses the role of market power and other contributors to the 2000-1 California electricity crisis; Ali Hortacsu and Steven Puller (11123) measure efficiency losses from strategic bidding in the Texas ERCOT market;

and Dae-Wook Kim and Chris Knittel (10895) compare direct measures of markups to those inferred from oligopoly models of market power in California generation markets. Wolak also describes market design and regulatory policies that limit the ability of suppliers to exercise unilateral market power — such as forward contracting, horizontal divestitures, demand-side participation, and local market power mitigation — and uses examples from worldwide wholesale electricity markets to illustrate the importance of effectively addressing each aspect of the market design process to ensure the maximum benefits of electricity restructuring.

While early empirical electricity research focused predominantly on generation markets, researchers increasingly have turned their attention to retail markets and demand-side policy. Peter Reiss and Matthew White (8687, 9986) use data from San Diego households to measure consumer responsiveness to changing electricity prices and conservation programs enacted during the California electricity crisis. They argue that consumers may be more responsive to price fluctuations than previously thought. Severin Borenstein and Stephen Holland (9922) suggest that substantial efficiency gains could be obtained from shifting even modest shares of relatively price-insensitive customers from fixed retail electricity prices to those that reflect time-varying wholesale electricity prices. Borenstein (11594) provides insight into continued res istance to real-time pricing, highlighting substantial distributional effects of real-time prices across heterogeneous industrial and commercial customers that may make it difficult to gain political support without some system to compensation losers.

For services such as transmission and distribution, which typically remain subject to regulation even in restructured markets, innovations have shifted the focus from cost-based price setting toward incentive mechanisms. Joskow provides a comprehensive review of the theory and complexities involved in applying incentive-based regulation. He then discusses applications of incentive mechanisms to the regulation of prices and service quality for "unbundled" electricity transmission and distribution networks. Further, he assesses the evidence on the performance of incentive regulation for electric distribution and transmission networks and describes challenges for future policy and research.

Among those challenges are determining the role of competition in electricity retailing and transmission. Joskow and Jean Tirole (9534) analyse the likely performance of competitive merchant transmission markets, and conclude that this model is likely to yield substantial investment inefficiencies. While their prognosis for retail electricity competition is more optimistic (10473), they note a variety of challenges and efficiency limitations of competitive outcomes. In their work on "Reliability and Competitive Electricity Markets" (10472), they analyse the complexity involved in integrating economists' approach to market design with engineering system design for reliability across the entire electricity network. Finally, they highlight the implications for system investment, operation, and reliability of interactions among competitive markets, operational constraints, and regulatory and administrative practices.

Telecommunications

The telecommunications sector similarly has undergone a dramatic transformation over the past quarter century. Although telecommunications regulators adopted various incentive-based policies early, "forward-looking" cost-based regulation still plays a prominent role in setting prices for unbundled network elements (UNEs) that must be leased by local telephone companies to their competitors. As noted by Robert Pindyck (10287, 11225), the typical pricing formulas used to set UNE lease rates induce substantial investment and entry inefficiencies by failing to account properly for the substantial sunk costs of telecomm investments. Jerry Hausman and Gregory Sidak compare the outcomes of regulatory approaches in the United States, the United Kingdom, and New Zealand. They conclude that in both the United States and the United Kingdom, unbundling may have caused an increase in competition if one measures competition by market share of entrants, at the cost of adverse investment effects by both incumbents and new entrants. In the last section of their paper, they argue that emerging facilities-based competition should allow the end of telecomm price regulation and the regulatory burden that it creates for both consumers and the economy. If the nature of local exchange competition during the 1990s is a guide to the future, then Shane Greenstein and Michael Mazzeo's (9761) research suggests that we may see increasing product differentiation as a result of local competition.

Cable Television

Greg Crawford's analysis of the cable television industry highlights the impact of economic regulation on product quality and innovation. Regulation in this industry has varied greatly over time, as federal legislation has deregulated, re-regulated, and deregulated consumer cable prices. More recently, penetration by Digital Broadcast Satellites raises questions about the need for regulation to constrain cable prices.

Crawford analyzes the interplay of price regulation and firm quality choices, with attention to the implications of satellite competition for performance in cable television markets. His work highlights ongoing concern over horizontal concentration and vertical integration in the programming market, and bundling by both cable systems and programmers, the latter being the subject of current policy debate at the Federal Communications Commission.

Airline Deregulation

In general, the empirical evidence on deregulation of structurally competitive industries suggests considerable gains from removal of price and entry regulation, although the transition from regulated to competitive markets may be longer and more costly than academics or policymakers originally envisioned. Borenstein and I describe the significant consumer benefits from reduced fares and increased flight frequencies and from nonstop service subsequent to airline deregulation, while acknowledging the industry's considerable financial volatility. We argue that market power concerns have diminished as growth by low-cost carriers now challenges legacy airlines in virtually all parts of the country.

Recent research by Goolsbee and Chad Syverson suggests that even the threat of entry by carriers such as Southwest may reduce incumbent prices (11072). This surge in competition, combined with adverse demand shocks, high fuel prices, and high labour costs, has contributed to current financial distress among many legacy airlines, though. Financial distress and accompanying bankruptcies have been costly for shareholders, high-wage workers, and the Pension Benefit Guaranty Corporation, although many costs and dislocations may be transitional.

For example, Borenstein and Rose (9636) show that schedule disruptions associated with airline bankruptcies are largely transitory; where they are more permanent, they appear to be modest relative to background fluctuations in flights and destinations served, and to be isolated to medium-sized airports. Overall airline investment and consumer benefits continue to be substantial. The greater long-run challenge may be the performance of government-controlled airports, air traffic control, and security infrastructure, which have not in general kept pace with the growth and changes in the industry.

Pharmaceutical Regulation

Pharmaceutical regulation has long generated concern over its effect on innovation incentives and product launch delays. Patricia

Danzon and Eric Keuffel tackle these and other issues in their analysis of pharmaceutical safety, price, and marketing regulations on a variety of industry performance measures. They note that regulatory reforms such as the adoption of user fees, fast track, and priority review may have reduced review-induced delays, especially for priority drugs. For example, Ernst Berndt et al. (10822) finds that implementation of performance goals and user fees for FDA drug applications substantially reduced approval lags — by an average of roughly six months. They estimate a net savings of more than 125,000 life-years from these reforms.

Discouragement of innovation also can be a significant hidden cost of price regulation. Price controls present in many countries may reduce the price of existing pharmaceuticals, but also appear to discourage the development and diffusion of innovative new treatments.

In their work on Medicaid prescription drug purchasing, Mark Duggan and Fiona Scott Morton (10930) highlight another indirect effect of price regulation: government rules that base Medicaid purchase price on the average price of that drug across private-sector purchasers increase equilibrium drug prices for non-Medicaid purchasers, and increase a firm's incentives to introduce new versions of a drug at higher prices.

Financial Services

Randall Kroszner and Phillip Strahan analyse the evolution of banking regulation of prices (interest rates), entry, capital, and investment decisions from the 1990s. to the last part of the twentieth century.

They note that while industry adaptations to constraints partially reduced the costs of regulatory distortions, banking efficiency improved following the removal of most price and entry controls, generating substantial real benefits for the economy as a whole. Patrick Bolton et al. (10571) show that opening the banking sector to price and product-offering competition also may improve information provision and consumer-product matching, given the superior information that financial services sellers may have about product suitability for buyers of those services.

Eric Zitzewitz analyzes the implications of such asymmetric information for the regulation of non-banking financial services firms. He argues that agency conflicts created by information asymmetries and consumer behavioural biases may impede market efficiency.

For example, asset management and financial advisor firms may have incentives to discriminate according to customer sophistication or search ability, offering low-price, high-quality products to sophisticated clients and high-price, low-quality products to the less sophisticated. Ali Hortacsu and Syverson (9728) provide some evidence of this phenomenon in research on product differentiation and search costs in the mutual fund industry. Zitzewitz too discusses the implications of these factors for regulatory and antitrust policy in this sector, with particular attention to recent interventions by the New York Attorney General and the SEC.

Antitrust Policy

In regulated industries, firms may be subject to overlapping jurisdiction by both regulators and antitrust authorities. Dennis Carlton and Randal Picker analyse the tension that this produces, describing the historical origin of antitrust and regulation policy and the ongoing struggles to define the appropriate mechanism and substantive scope for regulating competition. They note that debates over the role of antitrust and regulation continue with particular prominence in today's network industries, whether telecommunications, transportation, or electricity. Moreover, core issues such as interconnection and mandatory access have increased in salience as reform-induced restructuring has led to vertical disintegration of firms and increased competition with incumbents in many industry segments, while the Supreme Court's decision in *Trinko* leaves open substantial questions about how these relationships will be governed.

For most sectors of the economy, interactions among firms are governed by court interpretations of antitrust policy rather than by economic regulatory agency decisions. NBER researchers have explored a variety of aspects of antitrust policy, from theoretical and empirical analyses of merger policy to consideration of vertical restraints.

The appropriate role and application of antitrust policy in innovative sectors has attracted particular attention, both as a matter of principle and in the context of high-profile cases such as U.S. v. Microsoft. In these sectors, the tension between encouraging competition through entry and maintaining profit incentives for dynamic growth and efficiency is particularly acute.

Ilya Segal and Michael Whinston (11525) focus on this tension in research that analyzes a number of specific policies, highlighting those that benefit both entry and innovation. Carlton and Robert Gertner (8976) argue that dynamic efficiency requires coordination of antitrust policy with intellectual property laws in an attempt to resolve tensions created by the tendency for network industries to evolve toward closed systems. Michael Katz and Howard Shelanski (10710) argue that traditional merger analysis, based on static welfare analyses, may miss important dynamic efficiency implications of mergers in highly innovative sectors. Carlton (11645) emphasizes the importance of dynamic barrier-to-entry analysis as one component of this.

Pricing Behaviour in Oligopoly Markets

The behaviour of firms in oligopoly markets is one of the mainstays of IO research. NBER researchers have made considerable progress in better understanding firms' pricing decisions, particularly with reference to price dispersion. Although competitive models tend to assume that consumers are perfectly informed about each firm's single price, many markets deviate substantially from this description. The ability to price discriminate — charging different prices for a product either across firms or to different customers of the same firm— may enable firms to extract greater consumer value from a transaction or to expand the set of customers they serve. This phenomenon appears ubiquitous in the economy.

Consumer search costs may be an important source of sustained price variability in a market.

For example, cash prices for a given prescription drug vary widely across pharmacies within a particular geographic market. The magnitude of price dispersion is correlated with attributes that appear related to the costs and benefits of consumer search, for example, greater price variation for drugs prescribed for one-time use to treat an acute condition, relative to those prescribed for ongoing purchase as maintenance therapies.

Alan Sorensen (8548) uses information on retail price dispersion and prescription attributes to analyse the distribution of consumer search costs for these products. His estimated model of consumer pharmacy choice suggests that search intensities in this market are relatively low — implying that, on average, only 5 to 10 percent of prescriptions are comparison-price shopped.

One way to increase search intensity is to lower its cost. Internet retailing often has been cited as intensely price competitive in large part because of easy consumer search for low-price vendors. Joel Waldfogel and Lu Chen (9942) argue that this reduces the price advantage of brand-name retailers. They find that consumer exposure to price comparison sites such as DealTime.com reduces Amazon purchase shares for those consumers, and that reductions are roughly twice as large for sites that include retailer reliability information (which may substitute for retailer brand reputation) in addition to item price.

Goolsbee and Judith Chevalier (9085) develop a method of estimating price elasticities for online booksellers using publicly available data on Amazon and Barnes & Noble.com, and conclude that consumers are quite sensitive to prices, particularly at Barnes & Noble.com. Glenn Ellison and Sara Fisher Ellis on (10570) show that Internet retailers respond strategically to the increased pricing pressure imposed by these price comparison sites, though. Their analysis of the online computer components market demonstrates that retailers engage in a variety of practices to mitigate the extreme price-sensitivity that price comparison sites may induce, allowing firms to mark-up prices at least enough to cover fixed as well as marginal costs for efficient retailers.

Glenn Ellison (9721) provides a theoretical model of one such practice, "add-on pricing" — for example, advertising low prices for one good in the expectation of selling additional (or higher quality) products to consumers at a high price at the point of sale. His work shows that this practice can sustain softer price competition as a competitive equilibrium.

A rich body of research by Florian Zettelmeyer, Fiona Scott Morton, and Jorge Silva-Risso uses data on individual consumer automobile purchases to explore the interaction of retail auto pricing, consumer information, and Internet information and referral services. These researchers first document significant reductions in average automobile purchase price associated with using an Internet referral service (8667), on the order of 2.2 percent after controlling for selection effects in who uses the service.

They then show that Internet referrals disproportionately benefit minority buyers, offsetting the average 2 percent price disadvantage these groups incur because of their personal costs of search or negotiation for purchases made through traditional dealer channels (8668). In research that matches consumer survey and transactions data to explore the mechanism underlying these price effects, these researchers conclud e that increased transparency of dealer invoice costs combine with greater negotiating clout of the online referral service to reduce a customer's price by an average of 1.5 percent (11515).

Consumer information appears to be particularly important in extracting value from auto price negotiations.

For example, Megan Busse, Zettelmeyer, and Silva-Risso find that purchasers obtain 80 percent of the value of auto manufacturer promotions in the form of heavily promoted customer rebates, but only 35 percent of the value of promotions that are paid as dealer discounts (10887). This research agenda has provided unparalleled insights into pricing determinants in a significant consumer market, and generated important new findings for the role of the Internet in changing outcomes in conventional retail channels.

Auction Markets

While Internet retailing in general has attracted considerable attention and interest, the icon of Internet selling may well be eBay. Its popularity as a mechanism for matching buyers and sellers has spawned a rich economics literature as well as numerous competitors; much of this is described in Patrick Bajari and Ali Hortacsu's survey of Internet auctions research (10076).

The seeming ubiquity of auctions, for goods ranging from fine art to Beanie Babies, and in settings that range from government procurement to pollution permits, has prompted several NBER researchers to model the benefits of auctions over alternative market transaction mechanisms. Alexandre Ziegler and Edward Lazear (9795) analyse the choice between retail store-based and auction markets. They describe the relative benefits of each, and characterize the conditions that lead to more efficient market organization through retail stores relative to auctions.

Eduardo Engel, Ronald Fischer, and Alexander Galetovic (8869) analyse Demsetzian auctions for exclusive rights in settings that range from procurement to royalty contracts, and conclude that "competition for the field" through ex ante auctions welfare dominates duopoly competition whenever marginal revenue is decreasing in quantities sold. Bajari, Robert McMillan, and Steve Tadelis (9757) highlight limitations of auctions relative to negotiations in procurement settings, particularly those dominated by incomplete information. With Stephanie Houghton, Bajari and Tadelis estimate adaptation and renegotiation costs to procurement contracts awarded by auction mechanisms (12051).

As Susan Athey and Philip Haile point out (12126, p. 1), "auctions have provided a fruitful area for combining economic theory with econometric analysis ... to understand behaviour and inform policy."

Athey and Haile describe methodological innovations, many by NBER researchers, which have facilitated estimation of more realistic models and provided significant insights into auction market operation and performance. A significant thrust of this work has been to allow the data more freedom to drive results by relaxing parametric and functional form assumptions.

For example, Haile, Han Hong, and Matthew Shum (10105) develop nonparametric tests of one of the key valuation questions in auctions: are bidders' valuations generated by independent private values for the good, in which case bidders need not be concerned about the "winner's curse," or by common values, in which case bidders must optimally shade their bids knowing that winning means they had an excessively optimistic estimate of the good's true value. They apply this test to different types of U.S. Forest Service timber auctions, and find support for its ability to distinguish between settings in which common values are likely to be more or less significant.

Another approach to allaying concerns about constraints imposed by structural model estimates of auctions looks to experimental data. In this spirit, Bajari and Hortacsu (9889) use experimental data to calibrate the quality of structural estimation based on four alternative theoretical models of bidder behaviour. Andreas Lange, John List, and Michael Price (10639) develop an innovative combination of field data and lab experimental data to evaluate the impact of secondary resale markets for timber on bidding behaviour in timber auctions.

Improving the models and methods available to analyse auction markets can yield important economic insights into these markets, and can aid participants in developing appropriate bidding strategies. But an important policy goal is also to understand the performance of these markets. Mireia Jofre-Bonet and Martin Pesendorfer (8626) develop a method of estimating a dynamic model of behaviour in repeated highway construction procurement auctions with firm-level capacity constraints, and then quantify efficiency losses that result in this setting. In many repeated auctions settings, the potential for collusion among bidders may also be a significant concern. Ken Hendricks, Rob Porter, and Guofu Tan (9836) develop a theory of collusion in affiliated private value and common value auction environments, and use their model to test for bidding rings in federal offshore oil and gas lease auctions. They show that the winner's curse in common value settings works against bid rigging for marginal tracts. Bajari and Fox (11671) analyse potential collusion in FCC spectrum auctions; Orley Ashenfelter and Kathryn Graddy (10795) provide a case study of price-fixing in auctions using the Sotheby's/Christie's art auctions case, drawing out the lessons for auctions and competition policy from details of this case.

Conclusion

This report of necessity focuses on a fraction of the IO research conducted by NBER scholars, although I hope it provides an indication of the breadth and depth of contributions made in this area. Interested readers are encouraged to peruse the NBER website to access the entire body of scholarly work in this area.

6

Industrial Supervision

Supervision means the act of watching over the work or tasks of another who may lack full knowledge of the concept at hand. Supervision does not mean control of another but guidance in a work, professional or personal context. There are several interpretations of the term "supervision", but typically supervision is the activity carried out by supervisors to oversee the productivity and progress of employees who report directly to the supervisors. For example, first-level supervisors supervise entry-level employees. Depending on the size of the organization, middle-managers supervise first-level supervisors, chief executives supervise middle-managers, etc. Supervision is a management activity and supervisors have a management role in the organization.

Typical Experience of a First-Time Supervisor

Rarely have Adequate Training

Often, employees are promoted to supervision because of their strong technical expertise — expertise in building a product or providing a service. Suddenly, the new supervisor is now charged with a whole new range of responsibilities, many of which have little to do with technical expertise. Managers often deal with great deal of paperwork and people. Although paperwork is usually the most tedious, it's often the most predictable. People aren't predictable. They have moods, illnesses, career expectations, crises in their family lives, etc. The supervisor's technical expertise is often useless when it comes to supervising people.

Sometimes Intimidated by Wide Range of Policies and Procedures

The new supervisor is suddenly faced with a wide range of rules and regulations — each of which the supervisor is responsible to enforce.

The supervisor is responsible for signing time cards, authorizing overtime, granting compensation time, dealing with performance problems, developing job descriptions, following hiring procedures, dealing with grievances, conforming to a complicated pay system, and the list goes on. It can be quite difficult to conform to today's wide range of employee laws, rules and regulations — and at the same time, produce a product or service.

New Supervisors Rarely have Enough Time

No matter how many courses or degrees a new supervisor has completed, they're often surprised that management activities are so hectic and demanding. No matter how thorough the planning, managers rarely get to spend much time on any one activity. The role of most managers, whether new supervisors or executives, is interspersed with frequent interruptions. Any surprise in the work or lives of employees is a sudden demand on supervisors.

New supervisors often expect to have complete knowledge of everything that goes on in their group. They don't want to encounter any surprises. So they spend more time reading, thinking, planning, communicating with employees — new supervisors often spend 60 hours a week on the job. Still, they don't feel they have enough time to do the job right.

New Supervisors often Feel very Alone

Each manager has a unique role in the organization. Each organization is unique. Usually there are no clear procedures for dealing with the numerous challenges that suddenly face management. Ultimately, it's up to each manager to get through the day. Faced with a great deal of pressure, little time and continuing demands from other people, the new supervisor can feel quite alone. The supervisor is responsible to be an advocate for the organization and an advocate for the employee. For example, if the organization implements an unpopular new policy, the supervisor is often responsible to communicate and justify that new policy to the employee. In this case, management expects the supervisor to present and support the new policy, and the employee vents his or her frustration to the supervisor. However, if the supervisor wants to promote the employee or present some other reward, he or she is now representing the employee's case to the rest of management. The supervisor is often alone, stuck in the middle. The new supervisor wants to come across as having deserved their promotion, as being in control of the situation. It's difficult to seek help from others in the organization. Even when there is someone there to talk to, it's difficult to fully explain the situation — the new supervisor sometimes doesn't know how things got so hectic and confusing.

New Supervisors often Feel Overwhelmed, Stressed Out

The new supervisor is responsible, often for the first time, for the activities of another employee. The supervisor must ensure the employee knows his or her job, has the resources to do the job and does the job as effectively as possible. Until a new supervisor develops a "feeling for the territory", they often deal with the stresses of supervision by working harder, rather than smarter. They miss the comfort and predictability of their previous job. The stress and loneliness in the role of new supervisor can bring out the worst in a person. If they deal with stress by retreating, they'll retreat to their offices and close the door. If they deal with frustration, they'll become angry and unreasonable with their employees. If they are used to getting strong praise and high grades, they'll work harder and harder until their jobs become their lives.

Support and Development are Critical for New Supervisors

Courses in supervision, delegation, time management, stress management, etc., are not enough. New supervisors need ongoing coaching and support. They need someone whom they can confide in. Ideally, they have a mentor in the organization who remembers what it's like to be a first-time supervisor, someone who makes themselves available.

If the experience of first-time supervision is successful — it's challenging, but fulfilling — the supervisor goes on to become a progressive, supportive manager.

Impact of Individual Differences

Individual differences — the ways in which people differ from one another.

Personality — the pattern of relatively enduring ways that a person feels, thinks, and behaves.

Nature — biological heritage, genetic makeup.

Nurture — life experiences.

Attraction-selection-attrition (ASA) framework — the idea that an organization attracts and selects individuals with similar personalities and loses individuals with other types of personalities.

Trait — a specific component of personality.

The Big Five Personality Profile

Extraversion — the tendency to experience positive emotional states and feel good about oneself in the world around them, also called positive affectivity.

Neuroticism — the tendency to experience negative emotional states in the oneself in the world around one negatively, also called negative affectivity.

Agreeableness — the tendency to get along well with others.

Conscientiousness — the extent to which a person is careful, scrupulous, and preserving.

Openness to experience — the extent to which a person is original, has broad interests, and is willing to take risks.

Locus of Control

External locus of control — describes people who believe that fate, lot, or outside forces are responsible for happens to them.

Internal locus of control — describes people who believe that ability, effort, or their own actions determine what happens to them.

Self-monitoring — the extent to which people try to control the way they present themselves to others.

Self-esteem — the extent to which people have pride in themselves and their capabilities.

Cognitive Abilities

Verbal ability — ability to understand and use written and spoken language.

Numerical ability — ability to solve arithmetic problems and deal with numbers.

Reasoning ability — ability to come up with solutions for problems and understand the principles by which different problems can be solved.

Deductive ability — ability to reach of appropriate conclusions from an array of observations or evaluate the implications of a series of facts.

Ability to see relationships — the ability to see how two things are related to each other and then apply this knowledge to other relationships and situations.

Ability to remember — abilities to recall things ranging from simple associations to complex groups of statements or sentences.

Spatial ability — ability to determine the location or arrangement of two objects in relation to one's own position and to imagine how an object would appear if its position in space were altered.

Perceptual — ability to uncover visual patterns and see relationships within and across patterns.

Personality Types

Type a-a person who has an intense desire to achieve, is extremely competitive, it has a strong sense of urgency.

Type b-a person who tends to be easy-going and relaxed.

Need for achievement — the desire to perform challenging tasks well and to meet ones own high standards.

Need for affiliation — the desire to establish and maintain good relations with others.

Need for power — the desire to exert emotional and behavioural control or influence over other.

How personality is measured.

Ability — the mental or physical capacity to do something.

Physical Ability

Motor skills — the ability to physically manipulate objects in an environment physical skills — a person's fitness and strength.

Emotional intelligence — the ability to understand and manage one's own feelings and emotions and the feelings and emotions and other people.

Summary

The two main types of individual differences are personality differences and ability differences. Understanding the nature, determinants, and consequences of individual differences is essential for managing organizational behaviour. Because people differ so much from each other, an appreciation of the nature of individual differences is necessary to understand why people act the way they do in organizations.

Personality is the pattern of relatively enduring ways that a person feels, things, and behaves. Personality is determined both by nature (biological heritage) and nurture (situational factors). Organizational outcomes that have been shown to be predicted by personality include job satisfaction, work stress, and leadership effectiveness. Personality is not a useful predictor of organizational outcomes when there are strong situational constraints. Because personality tends to be stable over time, managers should not expect to change personality in the short run. Managers should except employees personalities as they are and develop effective ways to deal with people.

Feelings, thoughts, attitudes, and behaviours in an organization are determined by the interaction of personality and the situation.

The big five personality traits are extraversion, neuroticism, agreeableness, conscientiousness, and openness to experience. Other personality traits particularly relevant to organizational behaviour include locus of control, self-monitoring, self-esteem, type a & type b personalities, and the needs for achievement, affiliation, and power.

In addition to possessing different personalities, employees also differ in their abilities, or what they are capable of doing. The two major types of ability are cognitive ability and physical ability.

Types of cognitive ability can be arranged in a hierarchy with General intelligence at the top. Specific types of cognitive abilities are verbal ability, numerical ability, reasoning ability, deductive ability, ability to see relationships, ability to remember, spatial ability, and perceptual ability.

There are two types of physical ability, motor skills and physical skills. Both nature and nurture contribute to determining physical ability and cognitive ability. A third, recently identified, ability is emotional intelligence.

In organizations, ability can be measured by selecting individuals who have the abilities needed to compost tasks, placing employees in jobs that capitalize on their abilities, and training employees to enhance their ability levels.

Consistency vs. Individual Differences

Generally, human behaviour is not random. People behave in a particular way that they believe is in their best interest Following a systematic approach to the study of human behaviour will bring to light important facts and relationships that will, in turn, serve as a basis for more accurate predictions of behaviour.

Happy Workers need not be Productive

According to traditional theories in the study of organizational psychology and organizational behaviour, happy workers are more productive. These theories suggest that organizations should create a good work environment, offer fringe benefits and provide such facilities as to make the workers happy. However, a research study by psychologist, Dr. Robert Sinclair, along with his student, Carrie Lavis, at the University of Alberta refuted the traditional theories and proved the reverse: hard workers are more productive than happy workers.

Sinclair and Lavis created feelings of happiness and sadness in employees working on circuit boards. They observed that both sad and happy employees produced the same number of circuit boards, but the boards produced by happy employees bore more defects than those produced by sad employees. Sinclair and Lavis gave the following reason: Happy people did not want to disturb their pleasant feelings by being serious at work. They did not pay much attention to the task at hand as they were more concerned about their own happiness. But, sad people concentrated on their work and tried to perform their level best to overcome their somberness. In fact, recent studies in social psychology have also indicated that sad employees tend to reflect more deeper than do happy employees and thus are more rational and accurate in their judgments. Though these findings are contrary to the popular belief that happy workers are better workers, it does not imply that organizations should cease to provide amenities and employee benefits to make their employees sad and therefore more productive. The sad and happy moods observed in the employees in the above studies had nothing to do with the work or workplace. In their studies, Sinclair and Lavis found that people were dedicated to their job in the belief that their grievances would subside. Hence, organizations should strive to create such work environment (depending on the employee's nature and emotions) where people feel good by performing the task given to them. According to Sinclair, this practice will help organizations motivate employees and enhance their performance.

It may be interpreted that the organizations should take more care in making the task and its impact on the employee a pleasant experience rather than only focusing on improving the work/office environment in general.

Adapted from "Sad Workers May Make Better Workers," Science Daily, University of Alberta, June 14, 2001.

The knowledge about how a person perceives a particular situation can help predict his behaviour. Though a person's behaviour may appear rather irrational to others, it may seem perfectly rational to him This difference in perception arises because an outsider may not have access to the same information or may not perceive a given situation in the same way as the person whose behaviour is in consideration. However, certain consistencies can be identified in the behaviour of every individual. These consistencies are significant since they make room for accurate prediction of other's behaviour in specific situations.

For example, while driving a car, people make certain predictions regarding other drivers. The rules of driving give certain inputs that help people predict rather accurately that all drivers will stop at red signals, drive on the left side of the road, overtake from the right and never cross the solid double line on mountain roads. However, same cannot be said about the behaviour of people at work in an organization. For instance, consider a situation in which a manager lias passed inter-departmental transfer orders to a few employees to adjust the excess and under capacities existing in these departments. He may observe that some employees willingly accept the Liter-unit transfer and begin to receive training for the new job while some employees strongly resist the change and resort to strikes and violence. In this case, systematic study of the behaviour of employees would have helped the manager to make reasonably accurate predictions about their behaviour.

By systematic study, we mean a study based on viewing relationships, attributing causes and effects, and drawing conclusions on the basis of scientific evidence. For this, data should be gathered under controlled conditions and measured and interpreted rigorously.

Generalization about behaviour may be based on intuition. And intuition is a feeling that is not necessarily supported by research. Therefore, one of the challenges to the study of OB is to overcome the belief that behaviour is either the outcome of intuition or is based on common sense. Moreover, what might be common sense to one person may not be so to another. Thus, OB specialists seek to move away from intuitive views of behaviour to a systematic analysis that is essential for improving one's accuracy in the prediction and explanation of organizational behaviour.

You are interviewing a candidate for a position as a cashier in a supermarket. You need someone polite, courteous, patient, and dependable. The candidate you are talking to seems nice. But how do you know who is the right person for the job? Will the job candidate like the job or get bored? Will they have a lot of accidents on the job or be fired for misconduct? Don't you wish you knew before hiring? One company approaches this problem scientifically, saving companies time and money on hiring hourly wage employees.

Retail employers do a lot of hiring, given their growth and high turnover rate. According to one estimate, replacing an employee who leaves in retail costs companies around $4,000. High turnover also endangers customer service. Therefore, retail employers have an incentive to screen people carefully so that they hire people with the best chance of being successful and happy on the job. Unicru, an employee selection company, developed software that quickly became a market leader in screening of hourly workers. The company was acquired by Massachusetts-based Kronos Inc. in 2006.

The idea behind the software is simple: If you have a lot of employees and keep track of your data over time, you have access to an enormous resource. By analysing this data, you can specify the profile of the "ideal" employee. The software captures the profile of the potential high performers, and applicants are screened to assess their fit with this particular profile. More important, the profile is continuously updated as new employees are hired. As the database gets larger, the software does a better job of identifying the right people for the job. If you applied for a job in retail, you may have already been a part of this database: The users of this system include giants such as Albertsons, Universal Studios, Costco Wholesale Corporation, Macy's, Blockbuster Inc., Target Brands Inc., and other retailers and chain restaurants. In companies such as Target or Blockbuster, applicants use a kiosk in the store to answer a list of questions and to enter their background, salary history, and other information.

In other companies, such as some in the trucking industry, candidates enter the data through the Web site of the company they are applying to. The software screens people on basic criteria such as availability in scheduling as well as personality traits.

Candidates are asked to agree or disagree with statements such as "slow people irritate me" or "I don't act polite when I don't want to." After the candidates complete the questions, hiring managers are sent a report complete with a color-coded suggested course of action. Red means the candidate does not fit the job, yellow means proceed with caution, and green means the candidate can be hired on the spot. Interestingly, the company contends that faking answers to the questions of the software is not easy because it is difficult for candidates to predict the desired profile.

For example, according to their research, being a successful salesman has less to do with being an extraverted and sociable person and more to do with a passion for the company's product. Matching candidates to jobs has long been viewed as a key way of ensuring high performance and low turnover in the workplace, and advances in computer technology are making it easier and more efficient to assess candidate-job fit. Companies using such technology are cutting down the time it takes to hire people, and it is estimated that using such techniques lowers their turnover by 10%–30%.

Individuals bring a number of differences to work, such as unique personalities, values, emotions, and moods. When new employees enter organizations, their stable or transient characteristics affect how they behave and perform.

Moreover, companies hire people with the expectation that those individuals have certain skills, abilities, personalities, and values. Therefore, it is important to understand individual characteristics that matter for employee behaviours at work.

Psychological Testing and Measurement in Personnel Selection

Personality Tests: *A selection procedure measure the personality characteristics of applicants that are related to future job performance.* Personality tests typically measure one or more of five personality dimensions: extroversion, emotional stability, agreeableness, conscientiousness, and openness to experience.

Advantages;

- can result in lower turnover due if applicants are selected for traits that are highly correlated with employees who have high longevity within the organization
- can reveal more information about applicant's abilities and interests can identify interpersonal traits that may be needed for certain jobs.

Disadvantages,

- difficult to measure personality traits that may not be well defined
- applicant's training and experience may have greater impact on job performance than applicant's personality
- responses by applicant may may be altered by applicant's desire to respond in a way they feel would result in their selection
- lack of diversity if all selected applicants have same personality traits
- cost may be prohibitive for both the test and interpretation of results.

Tips

Select traits carefully An employer that selects applicants with high degree of 'assertiveness', 'independence', and 'self-confidence' may end up excluding females significantly more than males which would result in *adverse impact*. Select tests carefully Any tests should have been analysed for (high) reliability and (low) adverse impact. Not used exclusively Personality tests should not be the sole instrument used for selecting applicants. Rather, they should be used in conjunction with other procedures as one element of the selection process. Applicants should not be selected on the basis of personality tests alone.

Summary of Personality Tests

1. Since there is not a correct answer to personality tests, the scoring of the procedure could be questioned.
2. Recent litigation has suggested that some items for these types of tests may be too intrusive.
3. This technique lacks face validity. In other words, it would be difficult to show how individual questions on certain personality measures are job related even if the overall personality scale is a valid predictor of job performance.
4. Hooke and Krauss (1971) administered three (3) tests to sergeant candidates; the Minnesota Multiphasic Personality Inventory, the Allport-Vemon-Lindzey Study of Values, and the Gough Adjective Check List. These tests did not differentiate candidates rated as good sergeant material from those rates as poorer candidates. The researchers concluded that the groups may have been so similar that these tests were not sensitive enough to differentiate them.

Types of Personality Tests

1. Personal Attribute Inventory. An interpersonal assessment instrument which consists of 50 positive and 50 negative adjectives from Gough's Adjective Check List. The subject is to select 30 which are most descriptive of the taregt group or person in question. This instrument was specifically designed to tap affective reactions and may be used in either assessing attitudes toward others or as a self-concept scale.
2. Personality Adjective Checklist A comprehensive, objective measure of eight personality styles (which are closely aligned with DSM-III-R Axis II constructs). These eight personality styles are: introversive, inhibited, cooperative, sociable,

confident, forceful, respectful, and sensitive. This instrument is designed for use with nonpsychiatric patients and normal adults who read minimally at the eighth grade level. Test reports are computer-generated and are intended for use by qualified professionals only. Interpretive statements are based on empirical data and theoretical inference. They are considered probabilistic in nature and cannot be considered definitive. (2K)

3. Cross-Cultural Adaptability Inventory Self-scoring six-point rating scale is a training instrument designed to provide feedback to individuals about their potential for cross-cultural effectiveness. It is most effective when used as part of a training program. It can also be used as a team-building tool for culturally diverse work groups and as a counselling tool for people in the process of cross-cultural adjustment. The inventory contains 50 items, distributed among 4 subscales: emotional resilience, flexibility/openness, perceptual acuity, personal autonomy.

Materials

4. California Psychological Inventory Multipurpose questionnaire designed to assess normal personality characteristics important in everyday life that individuals make use of to understand, classify, and predict their own behaviours and that of others. In this revision, two new scales, empathy and independence, have been added; semantic changes were made in 29 items; and 18 items were eliminated. The inventory is applicable for use in a variety of settings, including business and industry, schools and colleges, clinics and counselling agencies, and for cross cultural and other research. May be used to advise employees/applicants about their vocational plans.

Personnel Selection Tests and Interviews

Personnel selection is the process used to hire (or, less commonly, promote) individuals.

Although the term can apply to all aspects of the process (recruitment, selection, hiring, acculturation, etc.) the most common meaning focuses on the selection of workers.

Overview

The professional standards of industrial psychologists require that any selection system be based on a job analysis to ensure that the selection criteria are job-related.

The requirements for a selection system are knowledge, skills, ability, and other characteristics, known as *KSAO's*. U.S. law also recognizes *bona fide occupational qualifications* (BFOQs), which are requirements for a job which would be discriminatory were they not necessary — such as only employing men as wardens of maximum-security male prisons, or enforcing a mandatory retirement age for airline pilots, or a religious college only employing professors of its religion to teach its theology.

The goal of personnel selection, as all business processes, is to ensure an adequate return on investment. In the case of selection, this entails assurances that the productivity of the new hires produce more value than the costs of recruiting, selecting, and training them. Within industrial psychology, the area of utility analysis specifically addresses this issue.

Several screening methods exist that may be used in personnel selection. Examples include the use of minimum or desired qualifications, resume/application review, scored biodata instruments, oral interviews, work performance measures (e.g., writing samples), and tests (cognitive ability, personality, job knowledge). Development and implementation of such screening methods is sometimes done by human resources departments; larger organizations hire consultants or firms that specialize in developing personnel selection systems.

Personnel Assessment Tools: Tests and Procedures

Any test or procedure used to measure an individual's employment or career-related qualifications and interests can be considered a personnel assessment tool. There are many types of personnel assessment tools. These include *traditional knowledge and ability tests, inventories, subjective procedures*, and *projective instruments*. In this guide, the term *test* will be used as a generic term to refer to any instrument or procedure that samples behaviour or performance. Personnel assessment tools differ in;

- Purpose, e.g., selection, placement, promotion, career counselling, or training
- What they are designed to measure, e.g., abilities, skills, work styles, work values, or vocational interests
- What they are designed to predict, e.g., job performance, managerial potential, career success, job satisfaction, or tenure
- Format, e.g., paper-and-pencil, work-sample, or computer simulation

- Level of standardization, objectivity, and quantifiability-Assessment tools and procedures vary greatly on these factors. For example, there are subjective evaluations of resumes, highly structured achievement tests, interviews having varying degrees of structure, and personality inventories with no specific right or wrong answers.

All assessment tools used to make employment decisions, regardless of their format, level of standardization, or objectivity, are subject to professional and legal standards. For example, both the evaluation of a resume and the use of a highly standardized achievement test must comply with applicable laws. Assessment tools used solely for career exploration or counselling are usually not held to the same legal standards.

Relationship between the Personnel Assessment Process and Tests and Procedures

A personnel test or a procedure provides only part of the picture about a person. On the other hand, the personnel assessment process combines and evaluates all the information gathered about a person to make career or employment-related decisions.

What do Tests Measure?

People differ on many psychological and physical characteristics. These characteristics are called *constructs*. For example, people skilful in verbal and mathematical reasoning are considered high on *mental ability*. Those who have little physical stamina and strength are labeled low on *endurance* and *physical strength*. The terms *mental ability, endurance* and *physical strength* are constructs. *Constructs* are used to identify personal characteristics and to sort people in terms of how much they possess of such characteristics.

Constructs cannot be seen or heard, but we can observe their effects on other variables. For example, we don't observe physical strength but we can observe people with great strength lifting heavy objects and people with limited strength attempting, but failing, to lift these

Tests, inventories, and procedures are assessment tools that may be used to measure an individual's abilities, values, and personality traits. They are components of the assessment process.

- observations
- resume evaluations
- application blanks/questionnaires

- biodata inventories
- interviews
- work samples/performance tests
- achievement tests
- general ability tests
- specific ability tests
- physical ability tests
- personality inventories
- honesty/integrity inventories
- interest inventories
- work values inventories
- assessment centers
- drug tests
- medical tests.

Assessment process Systematic approach to combining and evaluating all the information gained from testing and using it to make career or employment-related decisions.

Why do Organizations Conduct Assessment?

Organizations use assessment tools and procedures to help them perform the following human resource functions:

- Selection. Organizations want to be able to identify and hire the best people for the job and the organization in a fair and efficient manner. A properly developed assessment tool may provide a way to select successful sales people, concerned customer service representatives, and effective workers in many other occupations.
- Placement. Organizations also want to be able to assign people to the appropriate job level. For example, an organization may have several managerial positions, each having a different level of responsibility. Assessment may provide information that helps organizations achieve the best fit between employees and jobs.
- Training and development. Tests are used to find out whether employees have mastered training materials. They can help identify those applicants and employees who might benefit from either remedial or advanced training. Information gained from testing can be used to design or modify training programs. Test

results also help individuals identify areas in which self-development activities would be useful.

- Promotion. Organizations may use tests to identify employees who possess managerial potential or higher level capabilities, so that these employees can be promoted to assume greater duties and responsibilities.
- Career exploration and guidance. Tests are sometimes used to help people make educational and vocational choices. Tests may provide information that helps individuals choose occupations in which they are likely to be successful and satisfied.
- Program evaluation. Tests may provide information that the organization can use to determine whether employees are benefiting from training and development programs.

Some Situations in which an Organization may Benefit from Testing

Some situations include the following:

- Current selection or placement procedures result in poor hiring decisions.
- Employee productivity is low.
- Employee errors have serious financial, health, or safety consequences.
- There is high employee turnover or absenteeism.
- Present assessment procedures do not meet current legal and professional standards.

Importance of using Tests in a Purposeful Manner

Assessment instruments, like other tools, can be extremely helpful when used properly, but counter-productive when used inappropriately. Often inappropriate use stems from not having a clear understanding of what you want to measure and why you want to measure it. Having a clear understanding of the purpose of your assessment system is important in selecting the appropriate assessment tools to meet that purpose. This brings us to an important principle of assessment.

Principle of Assessment

Use assessment tools in a *purposeful manner*. It is critical to have a clear understanding of what needs to be measured and for what purpose.

Assessment strategies should be developed with a clear understanding of the knowledge, skills, abilities, characteristics, or personal traits you want to measure. It is also essential to have a clear idea of what each assessment tool you are considering using is designed to measure.

Limitations of Personnel Tests and Procedures-fallibility of Test Scores

Professionally developed tests and procedures that are used as part of a planned assessment program may help you select and hire more qualified and productive employees. However, it is essential to understand that *all assessment tools are subject to errors*, both in measuring a characteristic, such as verbal ability, and in predicting performance criteria, such as success on the job. This is true for all tests and procedures, regardless of how objective or standardized they might be.

- Do not expect any test or procedure to measure a personal trait or ability with perfect accuracy for every single person.
- Do not expect any test or procedure to be completely accurate in predicting performance.

There will be cases where a test score or procedure will predict someone to be a good worker, who, in fact, is not. There will also be cases where an individual receiving a low score will be rejected, who, in fact, would actually be capable and a good worker. Such errors in the assessment context are called selection errors. Selection errors cannot be completely avoided in any assessment program.

Why do organizations conduct testing despite these errors? The answer is that appropriate use of professionally developed assessment tools on average enables organizations to make more effective employment-related decisions than use of simple observations or random decision making. Using a single test or procedure will provide you with a limited view of a person's employment or career-related qualifications. Moreover, you may reach a mistaken conclusion by giving too much weight to a single test result. On the other hand, using a variety of assessment tools enables you to get a more complete picture of the individual. The practice of using a variety of tests and procedures to more fully assess people is referred to as the *whole-person approach* to personnel assessment. This will help reduce the number of selection errors made and will boost the effectiveness of your decision making. This leads to an important principle of assessment.

Principle of Assessment

Do not rely too much on any one test to make decisions. Use the *whole-person approach* to assessment.

Vocational Guidance

A vocation is a career or calling and the word is derived from the Latin *vocare*, which means "to call." Vocational guidance means helping someone find his or her calling or at least a suitable career choice. Vocations or careers can be loosely categorized into areas such as service, technical, mechanical, creative, health and business.

Vocational training rather than vocational guidance is available at career colleges and this is usually for entry-level careers. For example, a career college with a health vocational curriculum may offer education and training programs for nurse's aide and medical assistant careers, while business-oriented vocational schools may have marketing assistant and bookkeeping program offerings.

A career college or vocational school differs from regular colleges and universities as the focus isn't on academics, but rather on training students for a specific career. Vocational or career colleges are also sometimes referred to as community colleges or trade schools.

Vocational guidance is often started in high school although some high schools also have vocational training programs. Vocational exploration courses offer students the opportunity to research different career possibilities as well as learn which vocational areas they have aptitude or talent in. For instance, many vocational guidance classes give tests to the students that test their ability with numbers, words, mechanical concepts and many more subjects. Tests designed to measure an individual's personality traits, intelligence quotient (IQ) as well as his or her main values and interests are administered and analysed by career counsellors.

Once career counsellors and the students have looked over the test results, career options can be chosen that fit best with each individual. Vocational guidance doesn't stop there as many other considerations must be made when deciding on a career direction. The type and number of years of education must be considered. Salary and working conditions are other important considerations in career selection. The likely demand for the occupation in the next decade or more is a crucial element when choosing a vocation since this affects the likelihood of finding jobs in a certain career field.

Vocational guidance isn't just for high school students. Rather it's for anyone either starting a career or changing careers. Some people may have several different careers in their life, while others may stay in the same field during all their working years.

Personnel Selection : Job Analysis and Workers Analysis

What is Job Analysis? Job Analysis is a process to identify and determine in detail the particular job duties and requirements and the relative importance of these duties for a given job. Job Analysis is a process where judgements are made about data collected on a job.

Why is Job Analysis performed? What is the purpose of Job Analysis? Job Analysis is used to show the *relatedness* of employment procedures used by the employer. The procedures supported by job analysis include:

- Training
- Personnel Selection
- Job Evaluation, and
- Performance Appraisal.

Who conducts Job Analysis? Job Analysis may be conducted by the employer's Human Resources department or by a trained Job Analyst/Consultant.

How do I conduct a Job Analysis? The steps to conduct a Job Analysis are outlined below:

- Identify the Job(s) to be analysed.
- Determine the procedures to be used (methods) in collecting job data.
- Implement the job analysis methods.
- Review the data collected through Job Analysis.
- Summarize and document the data collected.

How are Jobs Analysed?

Who is involved in a Job Analysis? The Job Analysis may be conducted by a member of the employer's Human Resources department. This analysis may be in conjunction with the job incumbent (if the position is not vacant), the incumbent's supervisor, and possibly subject matter experts (SMEs).

Do I need a consultant for Job Analysis? When is a consultant needed for Job Analysis? A consultant is not necessary for Job Analysis. However, consultants may provide a more independent (unbiased) analysis of the job. Their analysis may not be affected by the internal politics of the organization. Also, a consultant may be needed for situations in which a large number of jobs will be analysed in a relatively short period of time. A consultant in this situation may be better able to concentrate on the job analysis task as their main function whereas internal employees probably still have their regular jobs to perform.

What are the products of a Job Analysis? A job description is the main product of a job analysis.

Can an employer be sued over inadequate or missing Job Analysis?

Are there Federal guidelines for Job Analysis? The Uniform Guidelines on Employee Selection Procedures states that a thorough job analysis is needed for supporting a selection procedure.

The Americans with Disabilities Act specifically states:

No covered entity shall discriminate against a qualified individual with a disability because of the disability of such individual in regard to job application procedures, the hiring, advancement, or discharge of employees, employee compensation, job training, and other terms, conditions, and privileges of employment.

The Act defines "*qualified individual with a disability*" as someone with a disability who: "with or without reasonable accommodation, can perform the essential functions of the employment position that such individual holds or desires." Essential functions may be determined through a Job Analysis.

Is there software to perform Job Analysis? HR-Guide offers an on-line form for creating Position Description Questionnaires. You may use this application to create the form that will be useful in collecting the job information. Is there software to help me manage Job Analysis? Yes. HR.Superb. Net allows you to access, store, create, and update job descriptions on-line.

What are sources of information for conducting a Job Analysis? Before a Job Analysis is conducted, the job analyst should review external sources if job information including:

- Dictionary of Occupational Titles
- U.S. Standard Occupational Classification System
- Other on-line job descriptions.

What methods are used for Job Analysis? The main methods of job analysis are:

- Interviews
- Questionnaires
- Observation.

What is Functional Job Analysis? Functional Job Analysis (FJA) was used by U.S. Employment Service job analysts to classify jobs for the DOT. The most recent version of FJA uses seven scales to describe what workers do in jobs:

1. Things,
2. Data,
3. People,
4. Worker Instructions,
5. Reasoning,
6. Math, and
7. Language.

What is the Position Analysis Questionnaire? This questionnaire, developed by McCormick, Jeanneret, and Mecham (1972), is a standardized job analysis instrument. It consists of 187 job elements that describe generic human work behaviours. This questionnaire was designed to be used for a wide variety of jobs.

What is the Critical Incident Technique? This method of Job Analysis focuses on identifying the *critical incidents* that distinguish satisfactory workers from unsatisfactory workers. This is based on the theory that certain tasks are crucial to satisfactory job performance, while others are not.

In this method, the job analyst interviews incumbents and/or supervisors to identify a list of critical incidents. The identification of required Knowledges, Skills, and Abilities (KSAs) is made by examining the incidents—their causes and solutions. This technique is useful for developing work sample tests.

What is the Job Element Method? This method of Job Analysis, developed by Ernest Primoff, is a worker oriented method and is used primarily with lesser skilled workers and industrial occupations. This method, like the Critical Incident Technique, focuses on satisfactory workers.

This method attempts to identify the characteristics of satisfactory workers (*job elements*). Once identified, these elements are used to develop appropriate selection tests. The steps to perform a Job Element job analysis are:

- Select a group of experts (may include incumbents and supervisors)
- Conduct brainstorming sessions to identify job elements (the KSA's of satisfactory workers).

- Assign weights to each of the elements based on the following criteria:
  a. proportion of barely acceptable workers who have the job element;
  b. effectiveness of the element in picking a superior worker;
  c. the trouble likely to occur if the element is not considered; and
  d. practicality—the effect of including the job element on the organization's ability to fill job openings.
- Analyse the Job Element data.

7

Industrial Organization

Price Discrimination

Price discrimination exists when sales of identical goods or services are transacted at different prices from the same provider. In a theoretical market with perfect information, no transaction costs or prohibition on secondary exchange (or re-selling) to prevent arbitrage, price discrimination can only be a feature of monopoly and oligopoly markets, where market power can be exercised. Otherwise, the moment the seller tries to sell the same good at different prices, the buyer at the lower price can arbitrage by selling to the consumer buying at the higher price but with a tiny discount.

However, market frictions in oligopolies such as the airlines and even in fully competitive retail or industrial markets allow for a limited degree of differential pricing to different consumers. Price discrimination also occurs when it costs more to supply one customer than it does another, and yet the supplier charges both the same price.

The effects of price discrimination on social efficiency are unclear; typically such behaviour leads to lower prices for some consumers and higher prices for others. Output can be expanded when price discrimination is very efficient, but output can also decline when discrimination is more effective at extracting surplus from high-valued users than expanding sales to low valued users. Even if output remains constant, price discrimination can reduce efficiency by misallocating output among consumers. Price discrimination requires market segmentation and some means to discourage discount customers from becoming resellers and, by extension, competitors. This usually entails using one or more means of preventing any resale, keeping the different price groups separate, making price comparisons difficult, or restricting pricing information. The boundary set up by the marketer to keep segments separate are referred to as a *rate fence*. Price discrimination is thus very common in services, where resale is not possible; an example is student discounts at museums.

Price discrimination can also be seen where the requirement that goods be identical is relaxed. For example, so-called "premium products" (including relatively simple products, such as cappuccino compared to regular coffee) have a price differential that is not explained by the cost of production. Some economists have argued that this is a form of price discrimination exercised by providing a means for consumers to reveal their willingness to pay.

Types of Price Discrimination

First Degree Price Discrimination

In first degree price discrimination, price varies by customer's willingness or ability to pay. This arises from the fact that the value of goods is subjective. A customer with low price elasticity is less deterred by a higher price than a customer with high price elasticity of demand. As long as the price elasticity (in absolute value) for a customer is less than one, it is very advantageous to increase the price: the seller gets more money for fewer goods. With an increase of the price elasticity tends to rise above one. One can show that in the optimum the price, as it varies by customer, is inversely proportional to one minus the reciprocal of the price elasticity of that customer at that price. This assumes that the consumer passively reacts to the price set by the seller, and that the seller knows the demand curve of the customer. In practice however there is a bargaining situation, which is more complex: the customer may try to influence the price, such as by pretending to like the product less than he or she really does or by threatening not to buy it. An alternative way to understand First Degree Price Discrimination is as follows: This type of price discrimination is primarily theoretical because it requires the seller of a good or service to know the absolute maximum price that every consumer is willing to pay. As above, it is true that consumers have different price elasticities, but the seller is not concerned with such. The seller is concerned with the maximum willingness to pay (or reservation price) of each customer. By knowing the reservation price, the seller is able to absorb the entire market surplus, thus taking all consumer surplus from the consumer and transforming it into revenues. From a social welfare perspective, first degree price discrimination is not undesirable. That is, the market is still entirely efficient and there is no deadweight loss to society. However, it is the complete opposite of a perfectly competitive market. In a perfectly competitive market, the consumers receive the bulk of surplus. In a market with first degree price discrimination, the seller(s) capture all surplus. Efficiency is unchanged but the wealth is transferred. This type of market does not much exist in reality, hence it is primarily theoretical. Examples of where this might be observed are in markets where consumers bid for tenders, though still, in this case, the practice of collusive tendering undermines efficiency.

Second Degree Price Discrimination

In second degree price discrimination, price varies according to quantity sold. Larger quantities are available at a lower unit price. This is particularly widespread in sales to industrial customers, where bulk buyers enjoy higher discounts. Additionally to second degree price discrimination, sellers are not able to differentiate between different types of consumers. Thus, the suppliers will provide incentives for the consumers to differentiate themselves according to preference. As above, quantity "discounts", or non-linear pricing, is a means by which suppliers use consumer preference to distinguish classes of consumers. This allows the supplier to set different prices to the different groups and capture a larger portion of the total market surplus.

Third Degree Price Discrimination

In third degree price discrimination, price varies by attributes such as location or by customer segment, or in the most extreme case, by the individual customer's identity; where the attribute in question is used as a proxy for ability/willingness to pay.

Additionally to third degree price discrimination, the supplier(s) of a market where this type of discrimination is exhibited are capable of differentiating between consumer classes. Examples of this differentiation are student or senior discounts.

For example, a student or a senior consumer will have a different willingness to pay than an average consumer, where the reservation price is presumably lower because of budget constraints.

Thus, the supplier sets a lower price for that consumer because the student or senior has a more elastic price elasticity of demand. The supplier is once again capable of capturing more market surplus than would be possible without price discrimination.

Note that it is not always advantageous to the company to price discriminate even if it is possible, especially for second and third degree discrimination. In some circumstances, the demands of different classes of consumers will encourage suppliers to simply ignore one/some class(es) and target entirely to the other(s). Whether it is profitable to price discriminate is determined by the specifics of a particular market.

Price Skimming

In price skimming, price varies over time. Typically a company starts selling a new product at a relatively high price then gradually reduces the price as the low price elasticity segment gets satiated. Price skimming is closely related to the concept of yield management.

Combination

These types are not mutually exclusive. Thus a company may vary pricing by location, but then offer bulk discounts as well. Airlines use several different types of price discrimination, including:

- Bulk discounts to wholesalers, consolidators, and tour operators
- Incentive discounts for higher sales volumes to travel agents and corporate buyers
- Seasonal discounts, incentive discounts, and even general prices that vary by location. The price of a flight from say, Singapore to Beijing can vary widely if one buys the ticket in Singapore compared to Beijing (or New York or Tokyo or elsewhere). In online ticket sales this is achieved by using the customer's credit card billing address to determine his location.
- Discounted tickets requiring advance purchase and/or Saturday stays. Both restrictions have the effect of excluding business travellers, who typically travel during the workweek and arrange trips on shorter notice.
- First degree price discrimination based on customer. It is not accidental that hotel or car rental firms may quote higher prices to their loyalty program's top tier members than to the general public.

Modern Taxonomy

The first/second/third degree taxonomy of price discrimination is due to Pigou (*Economics of Welfare*, 4th edition, 1932). However, these categories are not mutually exclusive or exhaustive. Ivan Png (*Managerial Economics*, 2nd edition, 2002) suggests an alternative taxonomy:

- Complete discrimination — where each user purchases up to the point where the user's marginal benefit equals the marginal cost of the item;

- Direct segmentation — where the seller can condition price on some attribute (like age or gender) that *directly* segments the buyers;
- Indirect segmentation — where the seller relies on some proxy (eg, package size, usage quantity, coupon) to structure a choice that *indirectly* segments the buyers.

The hierarchy—complete/direct/indirect—is in decreasing order of:

- profitability and.
- information requirement.

Complete price discrimination is most profitable, and requires the seller to have the most information about buyers. Indirect segmentation is least profitable, and requires the seller to have the least information about buyers.

Explanation

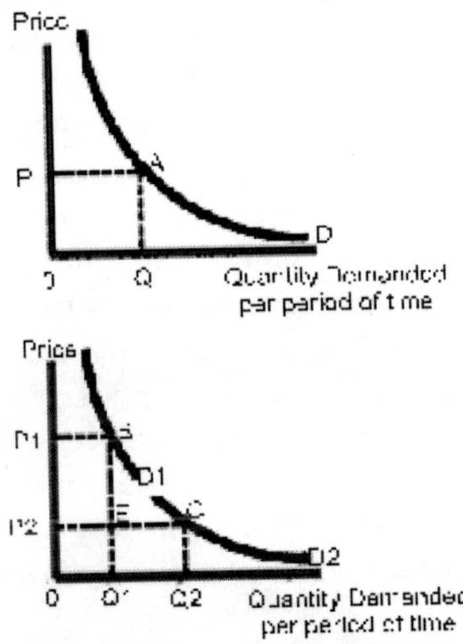

Figure: *Sales Revenue Without and with Price Discrimination*

The purpose of price discrimination is generally to capture the market's consumer surplus. This surplus arises because, in a market with a single clearing price, some customers (the very low price elasticity segment) would have been prepared to pay more than the single market price. Price discrimination transfers some of this surplus from the consumer to the producer/marketer. Strictly, a consumer surplus need not exist, for example where some below-cost selling is beneficial due to fixed costs or economies of scale. An example is a high-speed internet connection shared by two consumers in a single building; if one is willing to pay less than half the cost, and the other willing to make up the rest but not to pay the entire cost, then price discrimination is necessary for the purchase to take place.

It can be proved mathematically that a firm facing a downward sloping demand curve that is convex to the origin will always obtain higher revenues under price discrimination than under a single price strategy. This can also be shown diagrammatically. In the top diagram, a single price (P) is available to all customers. The amount of revenue is represented by area P, A,Q, O. The consumer surplus is the area above line segment P, A but below the demand curve (D).

With price discrimination, (the bottom diagram), the demand curve is divided into two segments (D1 and D2). A higher price (P1) is charged to the low elasticity segment, and a lower price (P2) is charged to the high elasticity segment. The total revenue from the first segment is equal to the area P1,B, Q1,O. The total revenue from the second segment is equal to the area E, C,Q2,Q1. The sum of these areas will always be greater than the area without discrimination assuming the demand curve resembles a rectangular hyperbola with unitary elasticity. The more prices that are introduced, the greater the sum of the revenue areas, and the more of the consumer surplus is captured by the producer. Note that the above requires both first and second degree price discrimination: the right segment corresponds partly to different people than the left segment, partly to the same people, willing to buy more if the product is cheaper. It is very useful for the price discriminator to determine the optimum prices in each market segment. This is done in the next diagram where each segment is considered as a separate market with its own demand curve. As usual, the profit maximizing output (Qt) is determined by the intersection of the marginal cost curve (MC) with the marginal revenue curve for the total market (MRt).

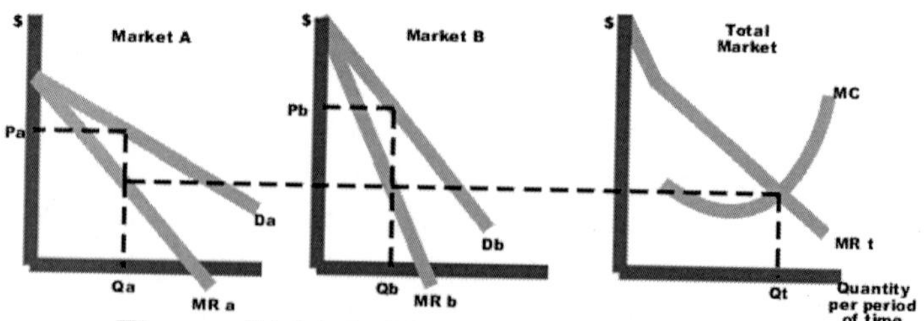

Figure: *Multiple Market Price Determination*

The firm decides what amount of the total output to sell in each market by looking at the intersection of marginal cost with marginal revenue (profit maximization). This output is then divided between the two markets, at the equilibrium marginal revenue level.

Therefore, the optimum outputs are Qa and Qb. From the demand curve in each market we can determine the profit maximizing prices of Pa and Pb.

It is also important to note that the marginal revenue in both markets at the optimal output levels must be equal, otherwise the firm could profit from transferring output over to whichever market is offering higher marginal revenue.

Given that Market 1 has a price elasticity of demand of E1 and Market of E2, the optimal pricing ration in Market 1 versus Market 2 is $P1/P2 = [1 - 1/E2]/[1 - 1/E1]$.

Examples of Price Discrimination

Retail Price Discrimination

In certain circumstances, it is a violation of the Robinson-Patman Act, (a 1936 Federal U.S. antitrust statute) for manufacturers of goods to sell their products to similarly situated retailers at different prices based solely on the volume of products purchased.

Travel Industry

Airlines and other travel companies use differentiated pricing regularly, as they sell travel products and services simultaneously to different market segments. This is often done by assigning capacity to various booking classes, which sell for different prices and which may be linked to fare restrictions. The restrictions or "fences" help ensure that market segments buy in the booking class range that has been established for them. For example, schedule-sensitive business passengers who are willing to pay $300 for a seat from city A to city B cannot purchase a $150 ticket because the $150 booking class contains a requirement for a Saturday night stay, or a 15-day advance purchase, or another fare rule that discourages, minimizes, or effectively prevents a sale to business passengers.

Notice however that in this example "the seat" is not really always the same product. That is, the business person who purchases the $300 ticket may be willing to do so in return for a seat on a high-demand morning flight, for full refundability if the ticket is not used, and for the ability to upgrade to first class if space is available for a nominal fee. On the same flight are price-sensitive passengers who are not willing to pay $300, but who are willing to fly on a lower-demand flight (say one leaving an hour earlier), or via a connection city (not a non-stop flight), and who are willing to forgo refundability.

On the other hand, an airline may also apply differential pricing to "the same seat" over time, e.g. by discounting the price for an early or late booking (without changing any other fare condition). This could present an arbitrage opportunity in the absence of any restriction on reselling. However, passenger name changes are typically prevented or financially penalized by contract.

Since airlines often fly multi-leg flights, and since no-show rates vary by segment, competition for the seat has to take in the spatial dynamics of the product. Someone trying to fly A-B is competing with people trying to fly A-C through city B on the same aircraft. This is one reason airlines use yield management technology to determine how many seats to allot for A-B passengers, B-C passengers, and A-B-C passengers, at their varying fares and with varying demands and no-show rates. With the rise of the Internet and the growth of low fare airlines, airfare pricing transparency has become far more pronounced. Passengers discovered it is quite easy to compare fares across different flights or different airlines. This helped put pressure on airlines to lower fares. Meanwhile, in the recession following the September 11, 2001, attacks on the U.S., business travellers and corporate buyers made it clear to airlines that they were not going to be buying air travel at rates high enough to subsidize lower fares for non-business travellers. This prediction has come true, as vast numbers of business travellers are buying airfares only in economy class for business travel. There are sometimes group discounts on rail tickets and passes. This may be in view of the alternative of going by car together.

Premium Pricing

For certain products, premium products are priced at a level (compared to "regular" or "economy" products) that is well beyond their marginal cost of production. For example, a coffee chain may price regular coffee at $1, but "premium" coffee at $2.50 (where the respective costs of production may be $0.90 and $1.25). Economists such as Tim Harford in the Undercover Economist have argued that this is a form of price discrimination: by providing a choice between a regular and premium product, consumers are being asked to reveal their degree of price sensitivity (or willingness to pay) for comparable products. Similar techniques are used in pricing business class airline tickets and premium alcoholic drinks, for example.

This effect can lead to (seemingly) perverse incentives for the producer. If, for example, potential business class customers will pay a large price differential only if economy class seats are uncomfortable while economy class customers are more sensitive to price than comfort, airlines may have substantial incentives to purposely make economy seating uncomfortable.

In the example of coffee, a restaurant may gain more economic profit by making poor quality regular coffee—more profit is gained from up-selling to premium customers than is lost from customers who refuse to purchase inexpensive but poor quality coffee. In such cases, the net social utility should also account for the "lost" utility to consumers of the regular product, although determining the magnitude of this foregone utility may not be feasible.

Segmentation by Age Group and Student Status

Many movie theatres, amusement parks, tourist attractions, and other places have different admission prices per market segment: typical groupings are Youth, Student, Adult, and Senior. Each of these groups typically have a much different demand curve. Children, people living on student wages, and people living on retirement generally have much less disposable income.

Discounts for Members of Certain Occupations

Many businesses, especially in the Southern United States, offer reduced prices to active military members. In addition to increased sales to the target group, businesses benefit from the resulting positive publicity, leading to increased sales to the general public. Less publicized are discounts to other service workers such as police; off-duty police customers in high-crime areas are said to constitute free security.

Employee Discounts

Discounts that businesses give to their own employees are also a form of price discrimination.

Retail Incentives

A variety of incentive techniques may be used to increase market share or revenues at the retail level. These include discount coupons, rebates, bulk and quantity pricing, seasonal discounts, and frequent buyer discounts.

Incentives for Industrial Buyers

Many methods exist to incentivize wholesale or industrial buyers. These may be quite targeted, as they are designed to generate specific activity, such as buying more frequently, buying more regularly, buying in bigger quantities, buying new products with established ones, and so on. Thus, there are bulk discounts, special pricing for long-term commitments, non-peak discounts, on high-demand goods to incentivize buying lower-demand goods, rebates, and many others. This can help the relations between the firms involved.

Gender-Based Examples

Many gender-based price differences are held to be illegal in countries such as the United States and the United Kingdom.

"Ladies' Night"

Many North American or European nightclubs feature a "ladies' night" in which women are offered discount or free drinks, or are absolved from payment of cover charges. This differs from conventional price discrimination in that the primary motive is not, usually, to increase revenue at the expense of consumer surplus.

Dry Cleaning

Dry cleaners typically charge higher prices for the laundering of women's clothes than for men's. Some US communities, have reacted by outlawing the practice. Dry cleaners justify the price differences because women's clothes typically require far more time to press than men's clothes due to more pleating.

Haircutting

Women's haircuts are often more expensive than men's haircuts which in past times could be accounted for as women generally had longer, more complex hairstyles whereas men generally had shorter hairstyles. Nowadays men's and women's styles are more varied but the price discrimination continues. Some salons have modified their pricing to reflect "long hair" versus "short hair" or style instead of gender.

Financial Aid in Education

Financial aid as offered by U.S. colleges and universities is a form of price discrimination that is widely accepted, and completely legal. Middle-and lower-income students may be offered discounts in the form of tuition waivers, scholarships, work-study programs that pay partly in free course hours, and government guaranteed loans.

Haggling

Many cultures involve haggling in market transactions — inflated prices are posted, but the customer can negotiate with the vendor. In the United States, haggling is rare to non-existent in retail, but common when automobiles and homes are sold. Negotiation often requires knowledge, confidence, and the ability to manage confrontational personalities, and vendors know that many customers will pay higher prices in order to avoid negotiating.

International Price Discrimination

Pharmaceutical companies may charge customers living in wealthier countries (such as the United States) a much higher price than for identical drugs in poorer nations, as is the case with the sale of anti-retroviral drugs in Africa. Since the purchasing power of African consumers is much lower, sales would be extremely limited without price discrimination. The ability of pharmaceutical companies to maintain price differences between countries is often reinforced by national drugs laws and regulations. (or lack thereof) Another example is textbooks. Publishers such as Prentice Hall and Pearson have low cost editions of textbooks for countries such as India. The textbooks are often printed on cheaper paper, are paperbacks and priced at 15-20% of the dollar price. This pricing has largely eliminated the practice of photo copying these books. Although not common in modern times, governments have traditionally raised revenues from tariffs. When these are not flat tariffs, the government effectively sets the prices of goods that are not produced locally and are only imported.

Even online sales for non material goods, which do not have to be shipped, may change according to the geographic location of the buyer. A song in Apple's iTunes costs 79 pence (1.49 USD) for Britons but only 99 cents for Americans. (~50% more for the same song) These differences may arise because of changes in exchange rates that occur much more frequently than changes in prices, or they may arise because the license-holders (in this case, record companies) are enforcing their existing pricing policy on new licensees or intermediaries.

Academic Pricing

Companies will often offer discounted software to students and faculty at K-12 and university levels. These may be labelled as academic versions, but perform the same as the full price retail software. Academic versions of the most expensive software suites may be priced as little as one fifth or less of retail price. Some academic software may have differing licenses than retail versions, usually disallowing their use in activities for profit or expiring the license after a given number of months. This also has the characteristics of an "initial offer"-that is, the profits from an academic customer may come partly in the form of future non-academic sales if they get "hooked" on the product.

Dual Pricing

Even within a country, differentiated pricing may be established to ensure that citizens receive lower prices than non-citizens; this is known as dual pricing. This is particularly common for goods that are subsidized or otherwise provided by the state (and hence paid by taxpayers). Thus Finns, Thais, and Indians (among others) may purchase special fare tickets for public transportation that are available only to citizens. Many countries also maintain separate admission charges for museums, national parks and similar facilities, the usually professed rationale being that citizens should be able to educate themselves and enjoy the country's natural wonders cheaply, but other visitors should pay the market rate.

Many publicly run universities in the United States are subsidized by taxpayers of the state in which they are located; residents of said state are frequently given a discount on tuition as a result.

Wage Discrimination

Wage discrimination is when the price of equivalent labour is discriminated among different groups of workers. This may be seen as just one kind of price discrimination or as an example of its inverse, one buyer buying identical goods at different rates.

Price Discrimination by Online Search Type

Some online stores and companies attempt to price discriminate between their customers by using information they gather about how a particular customer is searching for a product. For example, some travel firms have been shown to mark-up prices for all the holiday packages they list when a customer asks to see their holidays ranked with the most expensive package first (which suggests the customer may be price insensitive).

The same packages may be available for less if the customer changes their search type. Variants of this behaviour have been reported on other e-commerce sites, where the more specific your search for a particular good, the lower price is displayed for that good.

Universal Pricing

Universal pricing is the opposite of price discrimination — one price is offered for the good or service. This is usually preferred by consumers over tiered pricing For example, the European Union is currently making efforts to set a single-price protocol for automobile sales.

Two Necessary Conditions for Price Discrimination

There are two conditions that must be met if a price discrimination scheme is to work. First the firm must be able to identify market segments by their price elasticity of demand and second the firms must be able to enforce the scheme. For example, airlines routinely engage in price discrimination by charging high prices for customers with relatively inelastic demand-business travellers-and discount prices for tourist who have relatively elastic demand, The airlines enforce the scheme by making the tickets non-transferable thus preventing a tourist from buying a ticket at a discounted price and selling it to a business traveller (arbitrage).

Airlines must also prevent business travellers from directly buying discount tickets. Airlines accomplish this by imposing advance ticketing requirements or minimum stay requirements conditions that it would be difficult for average business traveller to meet.

Price Discrimination and Imperfect Competition

Firms frequently segment customers according to price sensitivity in order to price discriminate and increase profits. In some settings, consumer heterogeneity can be directly observed and a firm can base its pricing upon contractible consumer characteristics; in other settings, heterogeneity is not directly observable, but can be indirectly elicited by offering menus of products and prices and allowing consumers to self-select. In both cases, the firm seeks to price its wares as a function of each consumer's underlying demand elasticity, extracting more surplus and increasing sales to elastic customers in the process.

When the firm is a monopolist with market power, the underlying theory of price discrimination is now well understood, as explained, for example, by Varian (1989) in an earlier volume in this series. On the other extreme, when markets are perfectly competitive and firms have neither short-run nor long-run market power, the law of one price applies and price discrimination cannot exist. Economic reality, of course, largely lies somewhere in between the textbook extremes, and most economists agree that price discrimination arises in oligopoly settings. This chapter explores price discrimination in these imperfectly competitive markets, surveying the theoretical literature.

Price discrimination exists when prices vary across customer segments that cannot be entirely explained by variations in marginal cost. Stigler's (1987) definition makes this precise: a firm price discriminates when the ratio of prices is different from the ratio of marginal costs for two goods offered by a firm. Such a definition, of course, requires that one is careful in calculating marginal costs to include all relevant shadow costs. This is particularly true where costly capacity and aggregate demand uncertainty play critical roles, as discussed in section 8. Similarly, where discrimination occurs over the provision of quality, as reviewed in section 6, operationalizing this definition requires using the marginal prices of qualities and the associated marginal costs.

Even with this moderately narrow definition of price discrimination, there remains a considerable variety of theoretical models that address issues of rice discrimination and imperfect competition. We further limit attention in this survey to the straightforward setting of symmetric firms competing in a retail market; even here, there are numerous theories to explore. These include third-degree price discrimination (section 3), purchase-history price discrimination (section 4), intrapersonal price discrimination (section 5), second-degree price discrimination and nonlinear pricing (section 6), product bundling (section 7), and demand uncertainty and price rigidities (section 8). Unfortunately, we must prune a few additional areas of inquiry, leaving some models of imperfect competition and price discrimination unexamined. Among the more notable omissions in this chapter are price discrimination in vertical structures, imperfect information and costly search, the commitment effect of price discrimination policies, collusion and intertemporal price discrimination, and the strategic effect of product lines in imperfectly competitive settings.

It is well known that price discrimination is only feasible under certain conditions: (i) firm(s) have short-run market power, (ii) consumers can be segmented either directly or indirectly, and (iii) arbitrage across differently priced goods is infeasible. Given that these conditions are satisfied, an individual firm will typically have an incentive to price discriminate.

The form of price discrimination will depend importantly on the nature of market power, the form of consumer heterogeneity, and the availability of various segmenting mechanisms. A firm can typically extract greater consumer surplus by varying the marginal price and screening consumers according to their revealed consumptions. This use of nonlinear pricing as a sorting mechanism is typically referred to as second-degree price discrimination.

More generally, in a richer setting with heterogeneity over observable and unobservable characteristics, we expect that the monopolist will practice some combination of direct and indirect price discrimination—offering P(q, _o), but using the price schedule to sort over unobservable characteristics. While one can categorize price discrimination strategies as either direct or indirect, it is also useful to catalog strategies according to whether they discriminate across consumers (interpersonal price discrimination) or across units for the same consumer (intrapersonal price discrimination). Intrapersonal price discrimination is a variation of price/marginalcost ratios across the portfolio of goods purchased by a given consumer (i.e., cross-consumer heterogeneity is held constant). For example, suppose that there is no interconsumer heterogeneity so that _ is fixed. There will generally remain some intraconsumer heterogeneity over the marginal value of each unit of consumption so that a firm cannot extract all consumer surplus using a linear price. Here, a firm can capture the consumer surplus associated with intraconsumer heterogeneity, either by offering a nonlinear price schedule equal to the individual consumer's compensated demand curve or by offering a simpler two-part tariff. We will address these issues more in section 5.11 Elsewhere in this chapter, we will focus on interpersonal price discrimination, with the implicit recognition that intra-personal price discrimination often occurs simultaneously.

The methodology of monopoly price discrimination is both useful and misleading in illuminating the effects of discrimination by imperfectly competitive firms. It is useful because the monopoly methods can frequently be used to calculate each firm's best response to its competitors' policies. Just as one can solve for the best-response function in a Cournot quantity game by deriving a residual demand curve and proceeding as if the firm was a monopolist on this residual market, we can also solve for best responses in more complex price discrimination games by deriving residual market demand curves. Unfortunately, our intuitions from the monopoly models can be misleading, because we are ultimately interested in the equilibrium of the firms' best-response functions rather than a single optimal pricing strategy. For example, while it is certainly the case that, ceteris paribus, a single uniformpricing firm will weakly benefit by introducing price discrimination, if every firm were to switch from uniform pricing to price discrimination, profits may fall for the entire industry.

Whether profits fall depends upon whether the additional surplus extraction allowed by price discrimination (the standard effect in the monopoly setting) exceeds the additional competitive externality if discrimination increases the intensity of price competition. This comparison, in turn, depends upon the details of the markets, as will be explained. The pages that follow consist largely of evaluations of these interactions between price discrimination and imperfect competition.

When evaluating the impact of price discrimination in imperfectly competitive environments, two related comparisons are relevant. First, starting from a setting of imperfect competition and uniform pricing, what are the welfare changes from allowing firms to price discriminate? Second, starting from a setting of monopoly and price discrimination, what are the welfare effects of increasing competition? Because the theoretical predictions of the models often depend upon the nature of competition, consumer preferences and consumer heterogeneity, we shall pursue these questions by examining a collection of specialized models that illuminate the broad themes of this literature and illustrate how the implications of competitive price discrimination compare to uniform pricing and monopoly. In sections 2-7, we explore variations on these themes, by varying the forms of competition, preference heterogeneity, and segmenting devices. Initially in section 2, we begin with the benchmark of first-degree, perfect price discrimination. In section 3, we turn to the classic setting of third-degree price discrimination, applied to the case of imperfectly competitive firms. In section 4, we examine an important class of models that extends third-degree price discrimination to dynamic settings, where price offers may be conditioned on a consumer's purchase history from rivalsa form of price discrimination that can only exist under competition. In section 5, we study intrapersonal price discrimination. Section 6 brings together several diverse theoretical approaches to modelling imperfectly competitive second-degree price discrimination, comparing and contrasting the results to those under monopoly. Product bundling (as a form of price discrimination) in imperfectly competitive markets is reviewed in section 7. Models of demand uncertainty and price rigidities are introduced in section 8.

First-degree Price Discrimination

First-degree (or perfect) price discrimination—which arises when the seller can capture all consumer surplus by pricing each unit at precisely the consumer's marginal willingness to pay—serves as an important benchmark and starting point for exploring more subtle forms of pricing. When the seller controls a monopoly, the monopolist obtains the entire social surplus, and so profit maximization is synonymous with maximizing social welfare. How does the economic intuition of this simple model translate to oligopoly? The oligopoly game of perfect price discrimination is quite simple to analyse, even in its most general form. Following Spulber (1979), suppose that there are n firms, each selling a (possibly differentiated) product, but that each firm has the ability to price discriminate in the first degree and extract all of the consumer surplus under its residual demand curve.

In this oligopoly game of perfect price discrimination, the marginal consumer purchases at marginal cost, so, under mild technical assumptions, social surplus is maximized. In this setting, unlike the imperfect price discrimination settings which follow, the welfare effect of price discrimination is immediate, just as in monopoly perfect price discrimination. A few differences exist, however.

First, while consumers obtain none of the surplus under the residual demand curves, it does not follow that consumers obtain no surplus at all; rather, for each firm i, they obtain no surplus from the addition of the ith firm's product to the current availability of n"1 other goods. If the goods are close substitutes and marginal costs are constant, the residual demand curves are highly elastic and consumers may nonetheless obtain considerable non-residual surplus from the presence of competition. The net effect of price discrimination on total consumer surplus requires an explicit treatment of consumer demand.

Second, it may be the case that each firm's residual demand curve is more elastic when its rivals can perfectly price discriminate than when they are forced to price uniformly. Thus, while each firm prefers the ability to perfectly price discriminate itself, the total industry profit may fall when price discrimination is allowed, depending on the form of competition and consumer preferences.

We will see a clear example of this in the Hotelling demand model of These and Vives (1988) which examines discriminatory pricing based on observable location. In this simple setting, third-degree price discrimination is perfect, but firms are worse off and would prefer to commit collectively to uniform-pricing strategies. Third, if n is endogenous, if entry with fixed costs occurs until long-run profits are driven to zero, and if consumer surplus is entirely captured by price discrimination, then price discrimination lowers social welfare compared to uniform pricing. This conclusion follows immediately from the fact that consumer surplus is zero and entry dissipates profits, leading to zero social surplus from the presence of the market. Uniform pricing typically leaves some consumer surplus (and hence positive social welfare). Again, whether consumer surplus is entirely captured by price discrimination requires a more explicit analysis of demand. Rather than further explore the stylized setting of first-degree price discrimination, we instead turn to explicit analyses undertaken for each of the imperfect price discrimination strategies studied in the ensuing sections.

Third-degree price Discrimination

The classic theory of third-degree price discrimination by a monopolist selling to several distinct markets is straightforward: the optimal price-discriminating prices are found by applying the familiar inverse-elasticity rule to each market separately. If instead of monopoly, however, oligopolists compete in each market, then each firm applies the inverse-elasticity rule using its own residual demand curve—an equilibrium construction. Here, the crossprice elasticities of demand play a central role in determining equilibrium prices and outputs.

These cross-price elasticities, in turn, depend critically upon consumer preferences and the form of consumer heterogeneity.

Welfare Analysis

With third-degree price discrimination, there are three potential sources of social inefficiency.

First, aggregate output over all market segments may be too low if prices exceed marginal cost. To this end, we seek to understand the conditions for which price discrimination leads to an increase or decrease in aggregate output relative to uniform pricing.

Second, for a given level of aggregate consumption, price discrimination will typically generate interconsumer misallocations relative to uniform pricing; hence, aggregate output will not be efficiently distributed to the highest-value ends. And third, there may be inter-firm inefficiencies as a given consumer may be served by an inefficient firm, perhaps purchasing from a more distant or higher-cost firm to obtain a price discount. In the following, much is made of the relationship between aggregate output and welfare. If the same aggregate output is generated under uniform pricing as under price discrim-ination, then price discrimination must necessarily lower social welfare because output is allocated with multiple prices; with a uniform price, interconsumer misallocations are not possible. Therefore, holding production inefficiencies fixed, an increase in aggregate output is a necessary condition for price discrimination to increase welfare under monopoly. Varian (1985) made this point in the context of monopoly, but the economic logic applies more generally to imperfect competition, providing that the firms are equally efficient at production and the number of firms is fixed. Because we can easily make statements only about aggregate output for many models of third-degree price discrimination, this result will prove useful, giving us some limited power to draw welfare conclusions. There are two common approaches to modelling imperfect competition: quantity competition with homogeneous goods and price competition with product differentiation. The simple quantity-competition model of oligopoly price discrimination is presented in section

We then turn to price-setting models of competition. Within price-setting games, we further distinguish two sets of models based upon consumer demands. In the first setting (section 3.3), all firms agree in their ranking of high-demand (or "strong") markets and low-demand (or "weak") markets. Here, whether the strong markets are more competitive than the weak markets is critical for many economic conclusions. In the second setting (section 3.4), firms are asymmetric in their ranking of strong and weak markets; e.g., firm a's strong market is firm b's weak market and conversely. With asymmetry, equilibrium prices can move in patterns that are not possible under symmetric rankings and different economic insights present themselves. Following the treatment of price-setting games, we take up the topics of third-degree price discrimination with endogenous entry (section 3.5) and private restrictions on price discrimination (section 3.6).

Several observations regarding the effects of competition follow immediately from this framework. First, it follows that marginal revenues are also equal across market segments, just as in monopoly. Second, under mild assumptions, as the number of firms increases, the markup over marginal cost decreases in each market segment. From this comparative static, it follows that each firm's profit also decreases and consumer surplus increases as n increases. Third, if each market segment has a constant elasticity of demand, relative prices across segments are constant in n and, therefore, an increase in firms necessarily decreases absolute price dispersion. Finally, in the spirit of monopolistic competition, one can introduce a fixed cost of production and allow entry to drive long-run profits to zero, thereby making the size of the market endogenous. In such a setting, both long-term market power and economic profit are zero, but fixed costs of entry generate short-run market power, short-run economic rents, and prices above marginal cost. Aside from the effects of competition, one can also inquire about the welfare effects of price discrimination relative to uniform pricing. To this end, it is first helpful to review the setting of monopoly in Robinson (1933). In that work, Robinson concludes that whether aggregate output increases when a monopolist price discriminates depends upon the relative curvature of the segmented demand curves. Particularly in the case of two segments, if the "adjusted concavity" (an idea we will make precise below) of the more elastic market is greater than the adjusted concavity of the less elastic market at a uniform price, then output increases with price discrimination; when the reverse is true, aggregate output decreases.

When a market segment has linear demand, the adjusted concavity is zero. It follows that when demand curves are linear—providing all markets are served—price discrimination has no effect on aggregate output. In sum, to make a determination about the price discrimination effects on aggregate output under monopoly, one needs only to compare the adjusted concavities of each market segment.

A tale of two elasticities: best-response symmetry in price games In her study of third-degree price discrimination under monopoly, Robinson (1933) characterizes a monopolist's two markets as "strong" and "weak." By definition, a price discriminating monopolist always sets the higher price in the strong market, and the lower price in the weak market. It is useful to extend this ranking to imperfectly competitive markets.

Suppose that there are two markets, i = 1, 2. We say that market i is "weak" (and the other is "strong") for firm j if, for any uniform price(s) set by the other firm(s), the optimal price in market i is always lower than the optimal price in the other segment. Formally, if BRj i (p) is the best-response function of firm j in market i, given that its rival sets the price p, then market 1 is weak (and 2 is strong) if and only if BRj

1(p) < BRj

2(p) for all

We say that the market environment satisfies best-response symmetry (following Corts (1998)) if the weak and strong markets of each firm coincide; alternatively, if the weak and strong markets of each firm differ, then the environment exhibits best-response asymmetry.

As we will see, when firms commonly agree on their rankings of markets from strong to weak (i.e., best-response symmetry), there exists a useful result from Holmes (1989) which predicts when aggregate output will rise or fall with the introduction of price discrimination, and therefore provides some indication about its ultimate welfare effects. This result is not available when best responses are asymmetric, which creates a crucial distinction in what follows. In this section, we assume that there exists best-response symmetry; in the following section, we study best-response asymmetry.

Borenstein (1985) and Holmes (1989) extend the analysis of third-degree price discrimination to settings of imperfect competition with product differentiation, under scoring the significance of cross-price elasticities in predicting changes in profits and surplus. Specifically, Holmes (1989) builds upon the monopoly model of Robinson (1933) and demonstrates that under symmetric duopoly, it is crucial to know the ratio of market to cross-price elasticities, aside from the adjusted concavities of demand.

The curvatures of the demand curves are insufficient, by themselves, to predict changes in aggregate output when markets are imperfectly competitive.

Several results follow from this comparison and the presence of the cross-price elasticity.

- Price effects. From the above formulation of the inverse-elasticity rules, competition clearly lowers prices in both markets compared to monopoly, ceteris paribus, and therefore we expect competition to increase welfare in this simple third-degree price discrimination setting. It is also immediate that the effect of competition on price dispersion across markets is ambiguous and depends upon the cross-price elasticities. If the goods are close substitutes and market competition is fierce, prices will be close to marginal cost and competition will reduce price differentials across the markets. Alternatively, if consumers in the weak market find the goods to be close substitutes (their next best alternative is consuming from a rival firm) while consumers in the strong market exhibit powerful brand loyalties (their next best alternative is the outside good), then the firms choose highly competitive prices in the weak market and close-to-monopoly prices in the strong market. These choices lead to greater price differentials across markets. Unfortunately, no testable implications for price dispersion arise from the theory without additional information regarding the cross-price elasticities in each market.
- Output (and welfare) effects. A recurring policy question in the price discrimination literature is whether to allow third-degree

price discrimination or to enforce uniform pricing. A key ingredient to understanding this question in the context of imperfectly competitive markets is the impact of price discrimination on output.

We further assume that these marginal profit functions decrease in price for each market segment.

The first bracketed expression is a straightforward variation of Robinson's adjusted-concavity condition found in the case of monopoly. When demands are linear, the expression is zero. The second expression (the elasticity-ratio difference) is novel and due entirely to competition. If the strong market (market 2) is more sensitive to competition (i.e., "c 2/"m2 is larger in the strong market than the weak market), then price discrimination causes the output reduction in the strong market to be less than the output increase in the weak market; aggregate output rises accordingly. If this reduction in the strong market is sufficiently small relative to the weak market, then welfare will also rise. The point most worth stressing is that the effect of competition depends upon the size of the cross-price elasticity relative to the industry elasticity. When demands are linear (and adjusted concavities are zero), the elasticity ratio test gives a sufficient condition for increased output:

In words, price discrimination leads to an increase in output if the discrepancy in elasticities across the two markets is greater with respect to the outside option than with respect to the rival's good. Among other things, this condition implies that at the discriminating monopoly prices (where the left-hand ratio is 1), the strong market is "more competitive" than the weak market in the sense of cross-price elasticities. Profit effects. The profit effects of price discrimination are more difficult to predict. While any individual firm's profit rises when allowed to price discriminate, the entire industry profit may rise or fall when all firms add price discrimination to their strategic arsenals. Two papers have made significant findings in this direction. Holmes (1989) analyzes the case of linear demand functions and finds that when the elasticity ratio condition above is satisfied, profit (as well as output) increases. When the elasticity ratio is violated, however, the effect on profits is ambiguous although welfare necessarily falls. What is particularly interesting is that price discrimination decreases profits when the weak market has a higher cross-price elasticity but a lower market elasticity compared to the strong market. Because the market elasticity is lower in the weak market, a given increase in price would be more profitable (and more socially efficient) in the weak market than in the strong market. When profits fall due to price discrimination (which Holmes (1989) notes is never by more than a few percentage points), it is because the weak market's significantly higher cross-price elasticity outweighs its lower market elasticity, and therefore price discrimination reduces the weak-market price. From a profit perspective (and a social welfare perspective), this lower price is in the wrong market and thus profits decline relative to uniform pricing.

Related to this finding, Armstrong and Vickers (2001) consider a non-linear model of third-degree price discrimination in which each segment is a Hotelling linear market with uniformly distributed consumers, each of whom has identical downward-sloping demand.

The market segments differ only by the consumers' transportation costs. They demonstrate that when competition is sufficiently intense (specifically, each segment's transportation cost goes to zero while maintaining a constant cost ratio), industry profits increase under price discrimination and consumer surplus falls. This outcome suggests that Holmes's (1989) linear examples of slightly decreased profits from price discrimination may not be robust to nonlinear settings with intense competition. This finding, together with the other results of Holmes (1989), leads to a consensus that price discrimination increases profits in settings of best-response symmetry. In addition, Armstrong and Vickers (2001) find that when the segment with the lower market elasticity also has a sufficiently higher cross-price elasticity (i.e., low transportation costs), welfare falls under price discrimination. Interestingly, the economics underlying this result are similar to Holmes's (1989) linear model of decreased profits—price discrimination causes the prices to fall and rise in the wrong markets.

Inter-firm misallocations. The model examined in Holmes (1989) is symmetric across firms—no firm has a cost or product advantage over the other. This simplification obscures possibly significant, inter-firm misallocations that would arise in a model in which one firm has a comparative advantage in delivering utility to consumers. The change from uniform pricing to price discrimination may either mitigate or amplify these distortions. As an immediate illustration of this ambiguity, consider a duopoly setting in which both firms are local monopolists in the strong market and the strong-market demands are rectangular (although possibly different across firms).

In the weak market, suppose that the firms are Hotelling (1929) duopolists in a market which is covered in equilibrium. Given these assumptions, the only social inefficiency is that some consumers in the weak market purchase from the "wrong" firm; this situation arises when the price differential across firms in the weak market is not equal to the difference in marginal costs. Under price discrimination, our assumption of rectangular demand curves implies that the strong-market, inter-firm price differential depends entirely on the consumer's valuations for each product. In the weak market, however, it is easy to see that the resulting price differential between the firms is smaller than the difference in marginal costs; the price discrimination equilibrium results in the high-cost firm serving too much of the market. Compare this outcome to the uniformprice setting: If the strong market is sufficiently important relative to the weak market, then the uniform-price differential will be close to the price-discriminating, inter-firm differential in the strong market.

If the strong-market differential is close to the difference in marginal costs, then uniform pricing mitigates inefficiencies; if the differential in the strong market is smaller than the price-discriminating differential in the weak market, then uniform pricing amplifies the social distortions. In short, there are no robust conclusions regarding the effect of price discrimination on misallocated production.

When one firm's strength is a rival's weakness: best-response asymmetry in price games. The assumption that firms rank strong and weak markets symmetrically is restrictive, as it rules out most models with spatial demand systems in which price discrimination occurs over observable location; e.g., a weak (far away) market for firm a is a strong (close) market for firm b. The assumption of best-response symmetry in the previous analysis allowed us to conclude that the uniform price always lies between the strong market price and the weak market under discrimination. Without such symmetry, this conclusion does not exist. Indeed, it is possible that all prices rise or fall under price discrimination, depending on the underlying market demand curves. A simple model to illustrate recurring themes. We begin with a simple example of differentiated duopoly drawn from These and Vives (1988) to illustrate some of the consequences of price discrimination when firms have dissimilar strengths and weaknesses across market segments.

Consider a standard Hotelling (1929) model of duopoly in which two firms are located on the endpoints of a linear market. Each consumer has an observable location parameter, _ 2 (0, 1), which is drawn from a uniform distribution across the market; each consumer demands at most one unit of output.

Price Discrimination and Entry

The preceding analysis has largely taken the number of firms as exogenous. Given the possibility of entry with fixed costs, a new class of distortions arises: price discrimination may induce too much or too little entry relative to uniform pricing.

Monopolistic competition. If entry is unfettered and numerous potential entrants exist, entry occurs to the point where long-run profits are driven to zero. Under such models of monopolistic competition, social surplus is equated to consumer surplus. The question arises, with free entry does a change from uniform pricing to discrimination lead to higher or lower aggregate consumer surplus?

To answer this question, two effects must be resolved. First, by fixing the number of firms, does a change from uniform pricing to price discrimination lead to higher industry profits? We have already observed that price discrimination can either raise or lower industry profits, depending on the underlying system of demand. If price discrimination raises industry profits, then greater entry occurs; if price discrimination lowers profits, then fewer firms will operate in the market. Second, given that a move to price discrimination changes the size of the industry, will consumer surplus increase or decrease? Under uniform pricing, it is well known that the social and private values of entry may differ due to the effects of business stealing and product diversity; see, for example, Spence (1976) and Mankiw and Whinston (1986). Generally, when comparing price discrimination to uniform pricing, no clear welfare result about the social efficiency of free entry exists, although a few theoretical contributions are suggestive of the relative importance of various effects. Katz (1984), in a model of monopolistic competition with price discrimination, was one of the first to study how production inefficiencies from excessive entry may arise. He found that price discrimination's impact on social welfare is ambiguous and depends upon his model's demand parameters.

Rather than developing Katz's (1984) model, this ambiguity can be illustrated with a few simple examples. In our first example, price discrimination is shown to be beneficial through the extension of Hotelling's (1929) linear market to a circular setting, as in Salop (1979). Suppose that inelastic unit-demand consumers are uniformly distributed around a circular market. As entry occurs, assume firms automatically relocate equidistant from one another. When the market is covered, all potential consumers purchase a good from the nearest firm, so the optimal number of firms is that which minimizes the sum of transportation costs and the fixed costs of entry, K. As a counter-example, suppose that consumer preferences are entirely observable so that a third-degree price-discriminating monopolist would capture more of the consumer surplus than a uniform-pricing monopolist. To model imperfect competition, assume along the lines of Diamond (1971) that goods are homogeneous, but consumers must bear a small search cost for each visit to a store to obtain a price quote. There is then an equilibrium in which all firms offer the monopoly price schedule and consumers purchase from the first store they visit, providing that the resulting consumer surplus exceeds the cost of search. All firms follow identical pricing strategies, so there is no value to search, and each sells to an equal fraction of consumers. Because of ex ante competition, firms enter this market until long-run profits are dissipated. Because more consumer surplus remains under uniform pricing than under price discrimination, welfare is higher under uniform pricing while too much entry occurs under price discrimination.

Unfortunately, as these two examples suggest, we are left without any clear guidance regarding the effects of price discrimination on entry and the associated changes in social welfare under monopolistic competition.

Entry deterrence Allowing price discrimination by symmetric firms can increase the profitability of serving a market, and thereby generate more entry as shown in Katz (1984). On the other hand, one might imagine that firms are situated asymmetrically, as in Armstrong and Vickers (1993), where an incumbent firm serves two market segments, and potential entry can occur only in one of the segments. Here, price discrimination has no strategic value to the entrant given its limited access to a single market, but it does allow the incumbent to price lower in the newly entered market, while still maintaining monopoly profits from its captive segment. Hence, the incumbent's best-response discriminating prices following entry will generally result in a lower price in the attacked market than if uniform pricing across segments were required.

For sufficiently high capital costs, entry is blockaded whether or not the incumbent can price discriminate. For sufficiently low costs of entry, occurs regardless of whether the incumbent can price discriminate. For intermediate values, however, the availability of price discrimination leads to blockaded entry, while uniform price restrictions accommodate the entrant. Under uniform pricing, in Armstrong and Vickers's (1993) model, the prices in both markets are lower with entry than they would be with price discrimination and deterrence. Entrant profits and consumer surplus are also higher, while incumbent profits fall. This result is robust, providing that the monopoly price in the captive market exceeds the optimal discriminatory price in the competitive market. Armstrong and Vickers (1993) further demonstrate that the net welfare effects of uniform price restrictions are generally ambiguous, as the efficiencies from reduced prices must be offset against the inefficiencies from additional entry costs. The model in Armstrong and Vickers (1993) illustrates the possibility that uniform pricing reduces all prices relative to price discrimination, due entirely to entry effects. A restriction to uniform prices promotes entry, which in turn generates price reductions in both markets. A similar theme emerges in section 7 but for different economic reasons when we consider entry deterrence from bundling goods.

Restrictions Between Firms to Limit Price Discrimination

Using the example drawn from These and Vives (1988), we previously noted that when firms commit publicly to a pricing strategy (uniform or discriminating), it is possible that price discrimination becomes a dominant strategy and firms become trapped in a classic Prisoner's Dilemma—all firms would like to commit collectively to uniform pricing but, individually, each prefers to price discriminate. Of course, we have also seen settings in which price discrimination raises industry profits, as in Holmes (1989).28 At present, we do not have a general theory predicting when unilateral commitments to uniform pricing will be optimal. Such a theory would be directly useful for analyzing the conditions under which uniform pricing emerges without collective action. It would also be indirectly useful when studying strategic commitments in the face of entry. An incumbent monopolist may find, for example, that a commitment to uniform price is optimal if entry will occur regardless, but commitment to large price discounts (perhaps larger than the statically optimal price discriminating prices) will deter entry into the weak market.

We have more precise conclusions regarding collective restrictions, however, as well as a few useful insights regarding the control of price discrimination in vertical structures. We discuss each in turn.

Collective agreements to restrict price discrimination. It is difficult to obtain general results regarding the unilateral, multilateral and social incentives for price discrimination.

Fortunately, there are some clear cut cases: (i) best-response asymmetry with all-out competition, and (ii) best-response symmetry with linear demands. When all-out competition is present, price discrimination lowers prices and profits. Hence, a collective agreement by firms to restrict price discrimination has the effect of raising prices for all consumers, lowering aggregate output, and lowering consumer surplus and total welfare. In the second setting of best-response symmetry with linear demands, Holmes (1989) demonstrates that if the elasticity-ratio condition is satisfied, then price discrimination increases industry profits. Hence, with linear demands, firms have only a collective incentive to prohibit price discrimination if the elasticity-ratio condition fails. Given that demands are linear, violation of the elasticity-ratio condition implies that price discrimination lowers aggregate output and hence welfare. In this simple setting, it follows that welfare increases by allowing firms to agree collectively to limit price discrimination. There is still the possibility that the elasticity-ratio condition fails and welfare decreases, but industry profits still increase with price discrimination. Here, restrictions on welfare-reducing price discrimination must come from outside the industry. Winter (1997) considers a variation of Holmes's (1989) analysis in the context of collective agreements to limit (but not prohibit) price discrimination by restricting the difference between the high and low prices. His conclusion for linear demands is similar: when firms have a collective desire to restrict price discrimination, it is socially efficient for them to be allowed to do so. As an illustration, suppose an extreme case in which each half of the strong market is captive to one of the firms (therefore, "c 2 = 0), while the weak market has a positive cross-price elasticity of demand. In such a case, the elasticity-ratio test clearly fails. At the equilibrium prices, a slight restriction on price discrimination causes the weak-market price to rise slightly and the strong-market price to fall by a similar margin. Because the weak market price is below the collusive profit-maximizing price, this price increase helps the duopolists. Because the strong market's price is at the optimal monopoly price under discrimination (due to captive customers), a slight decrease causes only a second-order reduction in profits to the duopoly.

Hence, a slight restriction on price discrimination is jointly optimal for duopolists. In this case, where the elasticity-ratio condition is violated (and demands are linear), Holmes (1989) shows that Q0(r) < 0. As a consequence, a restriction on the price differential (a lowering of r) raises aggregate output. Since aggregate output increases and the price differential decreases, welfare necessarily increases. It follows that industry agreements to limit price discrimination arise only if price discrimination reduces welfare, providing that adjusted demand concavities are small. The results are less clear when demands are not linear and the adjusted concavity condition plays an important role.

In short, when profits are lower under price discrimination, firms in the industry would prefer to collude and commit to uniform pricing. Such collusion would decrease welfare if all-out competition would otherwise occur, and increase welfare when demand is linear and price discrimination would have reduced aggregate output. In more general settings, unfortunately, the results are ambiguous.

Vertical restraints and downstream price discrimination. Although this survey largely ignores the impact of price discrimination on competing vertical structures, it is worth mentioning a sample of work in this area. We have already mentioned one strategic effect of price discrimination via secret price discounts by wholesalers to downstream firms: price discrimination may induce the upstream firm to flood the downstream market. A legal requirement that the wholesaler offer a single price to all retailers may instead help the upstream firm to commit to not over supply the retail market, thereby raising profits and retail prices. In other settings of wholesale price discrimination, if downstream market segments have different elasticities of demand but third-degree price discrimination is illegal or otherwise impractical because of arbitrage, vertical integration can be used as a substitute for price discrimination. Tirole (1988) gives a simple model of such a vertical price squeeze. A monopoly wholesaler, selling to a strong market at price p2 and to a weak market at price p1 < p2, may suffer from arbitrage as the firms in the weak downstream market resell output to the strong segment. By vertically integrating into one of the weak-segment downstream firms, the wholesaler can now supply all output at the strong-segment price of p2 while producing in the weak segment and using an internal transfer price no greater than p1.

Other firms in the weak market will be squeezed by the vertically integrated rival due to higher wholesale prices. The wholesaler effectively reduces competition in the weak segment to prevent arbitrage and implement a uniform wholesale price.

Consider instead the case where it is the downstream retail firms that are the source of price discrimination. How do the various tools of resale price maintenance (RPM) by the upstream manufacturer impact profits and welfare when retailers engage in third-degree price discrimination? As the previous discussions suggested, a manufacturer who sells to imperfectly competitive, price-discriminating retailers would prefer to constrain retailers from discounting their prices to consumers who are highly cross-elastic, as this is just a businessstealing externality. On the other hand, the manufacturer would like to encourage price discrimination across the full range of cross-price inelastic consumers as this action raises profits to the industry. Hence, the combination of competition and price discrimination generates a unique conflict in the vertical chain.

Price Discrimination by Purchase History

Consumer price sensitivities are often revealed by past purchase decisions. For example, consumers may suffer exogenous switching costs in firms, so past customers may have more inelastic demands than new customers. Here, purchase history is useful because an otherwise homogeneous good becomes differentiated ex post due to exogenous switching costs. In other cases, it may be that no exogenous switching costs exist but that the products are inherently differentiated, with consumers having strong preferences for one product or the other. It follows that a customer who reveals a preference for firm a's product at current prices is precisely the person to whom firm b would like to offer a price reduction. In this case, purchase history operates through a different conduit of differentiation because it informs about a consumer's exogenous brand preference. Regardless, the strategies of "paying customers to switch" (Chen (1997b)) or "consumer poaching" (Fudenberg and Tirole (2000)) can be profitable because purchase history provides a valuable variable for the basis of dynamic third-degree price discrimination. It is not surprising, therefore, that such pricing is a well-known strategy among marketers. As the examples suggest, two approaches to modelling imperfect competition and purchase-history price discrimination have been taken in the literature. The first set of models, e.g., Nilssen (1992), Chen (1997b), Taylor (2003), et al., assumes that the goods are initially homogeneous in period 1, but after purchase the consumers are partially locked in with their sellers; exogenous switching costs must be paid to switch to different firms in future periods. The immediate result is that although prices rise over time as firms exploit the lock-in effects of switching costs, firms ultimately compete away in period 1 the long-run profits due to lock-in.

The second set of models assumes that products are horizontally differentiated in the initial period (e.g., Caminal and Matutes (1990), Villas-Boas (1999), Fudenberg and Tirole (2000), et al.). In the simplest variant, brand preferences are constant over time. It follows that a consumer who prefers firm a's product and reveals this preference through his purchase in period 1 will become identified as part of a's "strong" market segment (and firm b's "weak" market segment) in period 2. As we will see, when firms cannot commit to long-term prices, this form of unchanging product differentiation will generate prices that decrease over time, and competition intensifies in each segment.

The resulting price paths in the above settings rest on the assumption that firms cannot commit to future prices. This assumption may be inappropriate. One could easily imagine that firms commit in advance to reward loyal customers in the future with price reductions or other benefits (such as with frequent flyer programs). Such long-term commitments can be thought of as endogenous switching costs and have been studied in the context of horizontal differentiation by Banerjee and Summers (1987), Caminal and Matutes (1990), Villas-Boas (1999) and Fudenberg and Tirole (2000). Two cases have been studied: preferences that change over time and preferences that are static. In the first case, most papers assume that consumer valuations are independently distributed across the periods. If preferences change from period to period and firms cannot commit to future prices, there is no value to using purchase history as it is uninformative about current elasticities. Public, longterm contracts between, say, firm a and a consumer, however, can raise the joint surplus of the pair by making firm b price lower in the second period to induce switching, as in the models of Caminal and Matutes (1990) and Fudenberg and Tirole (2000). In equilibrium, social welfare may decrease as long-term contracts induce too little switching. In the second category of price-commitment models, preferences are assumed to be fixed across periods. When preferences are unchanging across time, Fudenberg and Tirole (2000) demonstrate a similar effect from long-term contracts: firm a locks in some of its customer base to generate lower second-period pricing for switching, and thereby encourages consumers to buy from firm a in the initial period. With long-term contracts, some inefficient switching still occurs but less than when firms cannot commit to long-term prices; hence welfare increases by allowing such contracts.

We consider both switching-cost and horizontal-differentiation models of pricing without commitment in the following two subsections. We then turn to the effects of long-term price commitments when discrimination on purchase history is allowed.

Exogenous Switching Costs and Homogeneous Goods

There are many important and subtle effects in switching-cost models. Farrell and Klemperer (2003), in this volume, provide a thorough treatment of switching costs, so we will limit our present attention to the very specific issues of price discrimination over purchase history under imperfect competition. One of the first discussions of purchase-history discrimination in a model of switching costs appears in Nilssen (1992).31 Chen (1997b), building on this approach, introduces a distribution of switching costs in a two-period model, resulting in some measure of equilibrium switching. We present a variant of Chen's (1997b) model here. Consider duopolists, j = a, b, selling identical homogeneous goods to a unit measure of potential consumers.

Discrimination over Revealed Preferences from First-period Choices

Instead of assuming exogenous switching costs arising after an initial purchase from either firm, one can suppose that consumers have exogenous preferences for brands that are present from the start, as in Fudenberg and Tirole (2000). To keep the analysis simple, they model such horizontal differentiation by imagining a Hotelling-style linear market of unit length with firms positioned at the endpoints, and by assuming that each consumer's uniformly distributed brand preference, _, remains fixed for both periods of consumption. Consumers have transportation costs of _ per unit distance, and firms produce with constant marginal and average costs of c per unit. In such a setting, consumers reveal information about their brand preference by their first-period choice, and firms set second-period prices accordingly.

Purchase-History Pricing with Long-term Commitment

Unlike the previous analyses which relied on short-term price agreements, we now ask what happens if a firm can write a long-term contract, committing to a second-period price so as to guarantee returning customers terms that differ from those offered to other customers. Banerjee and Summers (1987) and Caminal and Matutes (1990) were among the first to explore the use of long-term contracts to induce loyalty and generate endogenous switching costs. Consider the setting of Caminal and Matutes (1990). As before, there are two firms and two periods of competition. The market in each period consists of a linear city of unit length, with firm a located at 0 and firm b located at 1, and consumers uniformly distributed across the interval. The difference with the previous models is that the location of each consumer is independently distributed across periods. Thus, a consumer's location in period 1, _1, is statistically independent of the consumer's location in period 2, _2.

This independence assumption implies that there is no relevant second-period information contained in a consumer's first-period choice. It follows that if firms cannot commit to long-term prices, there is no value from price discrimination based upon purchase history. Caminal and Matutes (1990) find a few noteworthy results. First, equilibrium prices decline over time. Remarkably, the second-period commitment price is below even marginal cost. The reasoning of this is subtle. Suppose, for example, that firm b's poaching price in the second period was independent of firm a's second-period loyalty price. Because the consumer's second-period location is unknown at the time of long-term contracting, firm a maximizes the joint surplus of a consumer and itself by setting pj 2j = c and pricing efficiently in the second period. Given that firm b's poaching price in reality does depend positively on firm a's second-period loyalty price, firm a can obtain a first-order gain in joint surplus by reducing its price slightly below cost and thereby reducing firm b's second-period price.

This slight reduction in price incurs only a corresponding second-order loss in surplus since pricing was originally at the efficient level. Hence, a firm will commit to a follow-on price below marginal cost in the second-period as a way to increase the expected surplus going to the consumer, and hence raise the attractiveness of purchasing from the firm initially.

In this sense, the price commitment is similar to the analysis of Diamond and Maskin (1979) and Aghion and Bolton (1987), in which contractual commitments are used to extract a better price from an outside party. Of course, as Caminal and Matures (1990) confirm, when both firms undertake this strategy simultaneously, profits fall relative to the no-commitment case and firms are worse off. Welfare is also lower as too little switching takes place from a social viewpoint.

What are the effects of the presence of this commitment strategy? As is by now a familiar theme, although an individual firm will benefit from committing to a declining price path for returning customers, the firms are collectively worse off with the ability to write longterm price contracts. With commitment, it is also the case that there is too much lock-in or inertia in the second-period allocations.

Without commitment, social welfare would therefore be higher, as consumers would allocate themselves to firms over time to minimize transportation costs. The endogenous switching costs (created by the declining price path for returning consumers) decrease social welfare. As before, because market demand is inelastic in this model, there is an inherent bias against price discrimination, so we must carefully interpret the welfare conclusions. Closely related to Caminal and Matutes (1990), Fudenberg and Tirole (2000) also consider an environment in which price commitments can be made through long-term contracts, using an interesting variation in which consumer preferences are fixed across periods (i.e., location _ between firms a and b does not change). In this setting, there are no exogenous switching costs, but long-term contracts with breach penalties can be offered which introduce endogenous switching costs in the sense of Caminal and Matutes (1990). While such contracts could be effectively used to lock consumers into a firm and prevent poaching, the firms choose to offer both long-term and spot contracts in equilibrium so as to segment the marketplace. In equilibrium, consumers with strong preferences for one firm will purchase long-term contracts, while those with weaker preferences will select short-term contracts and switch suppliers in the second period. The firm utilizes long-term contracts to generate lower poaching prices, which benefit consumers located near the centre of the market. The firm can extract concessions in the first period by locking in some customers with long-term contracts, thereby generating more aggressive second-period pricing (similar in spirit to Caminal and Matutes (1990).) In addition, the long-term contracts also generate a singlecrossing property that segments first-period consumers: in equilibrium, consumers located near the middle of the market are more willing to purchase short-term contracts and switch in the second period to a lower-priced rival than consumers located at the extreme.

It is worth noting that a multi-plant monopolist would accomplish a similar sorting by selling long-term contracts for aa, bb and the switching bundles ab and ba. The monopolist can therefore segment the market, charging higher prices to the non-switchers and lower prices to the consumers who are willing to switch. The optimal amount of monopoly switching in the second period (given a uniform distribution) can be shown to be one-half of the consumers. Here, long-term contracts serve a similar segmentation function.

Interestingly, Fudenberg and Tirole (2000) show that if consumers are uniformly distributed, one-fourth of the consumers will switch in the long-term contracting equilibrium with duopoly—less switching than in the case of short-term contracts alone, and still less switching than under monopoly. Hence, given price discrimination is allowed, allowing firms to use long-term contracts improves social welfare. This finding emerges because demand is unchanging across periods, in contrast to Caminal and Matutes (1990), who find that long-term price commitments lead to too much lock-in and hence reduce social welfare when preferences vary over time.

Intrapersonal Price Discrimination

Intrapersonal price discrimination has received very little attention, partly because in the context of monopoly, the models and results are economically immediate. For example, consider a consumer with a known demand curve, p = D(q), and a constant marginal (and average) cost of production equal to c. Let q_ be the unique solution to c = D(q_). A monopolist can increase profits by offering any of a host of equally optimal but distinct mechanisms: a fixed bundle of q_ units at a bundle price of Rq_ 0 D(z)dz; a fully nonlinear tariff of P(q) = D(q); or a two-part tariff equal to P(q) = v(c)+cq where v(p) _ maxq u(q)" pq is the consumer's indirect utility of consuming at the linear price p. In all examples, the monopolist is effectively price discriminating in an intrapersonal manner: Different prices are charged to the same consumer for different units because the marginal values to the consumer for those units vary according to consumption. In this sense, it is closely related to third-degree price discrimination because the different units of consumption can be thought of as distinguishable market segments. Because there is no heterogeneity within each market segment—the reservation value is D(q) in the q-th unit market—price discrimination is perfect and social welfare is maximized.

When markets are imperfectly competitive, intrapersonal price discrimination using nonlinear prices allows firms to provide more efficiently a given level of consumer surplus and cover any fixed, per-consumer costs of production. This efficiency suggests that intrapersonal price discrimination may raise social welfare when firms compete. Following Armstrong and Vickers (2001), we address this possibility and related issues of consumer surplus and industry profit in the simplest discrete-choice setting in which there is a single market segment with homogeneous consumers.

Nonlinear Pricing (Second-Degree Price Discrimination)

Unlike the setting of third-degree price discrimination, indirect (second-degree) discrimination relies upon self-selection constraints, thus introducing an entirely new set of competitive issues.

In what follows we assume that firms compete via price schedules of the form Pj(qj), and consumers choose which (if any) firms to patronize and which product(s) from the offered lines they will purchase. To model imperfect competition we assume the product lines are differentiated.

The theoretical literature on second-degree price discrimination under imperfect competition has largely focused on characterizing equilibrium schedules and the efficiency consequences of competition; less attention has been spent on the desirability of enforcing uniform pricing in these environments. This is due in part to the extra technical complexity of second-degree price discrimination, and, to a lesser degree, to the impracticality of requiring uniform pricing when q refers to quality rather than quantity. The variety of consumer preferences and competitive environments make it useful to distinguish a few cases. First, two possible equilibrium configurations can arise: a consumer may purchase exclusively from one firm (referred to in the contract theory literature as exclusive agency) or may purchase different products from multiple firms (referred to as common agency). Second, within each setting, there are several possibilities regarding the unobservable heterogeneity of consumers. The two most common forms are what we will call vertical and horizontal heterogeneity. In the former, the consumer's marginal preferences for q (and absolute preferences for participating) are increasing in _ for each firm; in the latter, the consumer's marginal preferences for q and absolute preferences for participating are monotonic in _, but the direction varies across firms with the result that a high-demand type for firm j is a low-demand type for firm k and conversely. Under these definitions, vertical heterogeneity implies that firms agree in their ranking of type from high demand to low demand; under horizontal heterogeneity, two firms have reversed ranking for consumer types. In this sense, the taxonomy is similar in spirit to best-response symmetry and asymmetry under third-degree price discrimination.

Ideally, a general model of competition among second-degree price-discriminating firms should incorporate two dimensions of heterogeneity, one vertical and one horizontal, to capture both a common ranking of marginal valuations for quality among consumers (holding brand preferences fixed) and a variety of brand preferences (holding quality valuations fixed). Unfortunately, multidimensional self-selection models are considerably more difficult to study, as they introduce additional economic and technical subtleties. As a result, the economics literature has either relied upon one-dimensional models (either vertical or horizontal) for precise analytic results (e.g., Spulber (1989), Martimort (1992,1996), Stole (1991), Stole (1995), Martimort and Stole (2003a)), numerical simulations of multidimensional models (e.g., Borenstein (1985)), or further restrictions on preferences to simplify multidimensional settings to the point of analytical tractability (e.g., Armstrong and Vickers (2001), Rochet and Stole (2002a), Martimort and Ivaldi (1994)).

Before we survey the various approaches taken in the literature, we begin with a review of monopoly second-degree price discrimination to provide a benchmark and a vehicle to introduce notation.

Market Structure

In economics, market structure (also known as market form) describes the state of a market with respect to competition.

Basic Market Structures

- Perfect competition, in which the market consists of a very large number of firms producing a homogeneous product.
- Monopolistic competition, also called competitive market, where there are a large number of independent firms which have a very small proportion of the market share.
- Oligopoly, in which a market is dominated by a small number of firms which own more than 40% of the market share.
- Oligopsony, a market dominated by many sellers and a few buyers.
- Monopoly, where there is only one provider of a product or service.
- Natural monopoly, a monopoly in which economies of scale cause efficiency to increase continuously with the size of the firm. A firm is a natural monopoly if it is able to serve the entire market demand at a lower cost than any combination of two or more smaller, more specialized firms.
- Monopsony, when there is only one buyer in a market.

The imperfectly competitive structure is quite identical to the realistic market conditions where some monopolistic competitors, monopolists, oligopolists, and duopolists exist and dominate the market conditions. The elements of Market Structure include the number and size distribution of firms, entry conditions, and the extent of differentiation.

These somewhat abstract concerns tend to determine some but not all details of a specific concrete market system where buyers and sellers actually meet and commit to trade. Competition is useful because it reveals actual customer demand and induces the seller (operator) to provide service quality levels and price levels that buyers (customers) want, typically subject to the seller's financial need to cover its costs. In other words, competition can align the seller's interests with the buyer's interests and can cause the seller to reveal his true costs and other private information. In the absence of perfect competition, three basic approaches can be adopted to deal with problems related to the control of market power and an asymmetry between the government and the operator with respect to objectives and information: (a) subjecting the operator to competitive pressures, (b) gathering information on the operator and the market, and (c) applying incentive regulation.

Table: *Quick Reference to Basic Market Structures*

Market Structure	*Seller Entry Barriers*	*Seller Number*	*Buyer Entry Barriers*	*Buyer Number*
Perfect Competition	No	Many	No	Many
Monopolistic competition	No	Many	No	Many
Oligopoly	Yes	Few	No	Many
Oligopsony	No	Many	Yes	Few
Monopoly	Yes	One	No	Many
Monopsony	No	Many	Yes	One

The correct sequence of the market structure from most to least competitive is perfect competition, imperfect competition,oligopoly, and pure monopoly.

The main criteria by which one can distinguish between different market structures are: the number and size of producers and consumers in the market, the type of goods and services being traded, and the degree to which information can flow freely.

Perfect Competition

In neoclassical economics and microeconomics, perfect competition describes a market in which there are many small firms, all producing homogeneous goods. In the short term, such markets are productively inefficient as output will not occur where marginal cost is equal to average cost, but allocatively efficient, as output under perfect competition will always occur where marginal cost is equal to marginal revenue, and therefore where marginal cost equals average revenue. However, in the long term, such markets are both allocatively and productively efficient. In general a perfectly competitive market is characterized by the fact that no single firm has influence over the price of the product it sells. Because the conditions for perfect competition are very strict, there are few perfectly competitive markets.

A perfectly competitive market may have several distinguishing characteristics, including:

- Infinite Buyers/Infinite Sellers – Infinite consumers with the willingness and ability to buy the product at a certain price, Infinite producers with the willingness and ability to supply the product at a certain price.
- Zero Entry/Exit Barriers – It is relatively easy to enter or exit as a business in a perfectly competitive market.
- Perfect Information-Prices and quality of products are assumed to be known to all consumers and producers.
- Transactions are Costless-Buyers and sellers incur no costs in making an exchange.
- Firms Aim to Maximize Profits-Firms aim to sell where marginal costs meet marginal revenue, where they generate the most profit.
- Homogeneous Products – The characteristics of any given market good or service do not vary across suppliers.

Some subset of these conditions is presented in most textbooks as defining perfect competition. More advanced textbooks try to reconcile these conditions with the definition of perfect competition as equilibrium price taking; that is whether or not firms treat price as a parameter or a choice variable.

It is this distinction which differentiates perfectly competitive markets from imperfectly competitive ones. It should be noted that a general rigorous proof that the above conditions indeed suffice to guarantee price taking is still lacking (Kreps 1990, p. 265).

The importance of perfect competition derives from the fact that price taking by the firm guarantees that when firms maximize profits (by choosing quantity they wish to produce, and the combination of Factors of production to produce it with) the market price will be equal to marginal cost.

An implication of this is that a factor's price (wage, rent, etc.) equals the factor's marginal revenue product. This allows for derivation of the supply curve on which the neoclassical approach is based (note that this is also the reason why "a monopoly does not have a supply curve"). The abandonment of price taking creates considerable difficulties to the demonstration of existence of a general equilibrium except under other, very specific conditions such as that of monopolistic competition.

Approaches and Conditions

Historically, in neoclassical economics there have been two strands of looking at what perfect competition is. The first emphasis is on the inability of any one agent to affect prices. This is usually justified by the fact that any one firm or consumer is so small relative to the whole market that their presence or absence leaves the equilibrium price very nearly unaffected. This assumption of negligible impact of each agent on the equilibrium price has been formalized by Aumann (1964) by postulating a continuum of infinitesimal agents. The difference between Aumann's approach and that found in undergraduate textbooks is that in the first, agents have the power to choose their own prices but do not individually affect the market price, while in the second it is simply assumed that agents treat prices as parameters. Both approaches lead to the same result.

The second view of perfect competition conceives of it in terms of agents taking advantage of – and hence, eliminating – profitable exchange opportunities. The faster this arbitrage takes place, the more competitive a market is. The implication is that the more competitive a market is under this definition, the faster the average market price will adjust so as to equate supply and demand (and also equate price to marginal costs). In this view "perfect" competition means that this adjustment takes place instantaneously. This is usually modelled via the use of the Walrasian auctioneer. The widespread recourse to the auctioneer tale appears to have favoured an interpretation of perfect competition as meaning price taking *always*, i.e. also at non-equilibrium prices; but this is rejected e.g. by Arrow (1959) or Mas-Colell et al. Steve Keen notes, following George Stigler, that if firms do not react strategically to one another, the slope of the demand curve that a firm faces is the same as the slope of the market demand curve. Hence, if firms are to produce at a level that equates marginal cost and marginal revenue, the model of perfect competition must include at least an infinite number of firms, each producing an output quantity of zero. As noted above, an influential model of perfect competition in neoclassical economics assumes that the number of buyers and sellers are both of the power of the continuum, that is, an infinity even larger than the number of natural numbers. K. Vela Velupillai quotes Maury Osborne as noting the inapplicability of such models to actual economies since money and the commodities sold each have a smallest positive unit.

Thus nowadays the dominant intuitive idea of the conditions justifying price taking and thus rendering a market perfectly competitive is an amalgam of several different notions, not all present, nor given equal weight, in all treatments. Besides product homogeneity and absence of collusion, the notion more generally associated with perfect competition is the negligibility of the size of agents, which makes them believe that they can sell as much of the good as they wish at the equilibrium price but nothing at a higher price (in particular, firms are described as each one of them facing a horizontal demand curve).

However, also widely accepted as part of the notion of perfectly competitive market are perfect information about price distribution and very quick adjustments (whose joint operation establish the law of one price), to the point sometimes of identifying perfect competition with an essentially instantaneous reaching of equilibrium between supply and demand. Finally, the idea of free entry with free access to technology is also often listed as a characteristic of perfectly competitive markets, probably owing to a difficulty with abandoning completely the older conception of free competition. In recent decades it has been rediscovered that free entry can be a foundation of absence of market power, alternative to negligibility of agents (Novshek and Sonnenschein 1987.)

Free entry also makes it easier to justify the absence of collusion: any collusion by existing firms can be undermined by entry of new firms. The necessarily long-period nature of the analysis (entry requires time!) also allows a reconciliation of the horizontal demand curve facing each firm according to the theory, with the feeling of businessmen that "contrary to economic theory, sales are by no means unlimited at the current market price". Sraffian economists see the assumption of free entry and exit as characteristic of the theory of free competition in Classical economics, an approach that is not expressed in terms of schedules of supply and demand.

Results

In the short-run, it is possible for an individual firm to make a profit. This situation is shown in this diagram, as the price or average revenue, denoted by P, is above the average cost denoted by C.

However, in the long period, positive profit cannot be sustained. The arrival of new firms or expansion of existing firms (if returns to scale are constant) in the market causes the (horizontal) demand curve of each individual firm to shift downward, bringing down at the same time the price, the average revenue and marginal revenue curve. The final outcome is that, in the long run, the firm will make only normal profit (zero economic profit). Its horizontal demand curve will touch its average total cost curve at its lowest point.

In a perfectly competitive market, a firm's demand curve is perfectly elastic.

As mentioned above, the perfect competition model, if interpreted as applying also to short-period or very-short-period behaviour, is approximated only by markets of homogeneous products produced and purchased by very many sellers and buyers, usually organized markets for agricultural products or raw materials. In real-world markets, assumptions such as perfect information cannot be verified and are only approximated in organized double-auction markets where most agents wait and observe the behaviour of prices before deciding to exchange (but in the long-period interpretation perfect information is not necessary, the analysis only aims at determining the average around which market prices gravitate, and for gravitation to operate one does not need perfect information).

In the absence of externalities and public goods, perfectly competitive equilibria are Pareto-efficient, i.e. no improvement in the utility of a consumer is possible without a worsening of the utility of some other consumer. This is called the First Theorem of Welfare Economics. The basic reason is that no productive factor with a non-zero marginal product is left unutilized, and the units of each factor are so allocated as to yield the same indirect marginal utility in all uses, a basic efficiency condition (if this indirect marginal utility were higher in one use than in other ones, a Pareto improvement could be achieved by transferring a small amount of the factor to the use where it yields a higher marginal utility). A simple proof assuming differentiable utility functions and production functions is the following. Let w_j be the 'price' (the rental) of a certain factor j, let MP_{j1} and MP_{j2} be its marginal product in the production of goods 1 and 2, and let p_1 and p_2 be these goods' prices. In equilibrium these prices must equal the respective marginal costs MC_1 and MC_2; remember that marginal cost equals factor 'price' divided by factor marginal productivity (because increasing the production of good i by one very small unit through increase of the employment of factor j requires increasing the factor employment by $1/MP_{ji}$ and thus increasing the cost by w_j/MP_{ji}, and through the condition of cost minimization that marginal products must be proportional to factor 'prices' it can be shown that the cost increase is the same if the output increase is obtained by optimally varying all factors). Optimal factor employment by a price-taking firm requires equality of factor rental and factor marginal revenue product, $w_j=p_iMP_{ji}$, so we obtain $p_1=MC_1=w_j/MP_{j1}$, $p_2=MC_{j2}=w_j/MP_{j2}$.

Now choose any consumer purchasing both goods, and measure his utility in such units that in equilibrium his marginal utility of money (the increase in utility due to the last unit of money spent on each good), $MU_1/p_1=MU_2/p_2$, is 1. Then $p_1=MU_1$, $p_2=MU_2$. The indirect marginal utility of the factor is the increase in the utility of our consumer achieved by an increase in the employment of the factor by one (very small) unit; this increase in utility through allocating the small increase in factor utilization to good 1 is $MP_{j1}MU_1=MP_{j1}p_1=w_j$, and through allocating it to good 2 it is $MP_{j2}MU_2=MP_{j2}p_2=w_j$ again. With our choice of units the marginal utility of the amount of the factor consumed directly by the optimizing consumer is again w, so the amount supplied of the factor too satisfies the condition of optimal allocation. Monopoly violates this optimal allocation condition, because in a monopolized industry market price is above marginal cost, and this means that factors are underutilized in the monopolized industry, they have a higher indirect marginal utility than in their uses in competitive industries. Of course this theorem is considered irrelevant by economists who do not believe that general equilibrium theory correctly predicts the functioning of market economies; but it is given great importance by neoclassical economists and it is the theoretical reason given by them for combating monopolies and for antitrust legislation.

Profit

In contrast to a monopoly or oligopoly, it is impossible for a firm in perfect competition to earn economic profit in the long run, which is to say that a firm cannot make any more money than is necessary to cover its economic costs. In order not to misinterpret this zero-long-run-profits thesis, it must be remembered that the term 'profit' is also used in other ways. Neoclassical theory defines profit as what is left of revenue after all costs have been subtracted, including normal interest on capital plus the normal excess over it required to cover risk, and normal salary for managerial activity.

Classical economists on the contrary defined profit as what is left after subtracting costs except interest and risk coverage; thus, if one leaves aside risk coverage for simplicity, the neoclassical zero-long-run-profit thesis would be re-expressed in classical parlance as profits coinciding with interest in the long period, i.e. the rate of profit tending to coincide with the rate of interest. Profits in the classical meaning do not tend to disappear in the long period but tend to normal profit.

With this terminology, if a firm is earning abnormal profit in the short term, this will act as a trigger for other firms to enter the market. They will compete with the first firm, driving the market price down until all firms are earning normal profit only.

It is important to note that perfect competition is a sufficient condition for allocative and productive efficiency, but it is not a necessary condition. Laboratory experiments in which participants have significant price setting power and little or no information about their counterparts consistently produce efficient results given the proper trading institutions.

The Shutdown Point

When a firm is making a loss, it will have to decide whether to continue production or not. This decision will, in fact, depend on the different total costs levels and whether the firm is operating in the short run or in the long run.

If the firm is in the short run, and is Making a loss Where by:

- Total costs (TC) is greater than total revenue (TR)
- and whereby total revenue is greater or equal to total variable cost (TVC).

it is advisable for the firm to continue production. If it fails to achieve these conditions, it is advised to close down so that the only costs the firm will have to pay will be the fixed costs.

Even if the firm stops producing, it will have to continue to meet the level of fixed costs. Since whether the firm produces or not, it will have to pay fixed costs, it is better for it to continue production in an attempt to decrease total costs and increase total revenue, thus making profits. This can be done by:

- Increasing productivity. The most obvious methods involve automation and computerization which minimize the tasks that must be performed by employees. All else constant, it benefits a business to improve productivity, which over time lowers cost and (hopefully) improves ability to compete and make profit.
- Adopting new methods of production like Just In Time or lean manufacturing in an attempt to reduce costs and wastages.

In the long run, the condition to continue producing requires the price P to be higher than the ATC, i.e. the line representing market price should be above the minimum point of the ATC curve.

If P is equal to ATC, the firm is indifferent between shutting down and continuing to produce. This case is different from the short run shut down case because in long run there's no longer a fixed cost (everything is variable).

Short-run Supply Curve

The short run supply curve for a perfectly competitive firm is the MC curve at and above the shutdown point. Portions of the marginal cost curve below the shut down point are not part of the SR supply curve because the firm is not producing in that range. Technically the SR supply curve is a discontinuous function composed of the segment of the MC curve at and above minimum of the average variable cost curve and a segment that runs with the vertical axis from the origin to but not including a point "parallel" to minimum average variable costs.

Examples

Perhaps the closest thing to a perfectly competitive market would be a large auction of identical goods with all potential buyers and sellers present. By design, a stock exchange resembles this, not as a complete description (for no markets may satisfy all requirements of the model) but as an approximation. The flaw in considering the stock exchange as an example of Perfect Competition is the fact that large institutional investors (e.g. investment banks) may solely influence the market price. This, of course, violates the condition that "no one seller can influence market price".

Free software works along lines that approximate perfect competition. Anyone is free to enter and leave the market at no cost. All code is freely accessible and modifiable, and individuals are free to behave independently. Free software may be bought or sold at whatever price that the market may allow.

Some believe that one of the prime examples of a perfectly competitive market anywhere in the world is street food in developing countries. This is so since relatively few barriers to entry/exit exist for street vendors. Furthermore, there are often numerous buyers and sellers of a given street food, in addition to consumers/sellers possessing perfect information of the product in question. It is often the case that street vendors may serve a homogenous product, in which little to no variations in the product's nature exist. Another very near example of perfect competition would be the fish market and the vegetable or fruit vendors who sell at the same place.

1) There are large number of buyers and sellers.
2) There are no entry or exit barriers.

3) There is perfect mobility of the factors, i.e buyers can easily switch from one seller to the other.
4) The products are homogenous.

Criticisms

The use of the assumption of perfect competition as the foundation of price theory for product markets is often criticized as representing all agents as passive, thus removing the active attempts to increase one's welfare or profits by price undercutting, product design, advertising, innovation, activities that-the critics argue-characterize most industries and markets. These criticisms point to the frequent lack of realism of the assumptions of product homogeneity and impossibility to differentiate it, but apart from this the accusation of passivity appears correct only for short-period or very-short-period analyses, in long-period analyses the inability of price to diverge from the natural or long-period price is due to active reactions of entry or exit.

A frequent criticism is that it is often not true that in the short run differences between supply and demand cause changes in price; especially in manufacturing, the more common behaviour is alteration of production without nearly any alteration of price (Lee 1998). Anyway, the critics of the assumption of perfect competition in product markets seldom question the basic neoclassical view of the working of market economies for this reason. The Neo-Austrian school insists strongly on this criticism, and yet the neoclassical view of the working of market economies as fundamentally efficient, reflecting consumer choices and assigning to each agent his/her contribution to social welfare, is esteemed to be fundamentally correct (Kirzner 1981). Some non-neoclassical schools, like Post-Keynesians, reject the neoclassical approach to value and distribution, but not because of their rejection of perfect competition as a reasonable approximation to the working of most product markets; the reasons for rejection of the neoclassical 'vision' are different views of the determinants of income distribution and of aggregate demand (Petri 2004). In particular, the rejection of perfect competition does not generally entail the rejection of free competition as characterizing most product markets; indeed it has been argued (Clifton 1977) that competition is stronger nowadays than in 19th century capitalism, owing to the increasing capacity of big conglomerate firms to enter any industry: therefore the classical idea of a tendency toward a uniform rate of return on investment in all industries owing to free entry is even more valid today; and the reason why General Motors, Exxon or Nestle do not enter the computers or pharmaceutical industries is not insurmountable barriers to entry but rather that the rate of return in the latter industries is already sufficiently in line with the average rate of return elsewhere as not to justify entry. On this few economists, it would seem, would disagree, even among the neoclassical ones. Thus when the issue is normal, or long-period, product prices, differences on the validity of the perfect competition assumption do not appear to imply important differences on the existence or not of a tendency of rates of return toward uniformity as long as entry is possible, and what is found fundamentally lacking in the perfect competition model is the absence of marketing expenses and innovation as causes of costs that do enter normal average cost. The issue is different with respect to factor markets. Here the acceptance or denial of perfect competition in labour markets does make a big difference to the view of the working of market economies. One must distinguish neoclassical from non-neoclassical economists.

For the former, absence of perfect competition in labour markets, e.g. due to the existence of trade unions, impedes the smooth working of competition, which if left free to operate would cause a decrease of wages as long as there were unemployment, and would finally ensure the full employment of labour: labour unemployment is due to absence of perfect competition in labour markets.

Most non-neoclassical economists deny that a full flexibility of wages would ensure the full employment of labour and find a stickiness of wages an indispensable component of a market economy, without which the economy would lack the regularity and persistence indispensable to its smooth working. This was, for example, Keynes's opinion. Particularly radical is the view of the Sraffian school on this issue: the labour demand curve cannot be determined hence a level of wages ensuring the equality between supply and demand for labour does not exist, and economics should resume the viewpoint of the classical economists, according to whom competition in labour markets does not and cannot mean indefinite price flexibility as long as supply and demand are unequal, it only means a tendency to equality of wages for similar work, but the level of wages is necessarily determined by complex sociopolitical elements; custom, feelings of justice, informal allegiaces to classes, as well as overt coalitions such as trade unions, far from being impediments to a smooth working of labour markets that would be able to determine wages even without these elements, are on the contrary indispensable because without them there would be no way to determine wages (Garegnani 1990).

"Bizarre" Assumptions

A frequent criticism of perfect competition and the standard model is the absurdity of its assumptions. However, the reality of the assumptions is not the test of the validity of a scientific theory. It is whether the assumptions lead to refutable hypotheses that can survive empirical testing.

Some of the basic assumptions of perfect competition in its most pristine form are:

1. Consumers' sole motivation is to maximize utility-the satisfaction derived from the consumption of goods and services.
2. Producers maximize profits.
3. All economic actors are completely rational.
4. Only circumstances that can be quantified count.
5. All economic actors have perfect knowledge-they are omniscient and omniprescent.
6. All economic actors act independently; they are not affected by the actions of others.
7. Economic actors communicate only through price.
8. There are an infinite number of consumers and producers and infinite "supplies" of factors of production.
9. There are no barriers to entry, competition or mobility.
10. No market power

10a. No advertising

10b. No control over resources

10c. No proprietary technology,

10d. No patents

10e. No trademarks

10f. No copyrights

10g. No geographical advantages

10h. No customer loyalty

10i. No branding or marketing

10j. No government regulation

10k. No collusion

10l. No labour contracts or trade unions

10m. No research and development costs

10n. No sunk Costs

10o. No stocks of inputs

10p. No distribution networks

10q. No middle-men

10r. No economies of scale

10s. Each producer produces an infinitely small quantity of goods or services.

11. Free entry and exit-there is no need to build factories-they just pop up wherever needed. In fact, there are no factories, no workers and no consumers in any material physical sense-production materials, inputs (labour, materials, capital), are instantaneously transformed into products which are instantaneously consumed.
12. Free mobility of factors of production
13. No inventories
14. All goods are instantaneously consumed-all products are instantaneously produced.
15. All goods and services are perfectly homogeneous.
16. No government
17. Time does not exist.
18. System is closed and deterministic.
19. No transaction costs
20. No information costs
21. All economic activities are flows rather than stocks-production is similar to gauging the flow of a river past a point (i.e. gallons per minute).
22. The system's preferred state is equilibrium in all markets.
23. All economic activities-production, exchange, distribution and consumption-are perfectly efficient.
24. No externalities-good or bad.

Monopolistic Competition

Monopolistic competition is a common market structure where many competing producers sell products that are differentiated from one another (ie. the products are substitutes, but are not exactly alike).

Many markets are monopolistically competitive, common examples include the markets for restaurants, cereal, clothing, shoes and service industries in large cities. The "founding father" of the theory of monopolistic competition was Edward Hastings Chamberlin, in his pioneering book on the subject, *Theory of Monopolistic Competition* (1933).

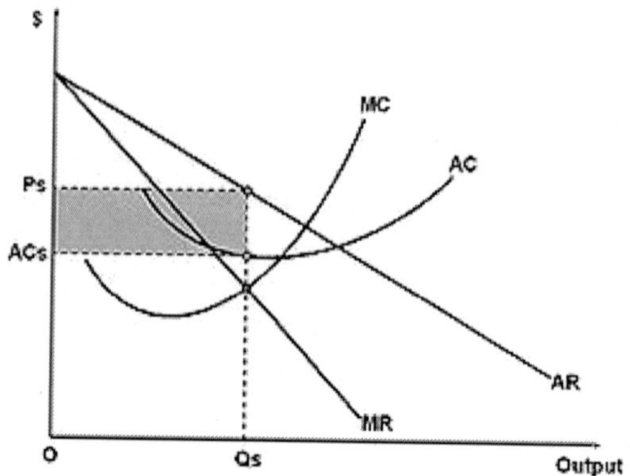

Figure: *Short-run equilibrium of the firm under monopolistic competition*

Monopolistically Competitive Markets have the Following Characteristics:

- There are many producers and many consumers in a given market, and no business has total control over the market price.
- Consumers perceive that there are non-price differences among the competitors' products.
- There are few barriers to entry and exit.
- Producers have a degree of control over price.

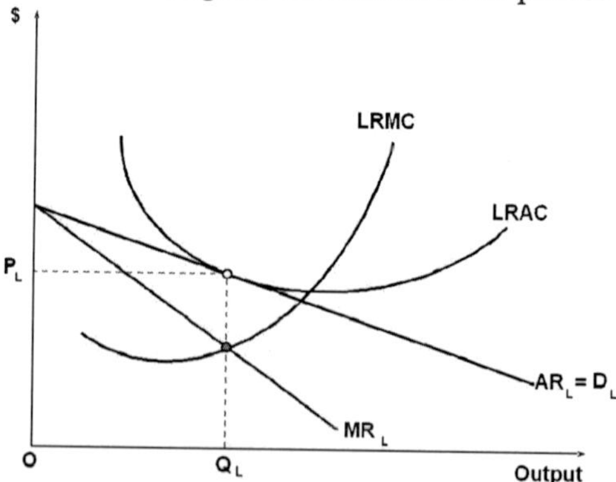

Figure: *Long-run equilibrium of the firm under monopolistic competition.*

The characteristics of a monopolistically competitive market are almost the same as in perfect competition, with the exception of monopolistic competition having heterogeneous products, and that monopolistic competition involves a great deal of non-price competition (based on subtle product differentiation). A firm making profits in the short run will break even in the long run because demand will decrease and average total cost will increase. This means in the long run, a monopolistically competitive firm will make zero economic profit. This gives the amount of influence over the market; because of brand loyalty, it can raise its prices without losing all of its customers. This means that an individual firm's demand curve is downward sloping, in contrast to perfect competition, which has a perfectly elastic demand schedule.

Major Characteristics

There are six Characteristics of Monopolistic Competition (MC)

- product differentiation
- many firms
- free entry and exit in long run
- Independent decision making
- Market Power
- Buyers and Sellers have perfect information.

Product Differentiation

MC firms sell products that have real or perceived non-price differences. However, the differences are not so great as to eliminate goods as substitutes. Technically the cross price elasticity of demand between goods would be positive. In fact the XED would he high.

MC goods are best described as close but imperfect subsitutes. The goods perform the same basic functions. The differences are in "qualities" and circumstances such as type, style, quality, reputation, appearance and location that tend to distinguish goods. For example, the function of motor vehilces is basically the same-to get from point A to B in reasonable comfort and safety. Yet there are many different types of motor vehicles, motor scooters, motor cycles, trucks, cars and SUV"s.

Many Firms

There are many firms in each MC product group and many firms on the side lines prepared to enter the market. A product group is a "collection of similar products" The fact that there are "many firms" gives each MC firm the freedom to set prices without engaging in strategic decision making. The requirements assures that each firm's actions have a negligible impact on the market. For example. a firm could cut prices and increase sales without fear that its actions will prompt retaliatory responses from competitors. How many firms will an MC market structure support at market equilibrium? The answer depends on factors such as fixed costs, economies of scale and the degree of product differentiation. For example, the higher the fixed costs the fewer firms the market will support.. Also the greater the degree of product differentiation-the more the firm can separate itself from the pack-the fewer firms there will be in market equilibrium.

Free Entry and Exit

In the long run there is free entry and exit. There are numerous firms awaiting to enter the market each with its own "unique" product or in pursuit of positive profits and any firm unable to cover its costs can leave the market without incurring liquidation costs. This assumption implies that there are low start up costs, no sunk costs and no exit costs.

Independent Decision Making

Each MC firm independently sets the terms of exchange for its product. The firm gives no consideration to what effect its decision may have on competitors. The theory is that any action will have such a negligible effect on the overall market demand that an MC firm can act without fear of prompting hightened competition. In other words each firm feels free to set prices as if it were a monopoly rather than an oligopoly.

Market Power

MC firms have some degree of market power. Market power means that the firm has control over the terms and conditions of exchange. An MC firm can raise it prices without losing all its customers. The firm can also lower prices without triggering a potentially ruinous price war with competitors. The source of an MC firm's market power is not barriers to entry since there are none. An MC firm derives it's market power from the fact that it has relatively few competitors, do not engage in strategic decision making and the firms sells differentiated product. Market power also means that an MC firm faces a downward sloping demand curve. The demand curve is highly elastic although not "flat".

Perfect Information

Buyers know exactly what goods are being offered, where the goods are being sold, all differentiating characteristics of the goods, the good's price, whether a firm is making a profit and if so how much.

Comparing Market Structures

Number of Firms

- PC: Infinite number of sellers
- MC: Many seller within each product group
- M: One seller.

Market Power

- PC: None
- MC: Some
- M: High.

Elasticity of Demand

- PC: Perfectly elastic
- MC: Highly elastic
- M:Relatively inelastic.

Product Differentiation

- PC: None
- MC:high
- M: Absolute.

Excess Profits

- PC: No
- MC: No
- M: Yes.

Efficiency

- PC: Yes
- MC: No
- M: No.

Profit Maximization Condition

- PC p =MR = MC
- MC MR = MC
- M MR = MC.

Ability to set Price

- PC Price taker
- MC price setter
- M price setter.

Inefficiency

There are two sources of inefficiency in the MC market structure. First, at its optimum output the firm charges a price that exceeds marginal costs, The MC firm maximizes profits where MR = MC. Since the MC firm's demand curve is downward sloping this means that the firm will be charging a price that exceeds marginal costs. The monopoly power possessed by an MC firm means that at its profit maximizing level of production there will be a net loss of consumer (and producer) surplus. The second source of inefficiency is the fact that MC firms operate with excess capacity. That is, the MC firm's profit maximizing output is less than the output associated with minimum average cost. Both a PC and MC firm will operate at a point where demand or price equals average cost. For a PC firm this equilibrium condition occurs where the perfectly elastic demand curve equals minimum average cost. An MC firm's demand curve is not flat but is downward sloping. Thus in the long run the demand curve will be tangent to the long run average cost curve at a point to the left of its minimum. The result is excess capacity.

Problems

While monopolistically competitive firms are inefficient, it is usually the case that the costs of regulating prices for every product that is sold in monopolistic competition by far exceed the benefits; the government would have to regulate all firms that sold heterogeneous products—an impossible proposition in a market economy.

A monopolistically competitive firm might be said to be marginally inefficient because the firm produces at an output where average total cost is not a minimum. A monopolistically competitive market might be said to be a marginally inefficient market structure because marginal cost is less than price in the long run.

Another concern of critics of monopolistic competition is that it fosters advertising and the creation of brand names. Critics argue that advertising induces customers into spending more on products because of the name associated with them rather than because of rational factors. This is disputed by defenders of advertising who argue that (1) brand names can represent a guarantee of quality, and (2) advertising helps reduce the cost to consumers of weighing the tradeoffs of numerous competing brands.

There are unique information and information processing costs associated with selecting a brand in a monopolistically competitive environment. In a monopoly industry, the consumer is faced with a single brand and so information gathering is relatively inexpensive. In a perfectly competitive industry, the consumer is faced with many brands. However, because the brands are virtually identical, again information gathering is relatively inexpensive. Faced with a monopolistically competitive industry, to select the best out of many brands the consumer must collect and process information on a large number of different brands. In many cases, the cost of gathering information necessary to selecting the best brand can exceed the benefit of consuming the best brand (versus a randomly selected brand). Evidence suggests that consumers use information obtained from advertising not only to assess the single brand advertised, but also to infer the possible existence of brands that the consumer has, heretofore, not observed, as well as to infer consumer satisfaction with brands similar to the advertised brand.

Examples

In many U.S. markets, producers practice product differentiation by altering the physical composition, using special packaging, or simply claiming to have superior products based on brand images and/or advertising. Toothpastes and toilet papers are examples of differentiated products.

Oligopoly

An oligopoly is a market form in which a market or industry is dominated by a small number of sellers (oligopolists). The word is derived, by analogy with "monopoly", from the Greek *oligoi* 'few' and *poleein* 'to sell'. Because there are few sellers, each oligopolist is likely to be aware of the actions of the others. The decisions of one firm influence, and are influenced by, the decisions of other firms. Strategic planning by oligopolists needs to take into account the likely responses of the other market participants. This causes oligopolistic markets and industries to be a high risk for collusion.

Description

Oligopoly is a common market form. As a quantitative description of oligopoly, the four-firm concentration ratio is often utilized. This measure expresses the market share of the four largest firms in an industry as a percentage (e.g. Target, Walmart and Bestbuy are viewed by some as having an oligopoly over their respective trades).

Oligopolistic competition can give rise to a wide range of different outcomes. In some situations, the firms may employ restrictive trade practices (collusion, market sharing etc.) to raise prices and restrict production in much the same way as a monopoly. Where there is a formal agreement for such collusion, this is known as a cartel. A primary example of such a cartel is OPEC which has a profound influence on the international price of oil. Firms often collude in an attempt to stabilize unstable markets, so as to reduce the risks inherent in these markets for investment and product development. There are legal restrictions on such collusion in most countries. There does not have to be a formal agreement for collusion to take place (although for the act to be illegal there must be actual communication between companies)-for example, in some industries, there may be an acknowledged market leader which informally sets prices to which other producers respond, known as price leadership.

In other situations, competition between sellers in an oligopoly can be fierce, with relatively low prices and high production. This could lead to an efficient outcome approaching perfect competition. The competition in an oligopoly can be greater than when there are more firms in an industry if, for example, the firms were only regionally based and did not compete directly with each other.

Thus the welfare analysis of oligopolies is sensitive to the parameter values used to define the market's structure. In particular, the level of dead weight loss is hard to measure. The study of product differentiation indicates that oligopolies might also create excessive levels of differentiation in order to stifle competition. Oligopoly theory makes heavy use of game theory to model the behaviour of oligopolies:

- Stackelberg's duopoly. In this model the firms move sequentially.
- Cournot's duopoly. In this model the firms simultaneously choose quantities.
- Bertrand's oligopoly. In this model the firms simultaneously choose prices.

Characteristics

Profit maximization conditions: An oligopoly maximizes profits by producing where marginal revenue equals marginal costs.

Ability to set price: Oliopolies are price setters rather than price takers.

Entry and Exit: Barriers to entry are high. The most important barriers are economies of scale, patents, access to expensive and complex technology and strategic actions by incumbent firms designed to discourage or destroy nascent firms. Number of firms: "Few"-a "handful" of sellers. There are so few firms that the actions of one firm can influence the actions of the other firms.

Long Run Profits: Oligopolies can retain long run positive profits. High barriers of entry prevent sideline firms from entering market to capture excess profits.

Product differentiation: Product may be standardized, steel, or differentiated, automobiles.

Perfect Knowledge Assumptions about perfect knowledge vary but the knowledge of various economic actors can be generally described as selective. Oligopolies have perfect knowledge of their own cost and demand functions but their inter-firm information may be incomplete. Buyers have only imperfect knowledge as to price, cost and product quality.

Interdependence: The distinctive feature of a monopoly is interdependence. Oligopolies are typically composed of a few large firms. Each firm is so large that its actions affect market conditions. Therefore the competing firms will be aware of a firm's market actions and will respond appropriately. This means that in contemplating a market action a firm must take into consideration the possible reactions of all competing firms and the firm's countermoves. It is very much like a game of chess or pool in which a player must anticipate a whole sequence of moves and countermoves in determining how to achieve his objectives. For example, an oligopoly that is considering a price reduction may wish to estimate the likelihood that competing firms would also lower their prices and possibly trigger a ruinous price war. Or if the firm is considering a price increase it may want to know whether other firms will also increase prices or hold existing prices constant. This high degree of interdependence and need to be aware of what the other guy is doing or might do is to be contrasted with lack of interdependence in other market structures. In a PC market there is zero interdependence because no firm is large enough to affect market price. All firm's in a PC market are price takers information which they robotically follow in maximizing profits. In a monopoly there is quite simply no competitors to be concerned about. In a monopolistically competitive market each firm's effects on market conditions is so negligible as to be safely ignored by competitors.

Modelling

There is no single model describing the operation of an oligopolistic market. The variety and complexity of the models is due to the fact that you can have two to 102 firms competing on the basis of price, quantity, technological innovations, marketing, advertising and reputation. Fortunately, there are a series of simplified models that attempt to describe market behaviour under certain circumstances. Some of the better known models are the dominant firm model, the Cournot-Nash model, the Bertrand model and the kinked demand model

Dominant Firm Model

In some markets there is a single firm that controls a dominant share of the market and a group of smaller firms. The dominant firm sets prices which are simply taken by the smaller firms in determining their profit maximizing levels of production. This type market is practically a monopoly and an attached perfectly competitive market in which price is set by the dominant firm rather than the market. The demand curve for the dominant firm is determined by subtracting the supply curves of all the small firms from the industry demand curve. After estimating its net demand curve (market demand less the supply curve of the small firms) the dominant firm maximizes profits by following the normal p-max rule of producing where marginal revenue equals marginal costs. The small firms maximize profits by acting as PC firms-equating price to marginal costs.

Cournot-Nash Model

The Cournot-Nash model is the simplest oligopoly model. The models assumes that there are two "equally positioned firms"; the firms compete on the basis of quantity rather than price and each firms makes an "output decision assuming that the other firm's behaviour is fixed." The market demand curve is assumed to be linear and marginal costs are constant. To find the Cournot-Nash equilibrium one determines how each firm reacts to a change in the output of the other firm. The path to equilibrium is a series of actions and reactions. The pattern continues until a point is reached where neither firm desires "to change what it is doing, given how it believes the other firm will react to any change." K 326. The equilibrium is the intersection of the two firm's reaction functions. The reaction function shows how one firm reacts to the quantity choice of the other firm.

For example, assume that the firm 1's demand function is $P = (60-Q_2) - Q_1$ where Q_2 is the quantity produced by the other firm and Q_1 is the amount produced by firm 1. Assume that marginal cost is 12. Firm 1 wants to know its maximizing quantity and price. Firm 1 begins the process by following the profit maximization rule of equating marginal revenue to marginal costs. Firm 1's total revenue function is $PQ = Q_1(60 - Q_2 - Q_1) = 60Q_1 - Q_1Q_2 - Q_1^2$. The marginal revenue function is $MR = 60 - Q_2 - 2Q$..

$MR = MC$

$60 - Q_2 - 2Q = 12$

$2Q = Q_2 - 60$

$Q_1 = 30 - 0.5Q_2$ [1.1]

$Q_2 = 30 - 0.5Q_1$ [1.2]

Equation 1.1 is the reaction function for firm 1. Equation 1.2 is the reaction function for firm 2.

To determine the Cournot-Nash equilibrium you can solve the equations simultaneously. The equilibrium quantities can also be determined graphically.

The equilibrium solution would be at the intersection of the two reaction functions. Note that if you graph the functions the axes represent quantities. The reaction functions are not necessarily symmetric. The firm's may face differing cost functions in which case the reaction functions would not be identical nor would the equilibrium quantities.

Bertrand Model

The Bertrand model is essentially the Cournot-Nash model except the strategic variable is price rather than quantity.

The Model Assumptions are:

There are two firms in the market.

They produce a homogeneous product.

They produce at a constant marginal cost.

Firms choose prices P_A and P_B simultaneously.

Firms outputs are perfect substitutes.

Sales are split evenly if $P_A = P_B$.

The only Nash equilibrium is $P_A = P_B = MC$.

Neither firm has any reason to change strategy if the firm raises prices it will lose all its customers. If the firm lowers price $P < MC$ then it will be losing money on every unit sold.

The Bertrand equilibrium is the same as the competitive result. Each firm will produce where P = marginal costs and there will be zero profits.

The Kinked Demand Curve Model

According to this model, each firm faces a demand curve kinked at the existing price. The conjectural assumptions of the model are (1) if a firm raises its price above the existing price competitor will not follow and the acting firm will lose market share (2) if a firm lowers price below the existing price then competitors will follow to preserve their market share and the acting frim's output will increase only slightly.

If the Assumptions Hold Then

The firm's marginal revenue curve is discontinuous, has a gap, at the kink.

For prices above the prevailing price the curve is relatively elastic.

For prices below the point the curve is relatively inelastic.

The gap in the marginal revenue curve means that marginal costs can fluctuate without changing equilibrium price and quantity. Thus prices tend to be rigid.

Examples

In industrialized economies, barriers to entry have resulted in oligopolies forming in many sectors, with unprecedented levels of competition, fueled by increasing globalization. Market shares in an oligopoly are typically determined by product development and advertising.

For example, there are now only a small number of manufacturers of civil passenger aircraft, though Brazil (Embraer) and Canada (Bombardier) have participated in the small passenger aircraft market sector. Oligopolies have also arisen in heavily regulated markets such as wireless communications: in some areas only two or three providers are licensed to operate.

Australia

- Most media outlets are owned either by News Corporation, Time Warner, or by Fairfax Media
- Retailing is dominated by Coles Group and Woolworths.

Canada

- Three companies (Rogers Wireless, Bell Mobility and Telus) share over 94% of Canada's wireless market. United Kingdom
- Four companies (Tesco, Sainsbury's, Asda and Morrisons) share 74.4% of the grocery market

- Scottish & Newcastle, Molson Coors, and Inbev control two thirds of the beer brewing industry.
- The detergent market is dominated by two players, Unilever and Procter & Gamble.

United States

- Anheuser-Busch and MillerCoors control about 80% of the beer industry.
- Many media industries today are essentially oligopolies. Six movie studios receive 90% of American film revenues, and four major music companies receive 80% of recording revenues. There are just six major book publishers, and the television industry was an oligopoly of three networks—ABC, CBS, and NBC—from the 1990s. through the 1970s. Television has diversified since then, especially because of cable, but today it is still mostly an oligopoly of five companies: Disney/ABC, CBS Corporation, NBC Universal, Time Warner, and News Corporation.
- Healthcare insurance in the United States consists of very few insurance companies controlling major market share in most states. For example, Calfornia's insured population of 20 million is the most competitive in the nation and 44% of that market is dominated by two insurance companies, Anthem and Kaiser Permanante.

Worldwide

- The accountancy market is controlled by Price Waterhouse Coopers, KPMG, Deloitte Touche Tohmatsu, and Ernst & Young (commonly known as the Big Four)
- Three leading food processing companies, Kraft Foods, PepsiCo and Nestle, together achieve a large proportion of global processed food sales. These three companies are often used as an example of "The rule of 3", which states that markets often become an oligopoly of three large firms.
- Boeing and Airbus have a duopoly over the airliner market.

Demand Curve

Above the kink, demand is relatively elastic because all other firms' prices remain unchanged. Below the kink, demand is relatively inelastic because all other firms will introduce a similar price cut, eventually leading to a price war. Therefore, the best option for the oligopolist is to produce at point E which is the equilibrium point and the kink point. This is a theoretical model proposed in 1947, which has failed to receive conclusive evidence for support.

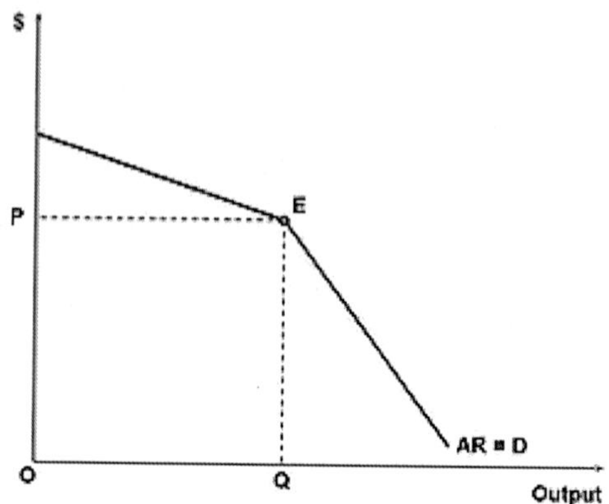

In an oligopoly, firms operate under imperfect competition. With the fierce price competitiveness created by this sticky-upward demand curve, firms use non-price competition in order to accrue greater revenue and market share. "Kinked" demand curves are similar to traditional demand curves, as they are downward-sloping. They are distinguished by a hypothesized convex bend with a discontinuity at the bend-the "kink." Thus the first derivative at that point is undefined and leads to a jump discontinuity in the marginal revenue curve.

Classical economic theory assumes that a profit-maximizing producer with some market power (either due to oligopoly or monopolistic competition) will set marginal costs equal to marginal revenue. This idea can be envisioned graphically by the intersection of an upward-sloping marginal cost curve and a downward-sloping marginal revenue curve (because the more one sells, the lower the price must be, so the less a producer earns per unit). In classical theory, any change in the marginal cost structure (how much it costs to make each additional unit) or the marginal revenue structure (how much people will pay for each additional unit) will be immediately reflected in a new price and/or quantity sold of the item. This result does not occur if a "kink" exists. Because of this jump discontinuity in the marginal revenue curve, marginal costs could change without necessarily changing the price or quantity.

The motivation behind this kink is the idea that in an oligopolistic or monopolistically competitive market, firms will not raise their prices because even a small price increase will lose many customers. This is because competitors will generally ignore price increases, with the hope of gaining a larger market share as a result of now having comparatively lower prices. However, even a large price decrease will gain only a few customers because such an action will begin a price war with other firms. The curve is therefore more price-elastic for price increases and less so for price decreases. Firms will often enter the industry in the long run.

Oligopsony

An oligopsony is a market form in which the number of buyers is small while the number of sellers in theory could be large. This typically happens in market for inputs where a small number of firms are competing to obtain factors of production. It contrasts with an oligopoly, where there are many buyers but just a few sellers. An oligopsony is a form of imperfect competition.

The terms monopoly (one seller), monopsony (one buyer), and bilateral monopoly have a similar relationship.

One example of an oligopsony in the world economy is cocoa, where three firms (Cargill, Archer Daniels Midland, and Callebaut) buy the vast majority of world cocoa bean production, mostly from small farmers in third-world countries. Likewise, American tobacco growers face an oligopsony of cigarette makers, where three companies (Altria, Brown & Williamson, and Lorillard Tobacco Company) buy almost 90% of all tobacco grown in the US.

In each of these cases, the buyers have a major advantage over the sellers. They can play off one supplier against another, thus lowering their costs. They can also dictate exact specifications to suppliers, for delivery schedules, quality, and (in the case of agricultural products) crop varieties. They also pass off much of the risks of overproduction, natural losses, and variations in cyclical demand to the suppliers.

Monopoly

In economics, a monopoly exists when a specific individual or an enterprise has sufficient control over a particular product or service to determine significantly the terms on which other individuals shall have access to it. Monopolies are thus characterized by a lack of economic competition for the good or service that they provide and a lack of viable substitute goods. The verb "monopolize" refers to the *process* by which a firm gains persistently greater market share than what is expected under perfect competition.

A monopoly must be distinguished from monopsony, in which there is only one *buyer* of a product or service ; a monopoly may also have monopsony control of a sector of a market. Likewise, a monopoly should be distinguished from a cartel (a form of oligopoly), in which several providers act together to coordinate services, prices or sale of goods. Monopolies can form naturally or through vertical or horizontal mergers. A monopoly is said to be coercive when the monopoly firm actively prohibits competitors from entering the field.

In many jurisdictions, competition laws place specific restrictions on monopolies. Holding a dominant position or a monopoly in the market is not illegal in itself, however certain categories of behaviour can, when a business is dominant, be considered abusive and therefore be met with legal sanctions.

A government-granted monopoly or *legal monopoly*, by contrast, is sanctioned by the state, often to provide an incentive to invest in a risky venture or enrich a domestic constituency. The government may also reserve the venture for itself, thus forming a government monopoly.

Economic Analysis

In economics, the study of market structures under imperfect competition begins with the analysis of Monopoly. If there is a single seller in a certain industry and there are no close substitutes for the goods being produced, then the market structure is that of a "pure monopoly". Sometimes, there are many sellers in an industry and/or there exist many close substitutes for the goods being produced, but nevertheless firms retain some market power. This is called monopolistic competition, whereas oligopoly refers to the case where the main theoretical framework revolves around firm's strategic interactions.

Basic Market Structures

There are four basic types of market structures under traditional economic analysis, perfect competition, monopolistic competition, oligopoly and monopoly.

A Monopoly is a market structure is which a single supplier produces and sells the product.

Characteristics of a Monopoly

- *Single Seller:* In a monopoly there is one seller of the monopolized good who produces all the output. The firm and industry are identical. In a PC market there are an infinite number of sellers each producing an infinitesimally small quantity of output.

- *Market Power:* Market Power is the ability to affect the terms and conditions of exchange. It is the ability to set your own price. Although a monopoly's market power is high it is not absolute. A monopoly faces a negatively sloped demand curve not a perfectly inelastic curve. Consequently, any price increase will result in the loss of some customers. The monopoly's objective is to maximize profits.
- *High Barriers to Entry and Competition:* Monopolies derive their market power from barriers to entry-circumstances that prevent or greatly impede a potential competitor's entry into the market or ability to compete in the market. There are three major types of barriers to entry; economic, legal and deliberate.

Economic Barriers: Economic barriers include economies of scale, capital requirements, cost advantages and technological superiority.

Economies of Scale: Monopolies are characterized by declining costs over a relatively large range of production. Declining costs coupled with large start up costs give monopolies an advantage over would be competitors. Monopolies are often in a position to cut prices below a new entrant's operating costs and drive them out of the industry.

Further the size of the industry relative to the minimum efficient scale may limit the number of firms that can effectively compete within the industry. If for example the industry is large enough to support one firm of minimum efficient scale then other firms entering the industry will operate at a size that is less than MES meaning that these firms cannot produce at an average cost that is competitive with the dominant industry.

Capital Requirements: Production processes that require large investments of capital, or large research and development costs or substantial sunk costs limit the number of firms in an industry. Large fixed costs also make it difficult for a small firm to enter an industry and expand.

Technological Superiority: A monopoly may be better able to acquire, integrate and use the best possible technology in producing its goods while entrants do not have the size or fiscal muscle to use the best available technology. In plain English one large firm can sometimes produce goods cheaper than several small firms.

No Substitute Goods: A monopoly sells a good for which there is no close substitutes. The absence of substitutes makes the demand for the good relatively inelastic enabling monopolies to extract positive profits.

Control of Natural Resources: A prime source of monopoly power is the control of resources that are critical to the production of a final good.

Legal Barriers: Legal rights can provide opportunity to monopolize the market in a good. Intellectual property rights, including patents and copyrights, give a monopolist exclusive control over the production and selling of certain goods. Property rights may give a firm the exclusive control over the materials necessary to produce a good.

Deliberate Actions: A firm wanting to monopolize a market may engage in various types of deliberate action to exclude competitors or eliminate competition. Such actions include collusion, lobbying governmental authorities, and force.

In addition to barriers to entry and competition, barriers to exit may be a source of market power. Barriers to exit are market conditions that make it difficult or expensive for a firm to leave the market. High liquidation costs are a primary barrier to exit. Market exit and shutdown are separate events. The decision whether to shut down or operate is not affected by exit barriers. A firm will shut down if price falls below minimum average variable costs.

Monopoly Versus Competitive Markets

While monopoly and perfect competition mark the extremes of market structures there are many point of similarity. The cost functions are the same. Both monopolies and perfectly competitive firms minimize cost and maximize profit. The shutdown decisions are the same. Both are assumed to face perfectly competitive factors markets. There are distinctions, some of the more important of which are as follows:

Market Power-market power is the ability to control the terms and condition of exchange. Specifically market power is the ability to raise prices without losing all one's customers to competitors. Perfectly competitive (PC) firms have zero market power when it comes to setting prices. All firms in a PC market are price takers. The price is set by the interaction of demand and supply at the market or aggregate level. Individual firms simply take the price determined by the market and produce that quantity of output that maximize the firm's profits. If a PC firm attempted to raise prices above the market level all its "customers" would abandon the firm and purchase at the market price from other firms. A monopoly has considerable although not unlimited market power. A monopoly has the power to set prices or quantities although not both. A monopoly is a price maker. The monopoly is the market and prices are set by the monopolist based on his circumstances and not the interaction of demand and supply. The two primary factors determining monopoly market power are the firm's demand curve and its cost structure.

Product Differentiation: There is zero product differentiation in a perfectly competitive market. Every product is perfectly homogeneous and a perfect substitute. With a monopoly there is high to absolute product differentiation in the sense that there is no available substitute for a monopolized good. The monopolist is the sole supplier of the good in question. A customer either buys from the monopolist on her terms or does without.

Number of Competitors: PC markets are populated by an infinite number of buyers and sellers. Monopoly involves a single seller.

Barriers to Entry-Barriers to entry are factors and circumstances that prevent entry into market by would be competitors and impediments to competition that limit new firm's from operating and expanding within the market. PC markets have free entry and exit. There are no barriers to entry, exit or competition. Monopolies have relatively high barriers to entry. The barriers must be strong enough to prevent or discourage any potential competitor from entering the market.

PED; the price elasticity of demand is the percentage change in demand caused by a one percent change in relative price. A successful monopoly would face a relatively inelastic demand curve. A high coefficient of elasticity is indicative of effective barriers to entry. A PC firm faces what it perceives to be perfectly elastic demand curve. The coefficient of elasticity for a perfectly competitive demand curve is infinite.

Excess Profits-Excess or positive profits are profit above the normal expected return on investment. A PC firm can make excess profits in the short run but excess profits attract competitors who can freely enter the market and drive down prices eventually reducing excess profits to zero. A monopoly can preserve excess profits because barriers to entry prevent competitors from entering the market.

Profit Maximization-A PC firm maximizes profits by producing where price equals marginal costs. A monopoly maximizes profits by producing where marginal revenue equals marginal costs. The rules are equivalent. The demand curve for a PC firm is perfectly elastic-flat. The demand curve is identical to the average revenue curve and the price line. Since the average revenue curve is constant the marginal revenue curve is also constant and equals the demand curve, Average revenue is the same as price (AR = TR/Q = P x Q/Q = P). Thus the price line is also identical to the demand curve. In sum, D = AR = MR = P.

P-Max quantity, price and profit: if a monopolist took over a perfectly competitive industry he would raise prices cut production and realize positive economic profits.

The most significant distinction between a PC firm and a monopoly is that the monopoly faces a downward sloping demand curve rather than the "perceived" perfectly elastic curve of the PC firm. Practically all the variations above mentioned relate to this fact. If there is a downward sloping demand curve then by necessity there is a distinct marginal revenue curve. The implications of this fact are best made manifest with a linear demand curve, Assume that the inverse demand curve is of the form x = a-by. Then the total revenue curve is TR = ay-by2 and the marginal revenue curve is thus MR = a-2by. From this several things are evident. First the marginal revenue curve has the same y intercept as the inverse demand curve. Second the slope of the marginal revenue curve is twice that of the inverse demand curve. Third the x intercept of the marginal revenue curve is half that of the inverse demand curve. What is not quite so evident is that the marginal revenue curve lies below the inverse demand curve at all points. Since all firms maximize profits by equating MR and MC it must be the case that at the profit maximizing quantity MR and MC are less than price which further implies that a monopoly produces less quantity at a higher price than if the market were perfectly competitive. A company with a monopoly does not undergo price pressure from competitors, although it may face pricing pressure from potential competition. If a company raises prices too high, then others may enter the market if they are able to provide the same good, or a substitute, at a lower price. The idea that monopolies in markets with easy entry need not be regulated against is known as the "revolution in monopoly theory".

A monopolist can extract only one premium, and getting into complementary markets does not pay. That is, the total profits a monopolist could earn if it sought to leverage its monopoly in one market by monopolizing a complementary market are equal to the extra profits it could earn anyway by charging more for the monopoly product itself. However, the one monopoly profit theorem does not hold true if customers in the monopoly good are stranded or poorly informed, or if the tied good has high fixed costs.

A pure monopoly follows the same economic rationality of firms under perfect competition, i.e. to optimize a profit function given some constraints. Under the assumptions of increasing marginal costs, exogenous inputs' prices, and control concentrated on a single agent or entrepreneur, the optimal decision is to equate the marginal cost and marginal revenue of production.

Nonetheless, a pure monopoly can-unlike a competitive firm-alter the market price for her own convenience: a decrease in the level of production results in a higher price. In the economics' jargon, it is said that pure monopolies "face a downward-sloping demand". An important consequence of such behaviour is worth noticing: typically a monopoly selects a higher price and lower quantity of output than a price-taking firm; again, less is available at a higher price. There are important points for one to remember when considering the monopoly model diagram (and its associated conclusions) displayed here. The result that monopoly prices are higher, and production output lower, than a competitive firm follow from a requirement that the monopoly not charge different prices for different customers. That is, the monopoly is restricted from engaging in price discrimination (this is called first degree price discrimination, where all customers are charged the same amount). If the monopoly were permitted to charge individualized prices (this is called third degree price discrimination), the quantity produced, and the price charged to the *marginal* customer, would be identical to a competitive firm, thus eliminating the deadweight loss; however, all gains from trade (social welfare) would accrue to the monopolist and none to the consumer. In essence, every consumer would be just indifferent between (1) going completely without the product or service and (2) being able to purchase it from the monopolist.

As long as the price elasticity of demand for most customers is less than one in absolute value, it is advantageous for a firm to increase its prices: it then receives more money for fewer goods. With a price increase, price elasticity tends to rise, and in the optimum case above it will be greater than one for most customers.

Monopoly and Efficiency

According to the standard model, in which a monopolist sets a single price for all consumers, the monopolist will sell a lower quantity of goods at a higher price than would firms under perfect competition. Because the monopolist ultimately forgoes transactions with consumers who value the product or service more than its cost, monopoly pricing creates a deadweight loss referring to potential gains that went neither to the monopolist or to consumers. Given the presence of this deadweight loss, the combined surplus (or wealth) for the monopolist and consumers is necessarily less than the total surplus obtained by consumers under perfect competition. Where efficiency is defined by the total gains from trade, the monopoly setting is less efficient than perfect competition.

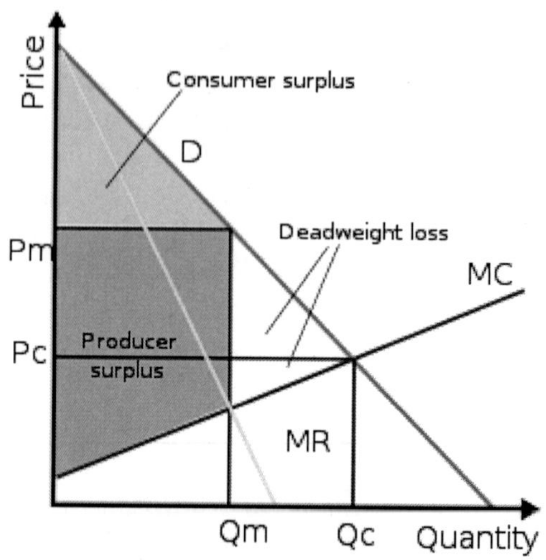

***Figure:** Surpluses and Deadweight loss Created by Monopoly price Setting*

It is often argued that monopolies tend to become less efficient and innovative over time, becoming "complacent giants", because they do not have to be efficient or innovative to compete in the marketplace. Sometimes this very loss of psychological efficiency can raise a potential competitor's value enough to overcome market entry barriers, or provide incentive for research and investment into new alternatives The theory of contestable markets argues that in some circumstances (private) monopolies are forced to behave *as if* there were competition because of the risk of losing their monopoly to new entrants. This is likely to happen where a market's barriers to entry are low. It might also be because of the availability in the longer term of substitutes in other markets. For example, a canal monopoly, while worth a great deal in the late eighteenth century United Kingdom, was worth much less in the late nineteenth century because of the introduction of railways as a substitute.

Natural Monopoly

A natural monopoly is a firm which experiences increasing returns to scale over the relevant range of output. A natural monopoly occurs where the average cost of production "declines throughout the relevant range of product demand." The relevant range of product demand is where the average cost curve is below the demand curve. When this situation occurs it is always cheaper for one large firm to supply the market than multiple smaller firms, In fact, absent government intervention such markets will naturally evolve into a monopoly. An early market entrant who takes advantage of the cost structure and can expand rapidly can exclude smaller firms from entering and can drive or buy out other firms. A natural monopoly suffers from the same inefficiencies as any other monopoly. Left to its own devices a profit seeking natural monopoly will produce where marginal revenue equals marginal costs. Regulation of natural monopolies is problematic. Breaking up such monopolies is counter productive. The most frequently used methods dealing with natural monopolies is government regulations and public ownership. Government regulation generally consists of regulatory commissions charged with the principal duty of setting prices. To reduce prices and increase output regulators often use average cost pricing. Under average cost pricing the price and quantity are determined by the intersection of the average cost curve and the demand curve. This pricing scheme eliminates any positive economic profits since price equals average cost. Average cost pricing in not perfect. Regulators must estimate average costs. Firms have a reduced incentive to lower costs. And regulation of this type has not been limited to natural monopolies.

Breaking up Monopolies

When monopolies are not broken through the open market, sometimes a government will step in, either to regulate the monopoly, turn it into a publicly owned monopoly environment, or forcibly break it up. Public utilities, often being naturally efficient with only one operator and therefore less susceptible to efficient breakup, are often strongly regulated or publicly owned. AT&T and Standard Oil are debatable examples of the breakup of a private monopoly: When AT&T was broken up into the "Baby Bell" components, MCI, Sprint, and other companies were able to compete effectively in the long distance phone market.

Law

The existence of a very high market share does not always mean consumers are paying excessive prices since the threat of new entrants to the market can restrain a high-market-share firm's price increases. Competition law does not make merely having a monopoly illegal, but rather abusing the power a monopoly may confer, for instance through exclusionary practices. First it is necessary to determine whether a firm is dominant, or whether it behaves "to an appreciable extent independently of its competitors, customers and ultimately of its consumer." As with collusive conduct, market shares are determined with reference to the particular market in which the firm and product in question is sold.

Under EU law, very large market shares raises a presumption that a firm is dominant, which may be rebuttable. If a firm has a dominant position, then there is "a special responsibility not to allow its conduct to impair competition on the common market". The lowest yet market share of a firm considered "dominant" in the EU was 39.7%. Certain categories of abusive conduct are usually prohibited under the country's legislation, though the lists are seldom closed. The main recognized categories are:

- Predatory pricing
- Tying (commerce) and product bundling
- Limiting supply
- Price discrimination
- Refusal to deal and exclusive dealing.

Despite wide agreement that the above constitute abusive practices, there is some debate about whether there needs to be a causal connection between the dominant position of a company and its actual abusive conduct. Furthermore, there has been some consideration of what happens when a firm merely attempts to abuse its dominant position.

Historical Monopolies

The term "monopoly" first appears in Aristotle's *Politics*, wherein Aristotle describes Thales of Miletus' cornering of the market in olive presses as a monopoly (*μουπωγλιυ*).

Common salt (sodium chloride) historically gave rise to natural monopolies. Until recently, a combination of strong sunshine and low humidity or an extension of peat marshes was necessary for winning salt from the sea, the most plentiful source. Changing sea levels periodically caused salt "famines" and communities were forced to depend upon those who controlled the scarce inland mines and salt springs, which were often in hostile areas (the Sahara desert) requiring well-organized security for transport, storage, and distribution. The "Gabelle", a notoriously high tax levied upon salt, played a role in the start of the French Revolution, when strict legal controls were in place over who was allowed to sell and distribute salt.

Robin Gollan argues in *The Coalminers of New South Wales* that anti-competitive practices developed in the Newcastle coal industry as a result of the business cycle. The monopoly was generated by formal meetings of the local management of coal companies agreeing to fix a minimum price for sale at dock. This collusion was known as "The Vend." The Vend collapsed and was reformed repeatedly throughout the late nineteenth century, cracking under recession in the business cycle. "The Vend" was able to maintain its monopoly due to trade union support, and material advantages (primarily coal geography). In the early twentieth century as a result of comparable monopolistic practices in the Australian coastal shipping business, the vend took on a new form as an informal and illegal collusion between the steamship owners and the coal industry, eventually going to the High Court as Adelaide Steamship Co. Ltd v. R. & AG.

Examples of Legal (and or) Illegal Monopolies

- The salt commission, a legal monopoly in China formed in 758.
- British East India Company; created as a legal trading monopoly in 1600.
- Standard Oil; broken up in 1911, two of its surviving "baby companies" are ExxonMobil and the Chevron Corporation.
- Major League Baseball; survived U.S. anti-trust litigation in 1922, though its special status is still in dispute as of 2009.
- Microsoft; settled anti-trust litigation in the U.S. in 2001; fined by the European Commission in 2004 for 497 million Euros, which was upheld for the most part by the Court of First Instance of the European Communities in 2007. The fine was 1.35 Billion USD in 2008 for noncompliance with the 2004 rule.
- Joint Commission; has a monopoly over whether or not US hospitals are able to participate in the Medicare and Medicaid programs.

Monopsony

In economics, a monopsony "single" is a market form in which only one buyer faces many sellers. It is an example of imperfect competition, similar to a monopoly, in which only one seller faces many buyers. As the only purchaser of a good or service, the "monopsonist" may dictate terms to its suppliers in the same manner that a monopolist controls the market for its buyers. The term was first introduced by Joan Robinson in her influential book, *The Economics of Imperfect Competition*. Robinson credits classics scholar Bertrand Hallward of Peterhouse College, Cambridge with coining the term. A single-payer health care system, in which the government is the only "buyer" of health care services, is an example of a monopsony. It has also been argued that Wal-Mart, in the United States, functions as a monopsony in certain market segments, as its buying power for a given item may dwarf the remaining market.

Overview

The term "monopsony power", in a manner similar to "monopoly power" is used by economists as a short hand reference to buyers who face an upwardly sloping supply curve but that are not the only buyer; better, but more cumbersome terms may be oligopsony or monopsonistic competition. A monopsonist may at the same time be a monopolist.

A monopsonist has market power, because it can affect the market price of the purchased good by varying the quantity bought. Formally, this is so because a monopsonist faces a supply curve with a *finite* (and generally positive) price elasticity. However, one can find this condition– and hence monopsony power – also in markets with more than one buyer. In all such cases the resulting market form is called an oligopsony.

For most practical purposes, what matters is monopsony power as such, whether it is exercised by one or more subjects. In standard microeconomics, where monopsonists or oligopsonists are assumed to be profit-maximizing firms, monopsony power leads to a market failure, due to a *restriction of the quantity purchased* relative to the (Pareto) optimal competitive outcome. Moreover, markets with monopsony power are predicted to react differently to public price regulations. Monopsony power is thus relevant from both the normative and positive points of view. The practical importance of its effects depends however on its actual *intensity*, measured by the size of the deviation from competitive outcomes.

Traditional microeconomics tended to assume that in most modern cases such intensity was small enough to be ignored, justifying as an acceptable approximation the general use of much simpler competitive models. The only and oft-quoted exception to this principle was assumed to be the labour markets of the nineteenth-century "company towns", which were isolated mining centres with only one employer (the mining company) for almost everybody.

This view has however been variously questioned by the more recent literature devoted to the actual *measurement* of monopsony power in observed markets. On the one hand, econometric exercises on the available data have apparently ruled out significant labour monopsony for the typical West Virginia "company towns" of the early twentieth century. On the other hand, many observations appear to suggest significant monopsony power in various *contemporary* labour markets, from baseball players to nurses, college professors and many others. There have also been attempts to measure possible monopsony power in some non-labour markets as well. Reasoning *a priori*, the specific dynamics of labour markets – and particularly search behaviour by workers – may indeed formally produce upward-sloping labour supply curves faced by most individual firms *in the short run*. On the longer-run supply behaviour of dynamic models, however, it is much more difficult to get simple general results on purely theoretical grounds, so that any firm conclusion must come from case-by-case empirical analysis. A wide and useful survey of both the theoretical and empirical literature on monopsony in labour markets may be found in Boal and Ransom (1997). The large bibliography provided at the end of Manning (2003).

Static Monopsony in a Labour Market

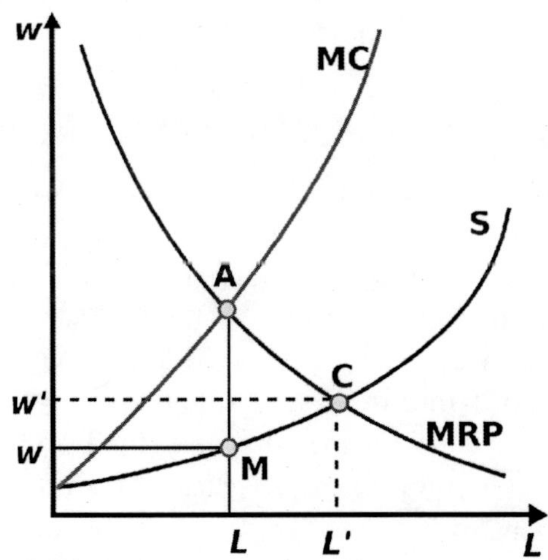

Figure: *A monopsonist employer maximizes profits with employment* L, *that equates demand, given by the* MRP *curve, to marginal cost* MC *at point* A. *The wage is then determined on the supply curve, at point* M, *and is equal to* w. *By contrast, a competitive labour market would reach equilibrium at point* C, *where supply* S *equals demand. This would lead to employment* L' *and wage* w'.

The standard textbook monopsony model refers to static partial equilibrium in a labour market with just one employer who pays the same wage to all its workers.

In this model, the employer is assumed to be a firm facing an upward-sloping *labour supply curve* (as generally contrasted with an infinitely elastic labour supply curve), represented by the S blue curve in the diagram on the right. This curve relates the wage paid, w, to the level of employment, L, and is denoted as the increasing function $w(L)$. Total labour costs are then given by $w(L)L$. Assume now that the firm has a total revenue R, which increases with L according to the concave function $R(L)$. It wants to choose L to maximize profits, which are given by:

$$R(L) - w(L)L..$$

This leads to the first-order condition:

$$R'(L) = w(L) + w'(L)L.$$

The left-hand side of this expression is the *marginal revenue product* of labour (roughly, the extra revenue produced by an extra worker) and is represented by the red *MRP* curve in the diagram. The right-hand side is the *marginal cost* of labour (roughly, the extra cost due to an extra worker) and is represented by the green *MC* curve in the diagram. It should be noticed that this marginal cost is *higher* than the wage $w(L)$ paid to the new worker by the amount

$$w'(L)L.$$

This is because the firm has to increase the wage paid to all the workers it already employs whenever it hires an extra worker. In the diagram, this leads to an *MC* curve that is *above* the supply curve S. The first-order condition for maximum profit is then satisfied at point A of the diagram, where the *MC* and *MRP* curves intersect. This determines the profit-maximising employment as L on the horizontal axis. The corresponding wage w is then obtained from the supply curve, through point M. The monopsonistic equilibrium at M should now be contrasted with the equilibrium that would obtain under competitive conditions. Suppose a competitor employer entered the market and offered a wage higher than that at M.

Then every employee of the first employer would choose instead to work for the competitor. Moreover, the competitor would gain all the former profits of the first employer, minus a less-than-offsetting amount from the wage increase of the first employer's employees, plus profits arising from additional employees who decided to work in the market because of the wage increase. But the first employer would respond by offering an even higher wage, poaching the new rival's employees, and so forth. In other words, a group of perfectly competitive firms would be forced, through competition, to intersection *C* rather than *M*. Just as a monopoly is thwarted by the competition to win sales, minimizing prices and maximizing output, competition for employees between the employers in this case would maximize both wages and employment, as shown in the graph.

Welfare Implications

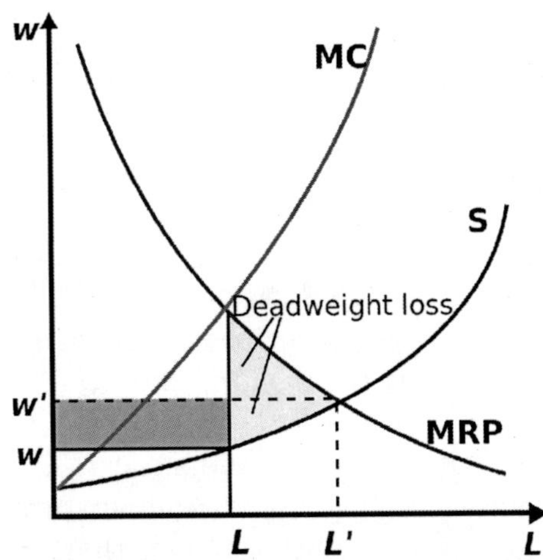

Figure: *The grey rectangle is a measure of the amount of economic welfare transferred from the workers to their employer(s) by monopsony power. The yellow triangle shows the* overall deadweight loss *inflicted on both groups by the monopsonistic restriction of employment. It is thus a measure of the* market failure *caused by monopsony.*

The lower employment and wage caused by monopsony power has two distinct effects on the economic welfare of the people involved. First, it redistributes welfare away from workers and to their employer(s). Secondly, it reduces the aggregate (or social) welfare enjoyed by both groups taken together, as the employers' net gain is smaller than the loss inflicted on workers. The diagram on the right illustrates both effects, using the standard approach based on the notion of economic surplus. According to this notion, the workers' economic surplus (or net gain from the exchange) is given by the area between the *S* curve and the horizontal line corresponding to the wage, up to the employment level. Similarly, the employers' surplus is the area between the horizontal line corresponding to the wage and the *MRP* curve, up to the employment level. The *social* surplus is then the sum of these two areas. Following such definitions, the grey rectangle in the diagram is the part of the competitive social surplus that has been redistributed from the workers to their employer(s) under monopsony. By contrast, the yellow triangle is the part of the competitive social surplus that has been lost by *both* parties, as a result of the monopsonistic restriction of employment. This is a net social loss and is called *deadweight loss*. It is a measure of the market failure caused by monopsony power, through a wasteful misallocation of resources.

As the diagram suggests, the size of both effects increases with the difference between the marginal revenue product *MRP* and the market wage determined on the supply curve *S*. This difference corresponds to the vertical side of the yellow triangle, and can be expressed as a proportion of the market wage, according to the formula:

$$e = \frac{R'(w) - w}{w}.$$

The ratio e has been called the rate of exploitation, and it can be easily shown that it equals the reciprocal of the elasticity of the labour supply curve faced by the firm. Thus the rate of exploitation is zero under competitive conditions, when this elasticity tends to infinity. Empirical estimates of e by various means are a common feature of the applied literature devoted to the measurement of observed monopsony power. Finally, it is important to notice that, while the gray-area redistribution effect could be reversed by fiscal policy (i.e., taxing employers and transferring the tax revenue to the workers), this is not so for the yellow-area deadweight loss. The market failure can only be addressed in one of two ways: either by breaking up the monopsony through anti-trust intervention, or by regulating the wage policy of firms. The most common kind of regulation is a binding minimum wage higher than the monopsonistic wage.

Minimum Wage

With a binding minimum wage of *w"* the marginal cost to the firm becomes the horizontal black *MC'* line, and the firm maximises profits at *A* with a higher employment *L"*. However in this example the minimum wage is higher than the competitive one, leading to *involuntary unemployment* equal to the segment *AB*. A binding minimum wage can be introduced either by law or through collective bargaining, and its possible effects in a special case are shown in the diagram on the right. Here the minimum wage is *w"*, higher than the monopsonistic w. At this given wage the firm can now hire all the workers it wants, up to the supply curve, so that in the relevant employment range its marginal cost of labour becomes effectively constant and equal to w'', as shown by the new black horizontal line *MC'*. Hence the firm maximizes profits at the new intersection point *A*, choosing the employment level L'', which is higher than the monopsonistic level L. As the reader can check, the rate of exploitation has been reduced to zero. More generally, a binding minimum wage modifies the form of the supply curve faced by the firm, which becomes:

$$w = \begin{cases} w_{min}, & \text{if } w_{min} \geq w(L) \\ w(L), & \text{if } w_{min} \leq w(L) \end{cases}$$

where $w(L)$ is the original supply curve and w_{min} is the minimum wage. The new curve has thus a horizontal first branch and a kink at the point

$$w(L) = w_{min}$$

as is shown in the diagram by the kinked black curve *MC' S*. The resulting equilibria can then fall into one of three classes or regimes, according to the value taken by the minimum wage, as is seen by the following table:

Minimum-wage regimes in monopsonistic labour markets

	Minimum wage	**Resulting equilibrium**
First regime	not higher than monopsony wage	unchanged from monopsony
Second regime	higher than monopsony wage but not higher than competitive wage	at kink of supply curve
Third regime	higher than competitive wage	at intersection where minimum wage equals *MRP*

As it is now seen, the example illustrated by the diagram belongs to the third regime. As a result, there is an excess supply of labour – i.e. *involuntary unemployment* – equal to the segment *AB*. So, although the exploitation rate has vanished, there is still a deadweight loss to society. This illustrates the problems that may arise when the proper level of the binding minimum wage is not exactly known, or cannot be enforced for political reasons.

Yet, even when it is sub-optimal, a minimum wage higher than the market rate raises the level of employment anyway. This is a highly remarkable result, because it only follows under monopsony. Indeed, under competitive conditions any minimum wage higher than the market rate would actually *reduce* employment, according to classical economic models. Thus, spotting the effects on employment of newly introduced minimum wage regulations is among the indirect ways economists use to pin down monopsony power in selected labour markets.

Wage Discrimination

Just like a monopolist, a monopsonistic employer may find that its profits are maximized if it *discriminates* prices. In this case this means paying different wages to different groups of workers even if their MRP is the same, with lower wages paid to the workers who have a lower elasticity of supply of their labour to the firm.

Some researchers have tried to use this fact to explain at least part of the observed wage differentials whereby women earn often less than men, even after controlling for observed productivity differentials. However, all such attempts have had to contend with the statistical fact that in most cases women actually display a *higher* labour supply elasticity than men.

Some authors have argued informally that, while this is so for *market* supply, the reverse may somehow be true of the supply to individual firms. In particular, Manning and others have shown that, in the case of the UK Equal Pay Act, implementation has led to higher employment of women. Since the Act was effectively minimum wage legislation for women, this might perhaps be interpreted as a symptom of monopsonistic discrimination.

Dynamic Problems

In many real-world situations a monopsonist firm will have to maximise its profits *through time*, rather than instantaneously as in the previous static model. In all such cases, any short-run outcomes will have to be balanced against longer-run ones, and the resulting equilibrium may differ. The simplest dynamic model to bring out this idea, used in Boal and Ransom (1997), is one where the supply of labour to the firm reacts to wage changes with a lag, due for instance to information costs and search behaviour. Assume hence that the supply function has a distributed-lag specification, leading to:

$$L_t = L(w_t, L_{t-1}),$$

where the subscript refers to the time period and L is increasing in both arguments. Inverting this function gives:

$$w_t = w_t(L_t, L_{t-1}),$$

with

$$\frac{\partial w_t}{\partial L_t} \geq 0 \quad \text{and} \quad \frac{\partial w_t}{\partial L_{t-1}} \leq 0.$$

If the firm has a time-discount rate r, the present value of profits is now given by:

$$\sum_{t=1}^{\infty}\left[R_t(L_t) - w_t(L_t, L_{t-1})L_t\right]\left(\frac{1}{1+r}\right)^{t-1}.$$

The tth first-order condition to maximise this present value is:

$$\frac{dR_t}{dL_t} - w_t - \frac{\partial w_t}{\partial L_t}L_t - \frac{\partial w_{t+1}}{\partial L_t}\frac{L_{t+1}}{1+r} = 0.$$

Define next the short-run simultaneous and lagged inverse supply elasticities respectively as:

$$\epsilon_{SR}^{-1} \overset{\text{def}}{=} \frac{\partial w_t}{\partial L_t}\frac{L_t}{w_t}, \qquad \epsilon_{SRL}^{-1} \overset{\text{def}}{=} \frac{\partial w_{t+1}}{\partial L_t}\frac{L_t}{w_{t+1}}.$$

Now, assume these elasticities to be constant over time. Assume further a steady state, with $L_t = L_{t+1}$ and $w_t = w_{t+1}$. Then the first-order condition gives the exploitation rate as:

$$e_t \overset{\text{def}}{=} \frac{MRP_t - w_t}{w_t} = \epsilon_{SR}^{-1} + \frac{\epsilon_{SRL}^{-1}}{1+r}.$$

Finally, the steady-state long-run inverse elasticity, ϵ_{LR}^{-1}, is given by the sum of the two short-run inverse elasticities defined above, and so one has:

$$e_t = \epsilon_{SR}^{-1}\left(\frac{r}{1+r}\right) + \epsilon_{LR}^{-1}\left(\frac{1}{1+r}\right).$$

The exploitation rate is thus a weighted average of the short-and long-run inverse supply elasticities, where the weight of the long-run one is much bigger, because r is much smaller than unity even when the discounting period is one year. It follows that, as the long-run (direct) supply elasticity of labour tends to be much higher than the short-run one, this very simple dynamic model predicts an exploitation rate which is much smaller than the one produced by static analysis.

However, less simplified dynamic models tell less simple stories. Even the employment effect of minimum wages is not as clear cut as static models would have.

Empirical Problems

The simplified dynamics sketched above suggests that the frequent observation of short-run relative inelasticity of labour supply to individual firms may not be very relevant to the diagnosis of significant monopsony power. Efforts to measure the size of the exploitation rate in specific labour markets have hence taken various forms:

- direct measurement of wage and MRP
- estimates of the long-run supply elasticity of labour to firms
- cross-sectional comparisons of wages and employer concentration
- correlations between wages and workers' mobility
- structural estimation of equilibrium search models
- employment effects of minimum wages.

The results of these empirical works are rarely unambiguous. However, even in cases such as coal miners or nurses, most US studies suggest rates of exploitation probably lower than marginal tax rates on workers' incomes, or union relative wage effects. The better documented instances of significant exploitation are found in the probably rare cases of explicit collusion, such as US baseball before the reserve clause.

The Sources of Labour Monopsony Power

The simpler explanation of monopsony power in labour markets is barriers to entry on the *demand* side. In all such cases, oligopsony would result from oligopoly in the product markets of the industries that use that type of labour as input. If the hypothesis was generally true, one would then find a positive statistical correlation between exploitation, on one side, and industry concentration and firm size on the other. However, numerous statistical studies document significant positive correlations between firm or establishment size and *wages*. These results, by themselves inconsistent with the oligopoly-oligopsony hypothesis, may be due to the prevalence of other factors, such as efficiency wages. However, monopsony power might also be due to circumstances affecting entry of workers on the *supply* side, directly reducing the elasticity of labour supply to firms. Paramount among these are moving costs for workers, which are also a cause of differentiation among potential employees, possibly leading to discrimination.

But a similar effect might also be produced by all the institutional factors that limit labour mobility between firms, including job protection legislation. The requirement that employees in the government or the defence sector is another source of monopsonistic competition, as are requirements for professional certification, for example, a medical degree. Finally, as already noticed, a significant reduction in the short-run elasticity of supply may come from information costs and search behaviour.

An alternative that has been suggested as a source of monopsony power is worker preferences over job characteristics (Bhaskar and To, 1999; Bhaskar, Manning and To, 2002). Such job characteristics can include distance from work, type of work, location, the social environment at work, etc. If different workers have different preferences, employers have local monopsony power over workers that strongly prefer working for them.

Monopsony in Public Administration and Product Markets

The same or similar empirical difficulties dog attempts to identify significant monopsony in non-labour markets, and specifically in markets for intermediate goods bought as inputs by very large firms. Among the most likely US candidates, one finds in the literature:

- trade in technological knowledge: Rodriguez (1975)
- tomatoes for tomato processing: Just and Chern (1980)
- beef for the beef packing industry: Schroeter (1988)
- western coal for electric utilities: Atkinson and Kerkvliet (1989)
- pulpwood and sawlogs: Murray (1995)
- sophisticated weaponry (i.e. jet fighters, tanks, artillery, etc.)
- global warming research funding.

A related issue is the role of monopsony power from the point of view of anti-trust policy affecting vertical integrations.

It has been argued that vertical integration by a monopsony– whereby the production of the previously bought input becomes an in-house operation – may reduce or eliminate the inefficiencies due to monopsonistic restriction of purchases.

In Australia, the Pharmaceutical Industry can be viewed as a kind of monopsony, as the Commonwealth government is the principal buyer of products through the Pharmaceutical Benefits Scheme (PBS) In the US, several, including *Harper's* and the PBS program *Frontline*, have made the case that Wal-Mart is a monopsonist, dictating terms to suppliers, whilst at the same time a monopolist dictating terms to consumers-at least in certain market segments.

Bilateral Monopoly

In a bilateral monopoly there is both a monopoly (a single seller) and monopsony (a single buyer) in the same market.

In such, market price and output will be determined by the non economic forces like bargaining power of both buyer and seller. A bilateral monopoly model is often used in situations where the switching costs of both sides are prohibitively high.

Bilateral monopoly situations are commonly analysed using the theory of Nash bargaining games.

An example of a bilateral monopoly would be when a labour union and a monopolist negotiate.

Bibliography

Arndt, William B. Jr.: *Theories of Personality*, Macmillan, New York, 1974.

Borcherding, K.,: *Contemporary Issues in Industrial Organization,* Amsterdam, North-Holland, 1990.

Boring, E.G.: *A History of Experimental Psychology*. New York: The Century Company, 1929.

Chaudhri, R.D.: *Herbal Drugs Industry: A Practical Approach to Industrial Pharmacognosy*, Eastern, Delhi, 1996.

Copeland, Tom, Tim Koller, and Jack Murrin, *Valuation: Measuring and Managing the Value of Companies,* New York, Wiley, 1994.

Dibbern, Jens: *The Sourcing of Application Software Services, Empirical Evidence of Cultural, Industry and Functional Differences,* Physica Verlag Heidelberg, 2004.

Dubey, K.C.: *Experimental and Developmental Psychology*, Omega Pub, Delhi, 2009.

Ellis, A. :*Humanistic Psychology, The Rational-emotive Approach,* Julian Press, New York, 1973.

Fruhan, W. E.: *Financial Strategy, Studies in the Creation, Transfer and Destruction of Shareholder Value*. Homewood, 1979.

Ginsburgh, Victor A.: *Economics of Art and Culture*, Contributions to Economic Analysis, Elsevier, 2004.

Grace, G.: *School Leadership: Beyond Educational Development*, London, Falmer, 1995.

Guala, F.: *The Methodology of Experimental Economics,* New York, Cambridge University Press, 2005.

Harold, L.: *Entertainment Industry Economics, A Guide for Financial Analysis,* Cambridge University Press, 2004.

Harvey, Francis: *A Primer of GIS, Fundamental Geographic and Cartographic Concepts,* The Guilford Press, 2008.

Hausman, D. M.: *The Inexact and Separate Science of Economics*, Cambridge, Cambridge University Press, 1992.

Jalan, P.K.: *Industrial Sector Reforms in Globalization Era*, Sarup, Delhi, 2004.

Kumar, Arvind: *Industrial Pollution and Management*, APH, Delhi, 2004.

Lindblom, C. E.: *A Strategy of Decision: Policy Evaluation as a Social Organization*, New York, The Free Press, 1970.

Loomes, G.: *Current Issues in Microeconomics*, New York: St. Martin's Press, 1989.

Marris, R. L., and Wood, A.: *The Corporate Economy*, London: Macmillan, 1971.

Mooney, J. D., and Reiley, A. C.: *Onward Industrial Organization*, New York, 1931.

Moustakas, S.: *Existential Psychotherapy and the Interpretation of Dreams*, J. Aronson, C., Northvale, NJ, 1994.

Rathod, P B: *Dynamics of Political Psychology*, ABD Pub, Delhi, 2008.

Santos, A.C.: *The Social Epistemology of Experimental Economics,* London, Routledge 2009.

Scott, W. R.: *Organizations: Rational, Natural, and Open Systems*, Englewood Cliffs, 1981.

Sharma, Ram Nath: *Advanced Industrial Psychology*, Atlantic, Delhi, 2004.

Suri, R.K.: *Dynamics of Industrial Relations*, Pentagon Press, Delhi, 2007.

Tinbergen, Jan.: *On the Theory of Economic Policy*; Amsterdam, North-Holland 1952.

Weber, M.: *The Theory of Social and Economic Organizations*, New York, Oxford University Press, 1947.

William, D.: *Social and Personality Development, Infancy through Adolescence*, New York: Norton, 1983.

Index

N

O

P

R

S

T

U

❑❑❑